THE HISTORY OF THE INDEPENDENT ORDER OF ODD FELLOWS IN THE CITY OF SAN FRANCISCO

An Early Fraternal Organization

—THE ODD FELLOWS STORY—

Peter V. Sellars

Acknowledgments

This project could not have been as thoroughly completed without the generosity and assistance of the following:

David W. Bandy, author and researcher (San Francisco), Laurie Prescott, Past President Rebekah Assembly (California), Christopher Craig (historian), John Meierdierks (Grand Scribe of the Grand Encampment of California), John Freeman and Darlene Thorne for use of their photographs and postcard collection, James Sossaman (Past Grand Master), Margareut K. Oleson (Secretary of the Rebekah Assembly of California), Jeremy Ritter for his mastery of digital imaging, Jane Hernandez for her direction and clarity conveying this writing, the Bancroft Library, San Francisco Public Library, San Francisco Historical Society, and IRIS Photo-Digital (San Francisco).

TABLE OF CONTENTS

INTRODUCTION

HISTORY OF ODD FELLOWS
FRATERNITY IN SAN FRANCISCO

Through photographs, images, and narrative accounts of the Independent Order of Odd Fellows in San Francisco, one might see the impact this organization made on just one city in America. The focus of this project is the historical perspective of the Independent Order of Odd Fellows and how it relates to the history of San Francisco.

The constant temptation to include more interesting information and other members from other areas of the state arose, but the story stayed on its scholarly track (focusing on San Francisco), with the exception of only one individual: Earl Warren is mentioned because he was one of the last notable public figures to hold membership in the Odd Fellows, and because he belonged to a lodge close in proximity to San Francisco. For his connection with the Odd Fellows, he is mentioned in the text of this project.

The discovery of gold not only brought most of the gold seekers to California via the docks of San Francisco, but it also brought people of all backgrounds and of different fraternal organizations. The Odd Fellows owes its early formation in San Francisco to the Gold Rush, as the city itself owes its rapid growth to the same.

The Independent Order of Odd Fellows was a powerful organization, having in its ranks notable figures. Its membership included congressmen, judges, police chiefs, attorneys, wealthy businessmen, newspaper moguls, blue-collar or white-collar workers, plus those of meager means. They all joined in the lodge room of Odd Fellowship.

In a letter dated May 23, 1934, from the American Trust Company to one of the Odd Fellows lodges inviting the members of the lodge to attend an Eightieth Anniversary of the bank, it was written, "your association reflects an important cross-section of our pioneer history." It was evident others saw the Odd fellows as being significant in the building of San Francisco.

The Great Earthquake & Fire affected the people of the city, as it affected its populace belonging to the Odd Fellows, and the organization itself. This story will relate that distressful time to the reader. While we almost lost a fraternity, the efforts of the Odd Fellows in 1906 helped to save the city. It provided relief to thousands of individuals, members and nonmembers alike. When martial law kept everyone out of the disaster area (the city), the Odd Fellows Relief Committee was given permission by the governor to access the city and provide help because it was already set up for this type of relief work.

The fact that most of the documents, photographs, literature, and other items were lost in 1906 due to the destruction of the Great Quake and the destruction of Odd Fellows Building made this project all the more challenging. However, with the kind assistance and direction by several friends and members of the Odd Fellows, enough information was put together to offer this insight of the early days of Odd Fellows in San Francisco.

Today, the Order is still in San Francisco. Although the organization has been swallowed up by an ever-growing modern society, it is still here. Some have incorrectly labeled the Odd Fellows as a "secret society," but that is far from the truth. Sadly, today it is—what many refer to as—"the best kept secret," but this is an unwelcome title and has deprived those in our communities the opportunity of personal enrichment through self-growth. Likewise, it has denied the Independent Order of Odd Fellows a potential membership that could lend its own experiences to the strength, will, and knowledge of this fellowship. There are no secrets for those interested in the Odd Fellows. The organization has been alive in San Francisco since 1849, officially instituted before California became a state.

Although the philosophical aspect of the Order is not the center of this work, some of the ideology does occasionally permeate the story. It is absurd to label the Independent Order of Odd Fellows as an "imitator" of the Freemasons, as is done from time to time by those individuals ignorant of its teachings. In fact, it was extremely commonplace in the late 1800s and early 1900s to find men belonging to both organizations, because these were, in fact, two very different groups having different practices and principles. Where the Masons were vastly different, the Odd Fellows only used their "secret signs" and passwords to dissuade imposters and to avoid distributing financial benefits to nonmembers.

Since 1849, the organization gave to its members, as well as nonmembers of San Francisco, a library, a literary club, and emergency relief funds. It also supported and participated in citywide-related events, welcomed dignitaries, buried the dead, provided a cemetery, aided the communities during times of disaster, provided a bank, and supported numerous other endeavors lending to the expansion of this great new "City-by-the-Bay."

This writing correlates the growth of San Francisco with those activities of the Independent Order of Odd Fellows. It also chronicles the activities and accomplishments of the Independent Order of Odd Fellows in San Francisco through historical documentation and related images. This book covering the period from 1849 to 1949 is a marker for historical measure and will appeal to audiences with an interest in or a love for San Francisco.

CHAPTER I

THE ORDER

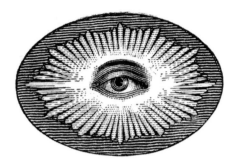

"All-Seeing Eye"

The all-seeing eye is watching you. This is what you believe if you are a member of the Independent Order of Odd Fellows. The eye reminds one that a Higher Being is always scrutinizing one's actions and thoughts. The skull and crossbones force one to be reminded of his or her mortality, and the duty to seek a proper burial or place of rest for a departed brother or sister. These symbols also encourage one to value the memory of that departed person's virtues. The scythe is the symbol of death. The serpent signifies wisdom; and the coffin is the final place of rest for a person. These are just a few symbols used by the Odd Fellows for hundreds of years.

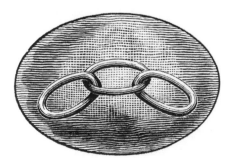

"Three-Links" and "Skull and Cross Bones"

"Symbols of the Independent Order of Odd Fellows"

The Odd Fellows live by the meanings of these mentioned symbols and act upon them to affect positive change in the world; each member of the Odd Fellows lives by this moral code daily. Was this a "secret organization"? Yes. But only secret in so far as to protect the Order from providing aid to imposters. It kept its organization's works secret like any corporation keeps its plans and strategies secret from competitors. Often, these imposters were caught and the membership was notified of the offense.

The Grand Lodge, I. O. O. F., of the State of California,

Office of the Grand Master,

San Diego, Cal., June 24, 1914.

IMPOSTER—WARNING TO LODGES AND MEMBERS

To all Subordinate Lodges, I. O. O. F., under the Jurisdiction of the Grand Lodge, I. O. O. F., of the State of California.
Dear Sirs and Brothers:

There is a man named George Krouse, traveling about the State representing himself as a member of Calumet Lodge, No. 601, I. O. O. F., of Hammond, Indiana, stating that he is without funds, has a family to support and a job to work if he can secure a loan of ten dollars for thirty days; he shows an Official Certificate, good for some months or about to the beginning of 1915. Said Krouse

442   JOURNAL OF PROCEEDINGS OF THE   [1915

was a member of Calumet Lodge, No. 601, but was expelled about one year ago, his receipt being dated to September 30, 1913. If he has a receipt dated in advance of that date, it is a forgery and he is obtaining money from the Lodges in this Jurisdiction under false pretenses; if you can locate him, I would advise having him arrested as an imposter and as a warning to others who may try this game. He is a man about 5-ft. 7-in., weighs about 165 or 170 pounds, full faced, some freckles, sandy complexion, and has a heavy beard but keeps it shaved off clean; has belonged to Subordinate Lodge, Encampment and Canton branches of the Order. He claims to be married. The last heard of him was in the vicinity of Los Angeles, where he received a loan of ten dollars from the General Relief Committee and which has not been returned.

Fraternally yours,

A. P. JOHNSON Jr.,
Grand Master.

Attest: H. D. RICHARDSON,
Grand Secretary.

The preceding two images are a description of an imposter (con man), trying to obtain money from lodges; from the 1915 Journal of Proceedings.

OFFICE OF THE GRAND MASTER

Grand Lodge, J. O. O. F.

of the State of California

GRANT BUILDING, COR. 7TH AND MARKET STS.

H. D. RICHARDSON
GRAND SECRETARY

San Francisco, Cal., July 25, 1907.

To all Lodges Subordinate to the Grand Lodge, I. O. O. F., of the State of California, Greeting:

We are in receipt of a letter from Orangedale Lodge, No. 211, I. O. O. F., Kings River, Cal., reciting that a Brother of that Lodge, named Charles J. Haywards, has disappeared. He had been acting as Treasurer and when he left in June last, is reported to have in his possession, $440.13 of the Lodge's money.

His description, as furnished by Orangedale Lodge, is as follows: "Charles J. Haywards, about 40 years of age, 6 feet 2 inches in height, large, raw-boned, slightly stooped, rough, quick-talking man; has his right hand crippled, as if crushed or drawn up by some accident, is light complected, weighs about 160 pounds. He left the station at Del Rey, on the Santa Fe, Sunday, June 10, 1907, and bought tickets for Oakland. He was accompanied by his wife and two children, a boy and girl about 12 and 14 years of age. They had worked, previous to coming to Kings River, at Point Richmond, and Watsonville. They are working people. The man likes to work around houses, is a good teamster, driving four to ten horses. They were seen in San Francisco, between the 11th and 15th of June, 1907."

If the brother should present himself at your Lodge, please report to the Grand Secretary.

Fraternally yours,

F. B. OGDEN,
Grand Master.

Attest:

H. D. RICHARDSON,
Grand Secretary.

A letter sent to all Odd Fellows Lodges, describing a thief. Letters warning against flim flam men and imposters were also mailed to and from other lodges, as these were regular occurrences in the order. This particular notice was sent out on July 25, 1907.

The main tenet of Odd Fellowship is to *"relieve the distressed, bury the dead, and educate the orphan."* The Order seeks *"to improve the character of mankind"* by employing its main principles of *Friendship, Love, and Truth.*

The name "Odd Fellows" is derived from England during an era when it was thought to be strange or "odd" for people to aid each other

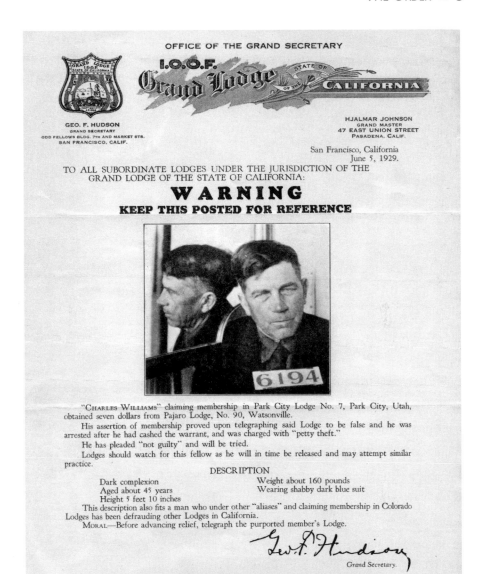

A rare "wanted" poster, with an image of an individual accused of defrauding lodges. 1929.

by means of mutual benefit. When the group organized officially, it named itself the Odd Fellows. Another factor lending to the name Odd Fellows was that, during the first half of the eighteenth century, tradesmen or professionals neither belonging to a union or guild were referred to as being "odd."

On April 26, 1819, after several years attempting to establish the fraternity in America, it finally established itself at the Seven Stars Inn, in Baltimore, Maryland. Thomas Wildey is recognized as the founder of the Independent Order of Odd Fellows in North America. Expansion continued across the country. As America grew, so did the Odd Fellowship. In 1849, it had taken hold in Yerba Buena, what is now called San Francisco. The rest is history.

"Thomas Wildey, the Founder of Odd Fellowship in America".

Because the focus of this book looks closely at the history of San Francisco Odd Fellows, it should be pointed out that the Order's history is every bit as rich in other cities and towns throughout country. The Order has enjoyed the memberships of four United States presidents, the latest being Franklin D. Roosevelt. Literally scores of prominent figures in U.S. history have been part of Odd Fellowship.

THE WHITE HOUSE
WASHINGTON

February 26, 1936

Dear Brother Deans:

Please accept my thanks for your kind letter of February twenty-fourth. As the years pass I am more and more convinced that the beneficent policy which has actuated our order was formulated on a sound basis and has been executed with true wisdom.

We have ever incorporated in our good works, education, establishment of homes for the aged, the indigent, the widow and the orphan so that it is our proud boast that every Grand Lodge in the United States has one or more of these institutions or has taken steps toward their establishment. So I think ours is a record to be proud of. I should greatly appreciate it if I may through you extend hearty felicitations to all members of our order.

Fraternally yours,

Franklin D. Roosevelt

Mr. Parke P. Deans,
Grand Sire,
Sovereign Grand Lodge of the I.O.O.F.,
State Office Building,
Richmond, Virginia.

Letter from Odd Fellow member Franklin D. Roosevelt, President of the United States.

CHAPTER 2

THE BEGINNING

The Gold Rush of 1849 brought more than gold seekers to California. It brought entrepreneurs of many trades, those dreaming of opportunities of wealth, fame, and fortune. It brought hordes of people to northern California, most of which came by way of sea on wooden ships, boats of all sizes, clippers, frigates, and even steamboats. These opportunists also traveled over the rough trail of what was then called the Kit Carson Pass. Today, it is simply called Carson Pass. Of course, the primary destinations were either Yerba Buena—later named San Francisco, or Sutter's Fort—later to become Sacramento.

"Forty-Niners". Many of these miners helped establish early lodges in California. Circa 1849. (Courtesy of Bancroft Library)

The Gold Rush of 1849 also brought many people who had belonged to clubs, social, and fraternal organizations back home in the eastern states. One of these groups was the Independent Order of Odd Fellows, an organization first originating in England and officially arriving in 1819 to Baltimore, Maryland. Many Odd Fellows, while traveling over the mountainous trails, would carve into the rocks or trees their three-links symbol. Along the pass they would also spread the goodwill of the Order.

Although several men attempted to establish an Odd Fellows lodge in San Francisco prior to the Gold Rush, none remained long enough in town to form a permanent lodge. However, Odd Fellowship in California would have to wait a little longer, as most of the new arrivals headed for the Sierra. It was not until after the Gold Rush had had time to cause miners to give up and return to the city that enough men would be available to institute a lodge. These so-called gold searchers met with hardships and would eventually return from the rivers, creeks, and mountains, searching for a place to settle.

Prior to being instituted in California, the few pioneer members hailing originally from other states tried in vain to find other members needed to establish a charter; at least five members were required. "In August, an attempt was made. A former member of the Order, walking the streets, ringing a bell, proclaiming in loud tones that all Odd Fellows were invited to assemble that evening in the little school house (located on Portsmouth Square) to organize a lodge."

Samuel Brannan's newspaper, the *California Star,* invited friends and Odd Fellows to gather at Portsmouth house. The ad read:

> "Notice.—The friends of the Independent Order of Odd Fellows are respectfully invited to attend a meeting of the Order on Tuesday evening next, at the Portsmouth house. Many Odd Fellows. San Francisco, December 4, 1847."

About a dozen Odd Fellows responded by showing up at the Portsmouth house. Although this group held no charter or dispensation, it still resolved to organize an Odd Fellows lodge in San Francisco. The members present selected Dr. E. P. Jones as their Noble Grand,

Samuel Brannan as the Vice Grand, and John Joice as Secretary of the lodge. For a period of time, the Odd Fellows met at the Portsmouth house until it "fitted up a lodge-room in a framed building at Clarke's Point." Clarke's Point was a rocky piece of landmass located just below Telegraph Hill running out into the San Francisco Bay, near what are now Broadway and Battery streets.

Then came the Gold Rush, where nearly everyone left town. The members had burnt all of the important documents and stored the regalia and other items to keep them from falling into the wrong hands. A later fire, as there were many in San Francisco, destroyed the stored lodge items. Another attempt was tried to establish Odd Fellows in the town, but could not keep enough men around long enough to stabilize a lodge.

Even though a dispensation, dated January 12, 1849, was issued by the Grand Lodge of the United States to form a new Odd Fellows lodge in San Francisco, it was not until September 9, 1849, and after many attempts of trying to keep enough members with current credentials around long enough, that California Lodge No. 1 was instituted. This was the first official Odd Fellows lodge in California.

James Smiley was one of the original five members allowed to institute the new lodge. On September 9, 1849, he instituted California Lodge No. 1. The charter members of this new lodge were R. H. Taylor, H. W. Herley, E. C. Franklin, John M. Coughlin, Julius Rose, William Burling, J. N. Dall, David Jobson, and Lewis Tramble. Exactly one year later, California was admitted into the Union as the thirty-first state. As the state grew, so did Odd Fellowship. From this first membership there would blossom a membership numbering approximately sixty thousand in the jurisdiction of California.

Not only did the Odd Fellowship rapidly spread east and north from San Francisco all the way into the mining areas, but also to the south, first springing up in San Jose on December 30, 1854, then arriving in Los Angeles three months later on March 29, 1855. The growth of the Odd Fellowship kept pace with the growth of humanity.

Once California Lodge had been instituted, Sacramento Lodge No. 2 was formed in Sacramento, another jump-off point to the gold mines. This was significant because the fraternity spread as the Gold Rush spread. The next several lodges came to Eureka, Stockton, Oak Park; then to places like Auburn, Diamond Springs, Sonora, Grass Valley, Nevada City, Tuolumne, and further into gold country. Wherever gold seekers went, Odd Fellowship spread.

Back in San Francisco, Odd Fellowship was growing exponentially. The Order had even been supplying the new members to these faraway places by financing and assisting them in their travels to the mines. Members from distant places sought relief and assistance almost as quickly as they departed the ships, and the number of lodges grew from a single lodge in 1849 to 120 lodges in only 15 years. The Order was flourishing.

Once the Order was established in California, it immediately went to work in practicing its doctrines of relieving the distressed, visiting the sick, and burying the dead. In 1849 and 1850, a young doctor, also an Odd Fellow, John Frederick Morse, took up the calling of helping those who suffered from "the terrible scourge of cholera," as it was called, a sickness never before seen in California.

It is a fact, "the I.O.O.F. [the Independent Order of Odd Fellows] was the first American fraternal order to offer its members financial benevolences with regard to relief of the sick, distressed, orphans and burial of deceased members."

In 1853, after the initial pioneer lodges had been instituted, Samuel Parker, a Past Grand Master from the East, came to San Francisco to establish a Grand Lodge in order to direct and assist the new lodges. Parker became the first Grand Master in California. "The preliminary meeting for the institution of the Grand Lodge of California was held in the old hall of the Order on Kearny Street, San Francisco on April 11, 1853, at 11 o'clock A M." Twenty-two lodges existed at this time. By 1899, 351 lodges were active in the state and there were over thirty thousand members.

As a characteristic, the Odd Fellows believed that the "Visiting Committee" (members of a lodge chosen to visit the sick) was its most important value. In an era where many men suffered while working under extreme conditions, it was not uncommon that many became very ill. Another characteristic was that when a member died, a proper burial would be provided and guaranteed. As once stated, [in] "our history no Odd Fellow has knowingly been permitted to be buried in an unknown grave." The Order acquired many plots in order to provide burial locations for members.

It was only natural for the organization to place its Grand Lodge in San Francisco, since this had been the place where it all began. The largest lodges in the state were in San Francisco. There were over thirty lodges in the city, an Odd Fellows cemetery, a Relief Association, a library, and a faction for women—called the Rebekahs. The fraternity had both its prominent members, as well as lesser-known members. There were judges, doctors, politicians, carpenters, and tradesmen of nearly all aspects of life. Past Grand Master William W. Morrow was appointed a U.S. district judge of California by President Harrison, and 6 years later became a U.S. circuit judge for the Ninth Judicial Circuit, appointed by President William McKinley.

In 1928, at the height of its membership in California, the Odd Fellows in San Francisco enjoyed a membership of 5,431 members. Of the 58,882, not including the Rebekahs, Encampments, and other bodies of the organization, approximately 10 percent were active in the San Francisco. Odin Lodge No. 393, a Swedish-speaking lodge, and Morse Lodge No. 257, named in honor of the late Dr. John Frederick Morse, boasted the largest memberships, with 608 and 438 members respectively.

The Relief Association was formed to assist those who became ill, as many people found themselves without the means to survive the ordeals of health problems associated with working in and around gold mines. When no one else seemed to be able to help these people, the Odd Fellows were there for them. The Relief Association was even committed to burying the dead. It is stated, "Men were still buried in the filth of an unattended sickness, and frequently without the benefit of being sewed up in a blanket for internment. . . . The Association of Odd

Fellows spent thousands of dollars for coffins alone; and, when General A. M. Winn [an Odd Fellow] became the executive officer of the city government, August 25th [1849], no man was denied a coffin burial."

The Odd Fellows in San Francisco worked in vain at times just to assist thousands of new arrivals who found themselves in a new land with no money, no family, and no one to assist them when they were ill. Many were in this predicament or worse even before stepping off the steamers. On occasion, the Relief Committee hired attorneys to defend Odd Fellows in courts of law; it also supplied clothing to needy, and it helped widows of members find homes.

It is a less-known fact that the Odd Fellows at Seventh & Market streets established an Odd Fellows Employment Club. In 1919, a committee had been tasked with gathering the names and skills of those members needing work, and then another list of employers seeking workers.

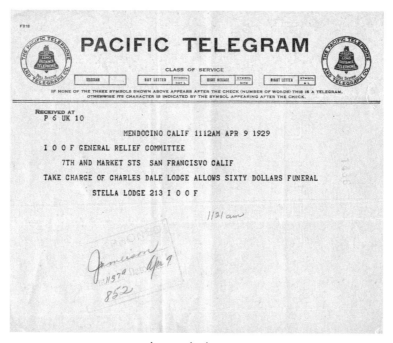

Assorted telegrams.

POSTAL TELEGRAPH – COMMERCIAL CABLES

CLARENCE H. MACKAY, PRESIDENT

RECEIVED AT

TELEGRAMS TO ALL AMERICA

CABLEGRAMS TO ALL THE WORLD

STANDARD TIME INDICATED ON THIS MESSAGE

BLUE	DAY LETTER
NL	NIGHT LETTER
NITE	NIGHT TELEGRAM
LCO	DEFERRED
NLT	CABLE LETTER
WLT	WEEK END LETTER

VRA236 64 NL

VANCOUVER BC 17

SECRETARY   1484

GEN RELIEF COMMITTEE IOOF ODDFELLOWS TEMPLE SANFRANCISCO CALIF

YOUR WIRE 16TH RECEIVED TERRY IS MEMBER FAIRVIEW NO 61 VANCOUVER

BC LODGE FUNERAL BENEFITS SEVENTY FIVE DOLLARS WIDOWS BENEFITS TWENTY

FIVE DOLLARS ALSO FUNERAL AID TWO HUNDRED AND FIFTY DOLLARS FAILING

FAMILY INSTRUCTIONS PLEASE HANDLE FUNERAL CHARGE TO FAIRVIEW NO 61

W ROMAIN 1562 8TH AVENUE WEST IS SECRETARY TO WHOM COMMUNICATIONS

SHOULD BE SENT

J J CHIPMAN NG.

POSTAL TELEGRAPH – COMMERCIAL CABLES

CLARENCE H. MACKAY, PRESIDENT

RECEIVED AT
21 TAYLOR ST.
BRANCH
KEARNY 1900   LOCAL 24

TELEGRAMS TO ALL AMERICA

CABLEGRAMS TO ALL THE WORLD

STANDARD TIME INDICATED ON THIS MESSAGE

BLUE	DAY LETTER
NL	NIGHT LETTER
NITE	NIGHT TELEGRAM
LCO	DEFERRED
NLT	CABLE LETTER
WLT	WEEK END LETTER

F37 SFFG 1145A 60 11 EXTRA BLUE

VANCOUVER BC APR 16 1929

SECRETARY GENERAL RELIEF COMMITTEE

I O O F ODDFELLOWS TEMPLE SANFRANCISCO CALIFORNIA

W S TERRY MEMBER FAIRVIEW   LODGE NO 61 VANCOUVER   BC DIED YESTERDAY

YOUR CITY AND REMAINS AT   HALSTED & CO 1123 SUTTER ST PLEASE LOOK AFTER

FUNERAL ARRANGEMENTS AND RE WIFE AND FAMILY ADVISING ALL PARTICULARS

HAVE WIRED HALSTED &CO TO CONFER WITH YOU

J J CHIPMAN N G

1195 HASTINGS ST W VANCOUVER BC

Assorted telegrams.

Assorted telegrams.

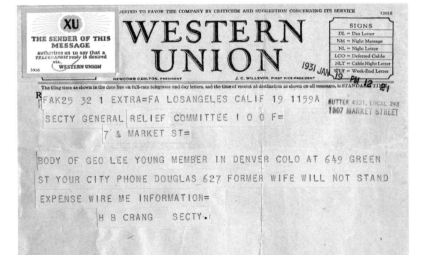

WESTERN UNION

SIGNS
DL = Day Letter
NM = Night Message
NL = Night Letter
LCO = Deferred Cable
NLT = Cable Night Letter
WLT = Week-End Letter

But why be prehistoric?
Don't write, TELEGRAPH

NEWCOMB CARLTON, PRESIDENT   J. C. WILLEVER, FIRST VICE-PRESIDENT

the date line on full-rate telegrams and day letters, and the time of receipt at destination as shown on all messages, is STANDARD TIME.

Market St., San Francisco, Calif.   Always Open

BA31 18 NM 4 EXTRA=NORTHFIELD VT 26   1931 MAR 26 PM 9 29

GENERAL RELIEF COMMITTEE IOOF=
SANFRANCISCO CALIF=

USE OUR FUNERAL BENEFITS $30 AND SEND BILL INVESTIGATE AND
WRITE CONDITIONS=
NORTHFIELD LODGE NO 19   L M PERVIER SECTY.

WESTERN UNION

XU
THE SENDER OF THIS MESSAGE
authorizes us to say that a TELEGRAPHIC reply is desired via
WESTERN UNION

SIGNS
DL = Day Letter
NM = Night Message
NL = Night Letter
LCO = Deferred Cable
NLT = Cable Night Letter
WLT = Week-End Letter

NEWCOMB CARLTON, PRESIDENT   J. C. WILLEVER, FIRST VICE-PRESIDENT

The filing time as shown in the date line on full-rate telegrams and day letters, and the time of receipt at destination as shown on all messages, is STANDARD TIME.

1931 JAN 19 PM 12 21

FAK25 32 1 EXTRA=FA LOSANGELES CALIF 19 1159A   SUTTER 4321, LOCAL 248
1807 MARKET STREET

SECTY GENERAL RELIEF COMMITTEE I O O F=
7 & MARKET ST=

BODY OF GEO LEE YOUNG MEMBER IN DENVER COLO AT 649 GREEN
ST YOUR CITY PHONE DOUGLAS 627 FORMER WIFE WILL NOT STAND
EXPENSE WIRE ME INFORMATION=
H B CRANG   SECTY.

Assorted telegrams.

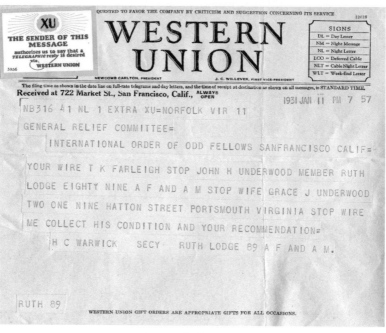

Assorted telegrams.

CHAPTER 3

THE NAMES

Templar Lodge No. 17 boasted many popular members who were society's elite, but lodges in the country had rich and poor, blue-collar and white-collar workers, and people of various backgrounds. Some of the better known members of San Francisco's Templar Lodge included Judge Lorenzo Sawyer, Honorable Charles A. Sumner (U.S. senator), Elias Driggs Farnsworth (Past Grand Sire, I.O.O.F.), Sheldon Gaylord Kellogg (famous attorney), Jacob Lorrilard van Bokkelen (once a member of the Committee of Vigilance of 1851 and the Sixth Grand Master, 1858–1859), Jacob Miller, William Chapman Ralston, founder of the Bank of California and noted as the "Man Who Built San Francisco," and Rueben Headley Lloyd, a pioneer lawyer of San Francisco who was a millionaire, having owned properties on Union Square Avenue, Front and Commercial streets, Sutter and Scott streets, Second and Folsom streets, Sutter, Mason and Geary streets, and Ellis and Hyde streets.

In fact, Rueben H. Lloyd served as Grand Marshal at the cornerstone ceremony on May 14, 1884, where the Odd Fellows Building was to be built at Seventh & Market streets.

Jacob L. van Bokkelen, Charles S. Eigenbrodt, and Samuel Brannan not only belonged to the same Odd Fellows lodge, but they were prominent members of the Committee of Vigilance of 1851 in the city, an organization which Brannan headed. Charter members of the Odd Fellows first lodge, California Lodge No. 1, John M. Coughlin, E. C. Franklin, and William Burling, were also members of the Committee of Vigilance of 1851. Richard Rust, an Odd Fellow belonging to yet another lodge in San Francisco, was a member as well. A. C. Russell of Yerba Buena No. 15 was a member of the committee. Many of these men were members of the Odd Fellows before they joined the Committee of Vigilance of 1851.

The Committee of Vigilance of 1851 was established to create order in San Francisco. The task of controlling the criminal element, particularly a local gang calling itself the *San Francisco Society of Regulators,* and later *The Hounds,* which was running rampant at the time, was monumental for the newly established law enforcers. The Committee of Vigilance of 1851 took it upon itself to handle all serious criminal activity in and around the city. Some individuals were even hanged by the committee for committing serious crimes.

Samuel Brannan was a charter member of Templar Lodge No. 17, which was instituted on October 22, 1853. Brannan was twenty-seven years of age when the ship called the *Brooklyn* sailed through the

Samuel Brannan was the first Treasurer of Templar Lodge No. 17.

Golden Gate on July 31, 1846. He was described as being a man "slightly above medium height, deep-chested, broad shouldered, hair rather shaggy, wearing sideburns and imperial. His eyes were dark and remarkably beautiful, flashing eyes that gave great animation to his face."

Aside from gaining notoriety for being an entrepreneur, Brannan was also remembered for his connection with the Mormons, where he had established a tie 4 years prior to arriving in San Francisco (then called Yerba Buena). In New York, he had published a weekly newspaper for the religious group called the *New York Messenger*. In fact, on the voyage to California, most of the 236 passengers he had brought with him on the *Brooklyn* were Mormons. He was the leader of the migration of Mormons to Yerba Buena, and eventually to other nearby areas.

According to a British bartender named Brown, "The first wedding which took place after this city was under the protection of the American flag was performed by Samuel Brannan, according to the Mormon faith. I was one of the guests, and never enjoyed myself at any gathering as I did there. There was a general invitation extended to all, a large quantity of refreshments had been prepared, and everyone returned to their homes perfectly satisfied and ready to pronounce the first wedding a grand success."

In 1848, after establishing a supply store at Mormon Island, which he named Natoma, Brannan convinced the Mormons who were now mining on the American River that they should pay him "The Lord's Tithes" on their earnings. Some people thought the Mormons were fools for paying such a "tax." In the meantime, word about this tax had reached Brigham Young. Young sent an Apostle to collect the taxes Brannan had been collecting from the Mormons in the "Lord's name"; however, when the Apostle arrived, Brannan told him to "go back and tell Young that I'll give up the Lord's money when he sends me a receipt signed by the Lord, and no sooner!" That was the end of Brannan's relationship with the Mormon faith.

Brannan delivered the first Protestant sermon in the English language on William A. Richardson's grounds on Dupont Street. On January 9, 1847, he published his first issue of *The California Star* with the printing equipment he had brought with him on the voyage in 1846.

It was Samuel Brannan, upon his return to San Francisco from the mining camp, who shouted, "Gold from the American River!" From his enthusiasm and announcement of the discovery of gold, only seven men remained in town. All others followed Sam back to the diggings. The Odd Fellows attempt at instituting the first lodge was put on hold during this time.

Of course, Brannan's partnership with Charles C. Smith of C.C. Smith and Company store prospered. He had previously purchased all of the tools such as shovels, picks, and iron pans in advance of announcing the news of gold being discovered, which did not hurt his future prospect of becoming wealthy.

Of his many purchases of land parcels in 1849 while he was a member of the first city council, Brannan eventually built a spectacular structure named the Express Building. It was four-stories tall and was located on the northeast corner of Montgomery & California streets. The top floor was reserved for the Society of California Pioneers. In 1853, after serving as its vice president for three years, Brannan became the Society's second president, replacing W. D. M. Howard.

On February 7, 1852, Samuel and Ann Lisa Brannan deeded property on Mission Street between Sixth & Seventh streets to the Trustees for the Independent Order of Odd Fellows of San Francisco. In his later years, when Samuel was at a financial low point in his life, the Odd Fellows rewarded him for his kindness by establishing an income fund in his name, where dividends were derived from the profits of the Odd Fellows Cemetery. Samuel had given the organization this land nearly twenty-five years earlier.

Through his many enterprises, Brannan became the richest man in California. However, on May 5, 1889, in Escondido, California, he passed away a broken and penniless man. However, before his passing, he managed to obtain money from the Mexican government for lands he had held south of the Rio Grande, whereby he returned to San Francisco and paid all his debts. He was a man of honor. His body was laid to rest at Mount Hope Cemetery in San Diego, California.

Today, the Odd Fellows still retain the property on Mission Street given to them by Mr. and Mrs. Samuel Brannan. It is set up as a trust, where each Odd Fellows lodge located in the city receives a share of the profit.

On May 17, 1853, Samuel H. Parker was elected as the first Grand Master in California. He was born in New Hampshire on July 23, 1818. Parker first joined the Odd Fellows on November 4, 1842, in Massachusetts, where at that time he was practicing law. When he came to California in 1852, he was commissioned as the Deputy Grand Sire, setting the stage for his election to Grand Master. His years were dedicated to the Odd Fellows. "He gave his time and money to the improvement of the Odd Fellows' Library of San Francisco, which for many years was the leading library of the City." Samuel Parker died on March 14, 1866. In later years, Parker Street in San Francisco was named in his honor. Samuel Parker was also the President of the Fireman's Fund Insurance.

Odd Fellow members Michael and Charles de Young had established themselves as being enterprising newspapermen in San Francisco. In 1865, they established the *Dramatic Chronicle,* later called the *Chronicle*. The publishing of this newspaper was a success for the brothers.

On April 23, 1880, Charles was killed by Isaac Milton Kalloch, the son of the newly elected San Francisco mayor, Rev. Isaac Smith Kalloch. It began when the *Chronicle* had run a story related to how Kalloch was forced to leave the Boston area for questionable activities. Kalloch, in turn, retaliated by insulting the character of the de Youngs' mother, causing an upset Charles to shoot and wound the mayoral candidate. Then, after the election, Isaac Milton Kalloch shot and killed Charles at the *Chronicle* office. His brother, Michael de Young, died in 1925 at the age of 75.

In 1869, it was William C. Ralston, president of the Bank of California, who guaranteed the expenses for a special train in order to bring dignitaries of the Grand Lodge on their last leg of a long journey from Omaha to San Francisco. This was the first time that the Grand Lodge of the United States was traveling such a far distance west, and it would be very costly. Once Union Railway Pacific and the Grand Lodge of the United States received the assurances, including a $10,000 guarantee from his bank for expenses, the trip was underway. This was the same

Samuel Hale Parker. Became California's first Grand Master on May 17, 1853. He was instrumental in starting the Odd Fellows Library of San Francisco, which for many years was the leading library of the city. Parker Street bears his name.

1869 trip that brought the beloved James L. Ridgely to San Francisco, as well as other prominent members of the Order.

In 1876, Ralston built his famous Palace Hotel in San Francisco. This would later prove to be a worthy accomplishment given it had withstood the 1906 earthquake when most other buildings in the area crumbled.

Any one of several Odd Fellows has been called the "Builder of San Francisco" or "The Man that Built San Francisco," and so on . . .

CHARLES DE YOUNG.
Houseworth, Photographer, 12 Montgomery St., San Francisco.

An early photograph of Charles De Young. Caption below image reads: "CHARLES DE YOUNG. Houseworth, Photographer, 12 Montgomery St., San Francisco". Louisiana born, he was the co-founder along with his brother, Michael Harry De Young of the *Daily Morning Chronicle* newspaper (1868). (Courtesy of Bancroft Library)

William Chatman Ralston. He was a member of Templar Lodge
No. 17. Also, founder of the Bank of California in San Francisco.
(Courtesy of Bancroft Library)

William Ralston, who has already been mentioned, was one of these
men; however, it is definite that Samuel Brannan laid the foundation
for San Francisco the moment he stepped off the boat in the 1840s.

Charley Darkey Parkhurst joined Soquel Lodge No. 137 on October 18, 1867, 16 years after arriving by steamship to San Francisco. In
1851, after disembarking the *R. B. Forbes,* which had come from
Boston, Parkhurst soon became one of the toughest, most popular
stagecoach drivers in the Wild West, first driving in the gold mining
areas in the Sierra foothills.

After his death from throat cancer on December 18, 1879, it was discovered that Charley Parkhurst was actually a woman who had been posing as a man for nearly three decades, a ruse so effective that on October 17, 1868, she registered to vote in Santa Clara County. This was a time when women were not allowed to vote. There was no proof that Parkhurst voted, but since she had taken the time to register, it is presumed she would have voted. This would, of course, make her the first woman to vote in the United States.

Parkhurst was buried at the Watsonville Pioneer Odd Fellows Cemetery. Later, her remains were exhumed and reburied, with a special marker placed on her grave.

General Albert Maver Winn joined the Odd Fellows in Sacramento, California. He was an important figurehead in the area before moving to San Francisco with his wife, Catherine, in 1860.

Daniel McLaren and General Albert Maver Winn. Noted I.O.O.F. figures of the Sacramento Odd Fellows Relief Association.

Winn was instrumental in heading a joint venture between the Odd Fellows and the Masons for establishing a hospital on land which he had donated. He founded the Native Sons of the Golden West (NSGW) and the Native Daughters of the Golden West. On July 11, 1879, the first NSGW meeting was called to order at Anthony's Hall on Bush Street.

The following year, Winn founded the Sons of the American Revolution, originally the Sons of the Revolutionary Sires. He was the organization's first president. This group marched in the Independence Day Parade in 1876, which was formed at the William Ralston's Palace Hotel in San Francisco.

In 1862, Winn's wife passed away and 3 years later, on September 16, 1865, he remarried to Charlotte L. King, the widow of the crusading editor of *The San Francisco Bulletin,* James King of William, who had been shot and killed by James P. Casay in 1856.

On August 26, 1883, General Winn died. He was buried in the Pioneer Plot of the Sacramento City Cemetery. At his funeral, in which many Odd Fellows attended, the Odd Fellows reflected on General Winn's life and his active participation in fraternalism. His grave was marked by the Grand Lodge of the I.O.O.F.

Leland Stanford, a member of Sacramento Lodge No. 2, established the Leland Stanford Jr. University in nearby Palo Alto. This was in honor of his late young son, to "benefit the children of his fellow men, and the most significant gift to the [human] race ever made by any single individual." Stanford University was built because of the values Leland Stanford practiced as an Odd Fellow. He gave with his heart and joined the Odd Fellows at Sacramento Lodge No. 2 on July 6, 1861.

After trying his luck at gold mining with his brothers, Stanford moved from the mining area to San Francisco in 1856 to expand his mercantile business. In 1861, he was elected governor of California, eventually becoming a U.S. senator (California).

By all accounts, and the fact that Leland Stanford was the principal of Central Pacific Railroad, he was the person that hammered the famous golden spike in Promontory, Utah, creating the first Transcontinental Railroad. He was well aware that a visit to San Francisco by the

Leland Stanford was a member of Sacramento Lodge No. 2, and also a frequent visitor to San Francisco and surrounding areas. Established Stanford University as a tribute to his late son, Leland Stanford, Jr. (Courtesy of Bancroft Library)

Odd Fellows' Grand Sire of the United States depended on the completion of the Transcontinental Railroad. The visit by the Grand Sire and his delegation took place in September of 1869, 2 months after the completion of the railroad.

Through the efforts of Ralston and Stanford, the Odd Fellows enjoyed one of the most important and celebrated events in the history of

California Odd Fellowship. In 1869, the Grand Sire of the Order came to visit San Francisco.

Earl Warren, a member of Oakland Lodge No. 3, had been a member of another lodge in Oakland before the new Lodge No. 3 was formed on July 10, 1945. San Francisco Lodge No. 3 became defunct in 1918; the old number three was taken by the two Oakland lodges which had consolidated in 1945, where Warren was a member of one of those lodges. He is remembered for his political achievements, having been the attorney general of California, elected as governor for three terms, and appointed as the chief justice of the United States. He retired as the chief justice in 1969.

Early notable figures in Odd Fellows included Wesley F. Norcross, publisher and editor of the *New Age* publication, who operated this company for over 21 years. He later relinquished it to Dewey & Company in 1887. James F. Thompson, another Past Grand Master, was the editor and proprietor of the *Daily Standard* paper, and eventually was elected president of the California Press Association. David Newell owned the Golden Gate Sal Soda Works. Dr. William M. Milton also served as superintendent of the Odd Fellows Home for the aged. Samuel Brannan, once a popular newspaper owner and land baron, was a charter member of the Odd Fellows Templar Lodge No. 17. John Bigler was the third governor of California. Colonel Richard Rust established the boundary line between the United States and Mexico; his son, also named Richard, was an attorney in San Francisco and eventually became a superior court judge. Lucius A. Booth was governor of California in 1871. There were other prominent members as well: Horatio Stockton Winn and his brother Major General Albert Maver Winn, who was the mayor of Sacramento in 1849; James Rolph Jr. was mayor of San Francisco; Charles de Young, popular businessman and cofounder of the *San Francisco Chronicle;* the great writer William H. Barnes, who wrote of many topics primarily dealing with fraternal organizations; Nathan Porter served as a state senator until his death in 1878; George Clement Perkins was the fourteenth governor of California. Superintendent of the California Street Cable Railroad in San Francisco, James W. Harris served in that capacity for 15 years; John Geary Jr., a prominent attorney in San Francisco, worked out of the third floor of the Parrott Building. The "who's who" of Odd Fellowship in the early formation of the state of California goes on and on. In fact, most—if not all—of the founding fathers of the early towns were Odd Fellows.

John Lawrence Geary, Jr., was a member of Parker Lodge No. 124. He was one of the founders of a fraternal group named "the Supreme Executive of the Sentinels of the Universe".

George C. Perkins, was a United States Senator for California, and once the Governor of California. He was initiated into the Odd Fellows Oroville Lodge No. 59 on December 4, 1865.

Louis Leander Alexander was the Seventh Grand Master of
California. He was a member of Yerba Buena Lodge No. 15 in San
Francisco. In 1850, on his way to California, he and thousands of
others were detained at Panama from the middle of April to the
last of July. He helped organize the Odd Fellows Association,
which cared for many of those who became ill, and buried those
that died while in Panama.

Frank D. Macbeth,

Grand Master 1915-1916

Frank D. Macbeth, Grand Master in 1915. He served as the
Grand Secretary of California from 1933 to 1957. He was a
member of Pacific Lodge No. 155.

Henry S. Martin served as Sheriff of the County of San
Francisco. On December 6, 1883, he joined Franco-American
Lodge No. 207.

In 1883, William W. Morrow was the thirty-first Grand Master of California. He was a member of Apollo Lodge No. 123. He was elected several times as a member of the United States Congress. In 1891 President Harrison appointed him the United States District Judge for the Northern District of California. On May 20, 1897, President McKinley appointed Judge Morrow a U.S. Circuit Judge for the Ninth Judicial Circuit. He died on July 24, 1929.

Dr. John Frederick Morse. Born in Essex, Vermont, in
1815. He was a doctor of medicine. In 1844 he
joined the Odd Fellows, later moving to California,
where he eventually transferred his membership to
that jurisdiction. In 1869, he personally led a
delegation to plant Odd Fellowship in Germany and
Switzerland. He succeeded, despite having been
taken prisoner in the, then, existing war between
Prussia and France. He died in San Francisco on
December 30, 1874.

Odd Fellow W.A.S. Nicholson was active in San Francisco politics. He served the city in many capacities, including two terms as prosecuting Attorney. He was a member of Golden West Lodge No. 322.

F. L. Turpin was born in Lebanon, Pennsylvania, in 1847. At the early age of seventeen, he enlisted in the Union Army. After serving for the time of his enlistment in the Infantry, he re-enlisted in the 21st Pennsylvania Calvary, where he served until the end of the civil war. He came to San Francisco and organized the Columbian Banking Company. He joined California Lodge No. 1 and eventually transferred to Pacific Lodge No. 155.

An ad for the "Upton Bros. Printers". Vernon was a member of Apollo Lodge No. 123, and Brother Thomas, a member of Yerba Buena Lodge No. 15.

Frank D. Worth arrived in San Francisco in April, 1859. In 1870, he established his upholstering and decorating business near Polk and Sutter Streets. In 1888, he joined Yerba Buena Lodge No. 15, and was appointed the Chairman of the Parade Committee of the Golden Jubilee Celebration of the I.O.O.F., held in San Francisco October 18, 19, 20, 1899.

Again, any one of many members of the San Francisco Odd Fellows could have been chosen as focal point of this chapter. Whatever endeavors these men may have chosen, all shared the same fraternal organization and its causes.

CHAPTER 4

THE MOVE

In the early days of trying to settle down into one place, the Odd Fellows and the California Lodge No. 1 seemed to keep searching for the right place to call home. They moved from one location to another for various reasons and eventually found a home for their Grand Lodge.

The first meeting place was set up in a framed building owned by Levi Stowell and was on the east side Montgomery Street, between Jackson and Washington. The Odd Fellows shared this building with the Masons, another growing fraternity.

Then, an offer by Colonel J. D. Stevenson to move into the Mason's building was accepted by the young fraternal organization. The Order moved into the three story on the east side of Kearny Street, between Pine and California. And once again, the Odd Fellows shared the space with the Masons. They also shared the building with the *California Star,* a newspaper company headed by an Odd Fellows member, Samuel Brannan. The building is pictured in a Wells Fargo poster.

Located across the street from the Odd Fellows meeting place was Portsmouth Plaza, the site of many historic gatherings and events. One of these events was the hanging of John Jenkins, who, on June 9, 1851, had been accused of stealing a safe from a merchant's store. Jenkins was caught, tried by the Committee, and hanged the same night at 2:00 a.m. The Committee of Vigilance of 1851 was led by Samuel Brannan.

A fire later ravished the area, as there were many in the new city during those early days, and destroyed the building, forcing the Odd Fellows to move again. They immediately found a new home at the Gianella Building on the east side of Montgomery, between Washington and Jackson streets. The 1855 city directory lists the address as "184 Montgomery

Street, 3rd Floor." Then on April 26, 1859, the organization moved yet again to larger quarters on the northeast corner of Bush and Kearny streets.

On May 6, 1863, the Odd Fellows dedicated the site for its new building at the "corner of Montgomery and Summer Street" in the city of San Francisco. The celebration included three thousand members, many banners, and a forty-four gun salute which was fired at "sunrise, noon, and sunset." The celebration wound up at the Metropolitan Theatre, where the crowd was overflowing. And in 1865, the organization moved into its new Odd Fellows Hall on the west side of Montgomery

Odd Fellows Building at 325 Montgomery Street, San Francisco. The group moved from the location to Seventh & Market Streets in 1884. Circa 1867. T. E. Hecht, photographer.
(Courtesy of San Francisco History Center, San Francisco Public Library)

(325 Montgomery Street), between Pine and California streets. The future would hold one final move for the group.

Just a short distance away from its meeting place at 325 Montgomery Street was the Odd Fellows Savings Bank located at 238 Montgomery Street. Its president was Martin Heller. The fate of the bank is not known, but most likely it ceased after the 1906 disaster.

In May of 1884, the Odd Fellows, with several of their lodges, completed the construction of a wonderful temple—the Odd Fellows Temple. It was at Seventh and Market streets. They were now in San Francisco for good. The Odd Fellows never again left that site.

Although numerous lodges met at the Seventh & Market streets location, many others met at other locations throughout San Francisco, as no building could house the thousands of members that resided in the city.

CHAPTER 5

THE LIBRARY

There is little information that remains concerning the Odd Fellows Library; however, the importance of such a endeavor deserves mention.

The Odd Fellows in San Francisco housed one of the largest libraries in the state. It was no wonder that they also had a literary club. There were no less than twenty-six thousand volumes within it. "The Odd Fellows' Library, founded in 1854, has about 27,000 volumes, including the most valuable and extensive collections of documents and books, relating to the history of the Pacific Coast, in the world."

The Odd Fellows actually did more to promote literacy in the gold mining areas, as most of the lodges provided small selections of reading materials in the meeting halls, with a limited amount of books available to the members. Reading and storytelling were some of the only forms of entertainment at the numerous mines. It was natural that the lodges in San Francisco would create a library for their members. In 1854, in San Francisco, during one of the sessions of the Grand Lodge, the membership approved the establishment of a new library.

Answering a challenge of what the Odd Fellows could do to encourage readers of young age to read "good" books, Mr. George A. Carnes, librarian, of the Odd Fellows Library Association of San Francisco, stated the following:

"Even a child knows that forbidden fruit is the sweetest on the branch. If you wish to compel a boy or girl to read a given book, strictly forbid him even to take it from the shelves. The tabooed books will somehow be secured in spite of their withdrawal."

No. 10739.8.

EXTRACT FROM THE

BY-LAWS

OF THE

Odd Fellows' Library

ASSOCIATION

OF SAN FRANCISCO.

———•◦•———

This Book may be kept Two Weeks.

For each day kept over the above time, the holder will be subject to a forfeit of five cents.

If a work of one volume be injured or lost, the same to be made good to the Librarian.

If a volume or more of a set of books be injured or lost, the full value of the set must be paid.

Press _____ Shelf _____

A rare label numbered "10739.S." from a book that once belonged to the Odd Fellows Library.

Much of the Odd Fellows' collection of books in San Francisco was destroyed in the earthquake and fire of 1906; however, books may still be found from time to time with the Odd Fellows Library label on the inside cover. There are only a few reminders of the great libraries that existed in the times prior to 1906.

Many of the Odd Fellows publications prior to the earthquake and fire of 1906 and after were printed by local member Joseph Winterburn, of Winterburn Company, Printers and Electrotypers, San Francisco, 417 Clay Street.

Joseph Winterburn was born in Northampton, England, March 9, 1836. He arrived in San Francisco on April 4, 1850, to seek his fortune. He learned the trade of printing with "Whitton, Towne, & Co.", and later established his own printing company: "Jos. Winterburn & Co." in 1866 at 417 Clay Street. His company printed many of the Odd Fellows booklets during the 1800's, where much of the material for this research was found.

CHAPTER 6

THE CEMETERY

Around 1850, member Samuel Brannan donated twenty-seven acres of land to the Odd Fellows for its first cemetery in San Francisco.

In 1865, with the approval of the Grand Lodge of California in keeping with its precept of "burying the dead," the Odd Fellows in San Francisco established a large cemetery with the founding of the Odd Fellows' Cemetery Association. On November 26, 1865, the newly acquired

Camp Merritt. Site of Odd Fellows cemetery is in far background, San Francisco. Circa 1898. (Courtesy of Bancroft Library)

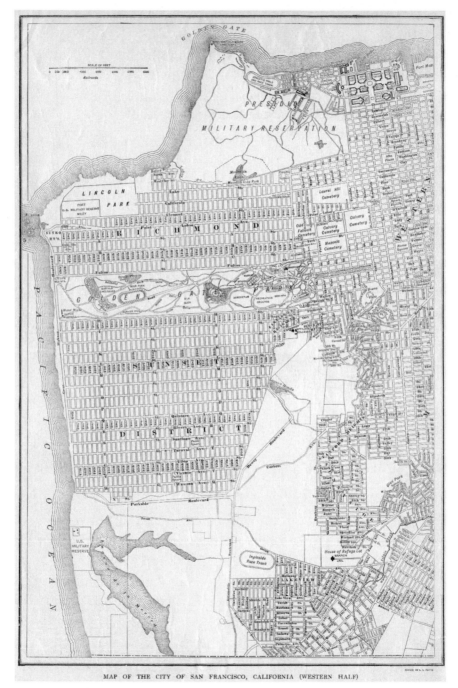

MAP OF THE CITY OF SAN FRANCISCO, CALIFORNIA (WESTERN HALF)

City of San Francisco map. Location of Odd Fellows cemetery is shown.

An entrance to the San Francisco Odd Fellows Cemetery. The Cemetery no longer exists. Today, only the Columbarium remains, which is now owned and operated by the Neptune Society.

grounds for the cemetery were dedicated. The master of ceremonies was Past Grand Master Samuel H. Parker. The Committee on Dedication included Charles Langley, George T. Bohen, Henry C. Squire, Henry B. Brooks, and James Adams. The listed location of the cemetery at the time of the dedication was Point Lobos Road, in San Francisco.

The cemetery surrounded the Odd Fellows Columbarium, built in 1898. This is the only remaining structure from the Richmond District cemeteries. The cemetery's boundaries were "irregular," falling between Arguello, Geary, Stanyan, Anza, Parker, and Turk streets.

At the time it was built, the Columbarium was considered the "finest" in the world. Today, the Columbarium is owned and operated by the Neptune Society. By definition, a columbarium houses numerous niches, which contain urns holding the ashes of cremated bodies.

In the 1890s, the corporation added a structure to handle the remains of those departed: a crematorium. The association strongly supported the idea of cremations, promoting the relatively new concept with a lengthy brochure. According to the California Genealogical

Image of the Odd Fellows Cemetery, San Francisco, circa 1900 (from "3D" stereoscope card).

Society, there were "10,000 records of cremations, dating 1895 to 1911," some of which included the cremating of disinterred burials from years earlier. The Odd Fellows Crematorium was busy.

Odd Fellow member George T. Bohen was the first president of The Odd Fellows Cemetery Association. Many prominent members of the Order were buried in the cemetery, as so stated in an excerpt from the book *Fifty Years of Odd Fellowship*. Facing the front of the Columbarium: "to the left [is] the last resting places of [Samuel] Parker, [George] Bohen, [Dr. John Frederick] Morse, and [Elias D.] Farnsworth." Also near the Columbarium was the sarcophagus of Congressman Piper.

This is a funeral, with James Harris wearing regalia on right side.

Bird's eye view of the San Francisco Odd Fellows Cemetery in 1899. The Columbarium still remains. Note the Crematorium in the right background. The cemetery was approximately located between Geary and Turk Streets.

The American Architect and Building News, February 4, 1899. No. 1206.

Copyright, 1899, by the American Architect and Building News Co.

COLUMBARIUM OF THE INDEPENDENT ORDER OF ODD FELLOWS, SAN FRANCISCO, CAL.

Columbarium of the Independent Order of Odd Fellows, San Francisco, 1906.
Today, surrounding graves no longer exist.

Interior of the Columbarium, 1899.

Crematorium.

Monument of Elias Driggs Farnsworth. In 1869, as Grand Sire of the Odd Fellows, he visited the State of California. He enjoyed his visits so much to the region that he retired to San Francisco after his term was completed. He lived in the city for 23 years before his passing.

Monument for Nathan Porter in the San Francisco Odd Fellows Cemetery. Nathan Porter was born in 1817. He was a longtime member of the Odd Fellows. He was once a member of Yerba Buena Lodge No. 15. At the time of his death on January 6, 1878, he was serving as a State Senator.

Brother Bohen arrived in San Francisco in November 1850. He transferred his membership from Baltimore, Maryland, and joined Yerba Buena Lodge No. 15 in 1853 (a lodge which still exists today). He was elected president of the Cemetery Association when it was organized and had been active in all aspects of the Odd Fellows' activities.

The Odd Fellows welcomed any religious denomination to use their chapel inside the Columbarium "free of charge, or restrictions of any character whatever."

"Odd Fellows do not feel the repugnance to death which is too often met with the thought coming to us through our ritual that those who have passed on are not dead, but simply asleep, to awake again in a better and purer environment." While the Odd Fellows Cemetery Association handled much of the business, the superintendent of the Odd Fellows' Cemetery, George R. Fletcher, a longtime member of the Odd Fellows, superintended the Columbarium and Crematorium. It was said he was dedicated to his work of overseeing the cremations. ". . . this man has made so careful a study of the entire subject-matter that from the time you enter the Crematorium with a body, until the entire work

George T. Bohen was the original President of the Odd Fellows Cemetery Association in San Francisco. In 1853, he became a member of Yerba Buena Lodge No. 15, before transferring his membership to another San Francisco Lodge—Pacific Lodge No. 155—in order to help institute that lodge. Mr. Bohen was one of the organizers and Commander of Golden Gate Battalion, Uniformed Patriarch. He was disappointed the Odd Fellows moved from its Montgomery Street property to Seventh & Market Streets. His remains rest in the San Francisco Columbarium, which was once in his charge.

Chapel.

of incineration has been performed, not a word is spoken, but everything is done automatically by the touch of a bell. You cannot fail to admire the genius of the man."

In the 1880s, the residential development had reached the cemetery and the San Francisco supervisors later established a law to prevent any further burials after 1901. After years of neglect and the damage from the 1906 earthquake and pressure from the local city government, twenty-eight thousand bodies were moved from the Odd Fellows Cemetery between 1929 and 1934. Today, many of these departed members rest in a mass grave on a neglected piece of land in Colma, California.

In 1904, the San Francisco Odd Fellows Cemetery Association purchased land in San Mateo County (Colma) from Mr. Morris Siminoff. A year later, the Odd Fellows Cemetery Association entered a highly controversial contract hiring the Golden Gate Land Association to lay out the new cemetery (Greenlawn), paying for this service with one-half of the proceeds from the sale of cemetery plots.

The general membership of the Order did not receive the arrangement between the Odd Fellows Cemetery Association and the Golden Gate Land Association very well. In fact, the membership ordered an

George T. Fletcher, was elected to the position of Superintendent of the Odd Fellows Cemetery in 1885. He was a member of the Alta Lodge No. 205.

H. E. SNOOK,
Apollo Lodge, No. 123

G. W. KEELER,
Excelsior Lodge, No. 310

G. P. PRECHTEL
Unity Lodge, No. 131

Golden Gate Undertaking Company

FUNERAL DIRECTORS

×————AND————×

PRACTICAL EMBALMERS

Special Attention Given to Shipping Bodies.

Every Requisite for First - class Funerals.

Lady Attendants at all hours.

2425=2429 Mission Street

NORTH OF TWENTY-FIRST

❧ ❧ ❧

THE FINEST PRIVATE PARLORS IN THE CITY

OPEN DAY AND NIGHT

❧ ❧ ❧

Telephone Mission 102

An ad for the Golden Gate Undertaking Company. All three proprietors are members of different Odd Fellows Lodges in San Francisco.

investigation of the transaction of both these corporations. It turned out the Odd Fellows Cemetery Association essentially gave away its total control of the new cemetery by allowing the Land Association one-half of the proceeds, whereby the Golden Gate Land Association was using the name of "Odd Fellows" to promote the sales of plots. It allowed those not belonging to the Order to purchase these plots, but little could be done and the Odd Fellows Cemetery Association endured harsh skepticism ever since.

The resulting dilemma between the Odd Fellows Cemetery Association and the Golden Gate Land Association was finally resolved through a Special Committee for the Odd Fellows Cemetery Association. In its 1906 report, it was stated the Odd Fellows' Cemetery Association had "no legal relations or affiliations with the Order."

San Franciscan Charles De Young was a prominent member of the Odd Fellows. Lower portion of monument was left behind when it moved to Cypress Lawn Memorial Park in Colma, CA. (Courtesy of San Francisco History Center, San Francisco Public Library)

This report was approved, despite the fact that the land had been purchased by the Odd Fellows, dedicated by the Odd Fellows in 1865, named the Odd Fellows Cemetery, held the graves of thousands of Odd Fellows, and was managed exclusively by members of Odd Fellows. The name of the cemetery had always been the Odd Fellows Cemetery. Never was its relationship to the Order questioned, not until the dealings with an outside organization such as Golden Gate Land Association in 1904. Regardless, the Odd Fellows Cemetery was always under the auspices of the Order until it was divorced by the Order.

In 1851, years prior to the establishment of a cemetery at Geary and Masonic streets, the Odd Fellows selected a piece of land between Sixth & Seventh streets, on Mission Street, to be used as a cemetery. It was Noble Grand Samuel Brannan who kindly donated this plot of land for that purpose. However, no one was ever buried at this location and the property eventually became a source of revenue for lodges in the city, being set up as a trust after a court battle years later between relatives of the late Samuel Brannan and the Odd Fellows.

CHAPTER 7

THE ODD FELLOWS BUILDING—1884

O n December 1, 1884, after construction of the new Odd Fellows Building at Seventh & Market streets, the Odd Fellows had found their permanent home. The Odd Fellows Building was a beautiful structure made of bright red brick. It was the flagship home for the organization. The Odd Fellows Hall Association of San Francisco was created to maintain and care for the building. It was comprised of many representatives and shareholders from each of the lodges in the city.

Michael H. de Young, for whom the de Young Museum was named, and the owner of the San Francisco *Chronicle* newspaper, was the chairman of the dedication ceremony of the new Odd Fellows Building.

The Odd Fellows Building housed the Odd Fellows Literary and Social Club at Seventh & Market streets. The objective was the improvement of members' knowledge about the work of the Order, as well as for social and literary purposes.

There is very little written history about the Odd Fellows Building at Seventh & Market streets because most—if not all—of the records were destroyed almost immediately after the earthquake in 1906. What records do exist are a few scattered years of annual recordings of the Odd Fellows Hall Association, most likely finding their way back to the Odd Fellows via members of the Order, after the Great Quake. The chairman of the building committee, Mr. Jules Cerf, spent 2 years overseeing the construction of the Odd Fellows Temple until the new building was finished.

"Our Temple is completed; may it always be the fountain from which shall continuously flow living streams of relief to the distressed

Drawing of the original Odd Fellows building in the 1880's, at Seventh & Market Streets.

and afflicted ones of our Order; and may it be the magnet that draw to our folds all the right-thinking, pure-minded men of our city" (A. W. Scott, president of the Odd Fellows Hall Association).

In the year 1887, twenty-three Odd Fellows lodges, three Rebekah [Degree] lodges, five I.O.O.F. Encampments, the Odd Fellows Literary and Social Club, a Degree Lodge, three Parlors Native Sons of the Golden West, one Court of the Ancient Order of Foresters, and one

Great image of the Odd Fellows Building at Seventh & Market Streets, in 1904.

Union of the Brotherhood of Carpenters and Joiners met in the large lodge rooms above the ground floor.

Some various craftsmen were selected for their expertise to construct the Odd Fellows Building at Seventh & Market streets during the year of 1885 to 1887; the following is a listing of these early San Franciscans:

Will & Finck: switch to annunciator and installation of brass bars at
    windows
J. H. Jackson: installation of lights in basement
P. H. Jackson: two hitching posts (for horses)

Stationery depicting Odd Fellows Building, dated May 2, 1899.

Ames & Detrick: awnings
E. H. Black: painting section letters
Wright & Sanders: balance of commissions
J. G. Leibert: brickwork
E. Farrell: carpenter
G. Griffiths: granite
R. Llewellyn: cast Iron
E. A. Rix: wrought Iron
Cronin & Dunbar: tin and slate
Geo. Milne: plumber
A. C. Corbett: plasterer
E. M. Gallagher: painting
Davis & Cowell: cement

On May 14, 1884, the cornerstone of the new foundation was laid.

In 1888, while the building was still new, it was reported that there were several problems relating to the plumbing and many costly repairs that had to be tended. The repairs "being upwards of $600, or

1884 dedication coin of the Odd Fellows Building
at Seventh & Market Streets.

Ribbon celebrating the laying of the
cornerstone of the new Odd Fellows
Building, May 14, 1884.

nearly as much as was expended the preceding year for all repairs. This indicates either defective work or defective material, or both, done during the progress of construction."

Odd Fellow John Daly, for whom a nearby city is now named, was one of the association's thirty-six directors for many years.

As the years passed, the condition of the building was often noted in the Hall Association's reports. It seems the Hall Association, with this "new building," continually had to deal with many ongoing issues. One of them was the flooding of the basement due to the cutting of a main drain by the sidewalk elevator installers—A. J. McNicoll & Co. They had tried to conceal it before the Odd Fellows could make the discovery, but eventually, this would be repaired.

> "I feel compelled to call attention to the condition of the walls throughout the building, especially the whitewalls. They are in exceedingly dirty condition, and such walls are studded and badly cracked; owing, I presume, to the shrinkage of the timber."

In 1892, it was reported that forty-nine organizations now used the floors above the street level. While the needs of the building were always demanding, use of the building never diminished.

Later, in that same year, new lighting was being installed; this was the Welsbach light.

The Odd Fellows basement was called the Good Fellows' Grotto. According to the *Daily Alta Newspaper,* dated May 7, 1891, the Grotto was a "first class restaurant."

Much work was done to the basement. Some of the contractors who worked on the facility were as follows:

Joseph Musto, marble work; G. Eastman, plumbing; A. M. Bruce, iron work; and L. Schmidt, carpentering.

It is ironic that in 1899, just as today, the Odd Fellows Hall Association hoped for improvement in the area. "The construction of the new Post Office and Federal Court building on Seventh Street, which

Moses Greenbaum was born in Germany in 1833. He
came to the United States in 1847. Upon moving to San
Francisco five years later, he transferred to the Bay City
Lodge No. 71. For fifteen years, he served as a Director
for the San Francisco Odd Fellows Hall Association. In
1895, he was elected Grand Treasurer for the Grand
Lodge of California.

is, at last, proceeding with some degree of rapidity, will greatly improve
the neighborhood."

For the next several years, the Odd Fellows Building stood as a
jewel in the city of San Francisco. The Order was thriving and membership growing to its highest levels ever. Nothing it seemed could slow
down the expansion of the Odd Fellowship. Everything was good—
until April 18, 1906.

Evidence of a one-time active order. Picture taken at the Odd Fellows Building at Seventh & Market Streets, 1904.

Many other organizations, businesses, clubs, and fraternal organizations grew in San Francisco, and the Odd Fellows soon faced the realization that their existence was in serious jeopardy because after residing in the City-by-the-Bay for 57 years, there occurred the worst catastrophic event on historical record in the state of California. Saving the organization would take a miracle—and a bit of pure determination.

CHAPTER 8

THE EVENTS

Many significant events—literally hundreds—which were reported in every local newspaper, took place at the Odd Fellows Building and in the city of San Francisco. There were weekly dances, plays, skits, and theater-types of entertainment at the Odd Fellows Building. Outside organizations also used available spaces for events. In most cases, these events were opened to everyone—members and nonmembers alike.

Events included acts by local entertainers such as "Frankie & Johnnie," who always promised to get the audience singing before they finished a show. Artists' performances were provided by the National Broadcasting Service, whose offices were located at 111 Sutter Street in San Francisco; and various movies were provided by Ford Motor Company. Only a handful of these events are mentioned in this text.

THURSDAY DECEMBER 10, 1936
SPECIAL COLLAR AND JEWEL
DINNER AND WHIST PARTY
THURSDAY DECEMBER 10th 6 P. M.
IN ODD FELLOWS BUILDING
BY BAY VIEW REBEKAH LODGE No. 317
DINNER AND WHIST 50 CENTS
DINNER 35 CENTS
WHIST 25 CENTS
FIRST PRIZE $5.00
DONT FORGET THE DATE DECEMBER 10, 1936

Dinners, parties, and other events were a regular occurrence at the Odd Fellows Building.

The events change as the times change, circa 1920. This event was hosted by the Loyal Rebekah Lodge No. 215.

FRANKIE and JOHNNIE

Sensational Singing Act

In the Gay Nineties

A Sure-fire Attraction

Featuring Oldtime Songs and Community Singing, Solos and Harmony Numbers

▼

An Earful of Excellent Entertainment

▲

Under Exclusive Management of

Phone GArfield 0515   **MARIE HURSEY**   Res. PRospect 8705

BRADBURY AGENCY

68 POST STREET, Suite 217   SAN FRANCISCO, CALIF.

An advertisement for "Frankie and Johnnie", a popular act in the era of vaudeville. They performed at the Odd Fellows Building.

Amity Rebekah Lodge, No. 161, I.O.O.F.

Memorial Hall, Odd Fellows Building

We cordially invite you and your friends to attend a,

Night in Japan, Saturday Evening

Saturday – June 8 , 191 2.

Admission 25 cents

Drill by 12 Giesha Girls

Entertainment Committee

"Night in Japan" event, hosted by Amity Rebekah Lodge No. 161. 1912.

GOLDEN WEST ATHLETIC CLUB

BENEFIT

CARNIVAL AND WHIST

WHIST PRIZES	DOOR PRIZES
$10.00 CASH	$10.00 FIRST PRIZE
& MERCHANDISE	SEVERAL OTHERS

GIRLS POPULARITY CONTEST
WINGO AND OTHER GAMES

TO BE HELD

THURSDAY EVENING, APRIL 30, 1936

ODD FELLOWS BLDG.

26 - 7TH ST.

STARTING 8 P. M.

Games at the I.O.O.F. building.

S. F. Theta Rho Girls Club No. 11
S. F. Lodge Junior Order No. 11
J. O. O. F.
cordially invites you to attend the
Joint Public Installation of Officers
Saturday Evening, October 9, 1937
at eight o'clock
Memorial Hall J. O. O. F. Building
7th and Market Street
San Francisco, California
Dancing, with Krausgrill's Orchestra

The children of the Odd Fellows thrived in the 1930's in San Francisco. Circa 1937.

DON'T MISS

Something doing every minute

~GAMES~
VAUDEVILLE ACTS
FREE DANCING
GOOD MUSIC
FREE GATE PRIZE

CARNIVAL
AND
BAZAAR

GIVEN BY
Morse Lodge No. 257
and
Golden Gate Encampment No. 1
Benefit of S. F. Junior Lodge No. 11
ENCAMPMENT HALL 6th FLOOR

SATURDAY

SEPTEMBER 25

8:30 P. M.
ADMISSION FREE

Event to benefit San Francisco Junior
Lodge No. 11. Circa 1940.

OFFICERS AND COMMITTEES
For Term Ending June 30,
1937

Noble Grand...................F. R. MacCubbin
3332 Twenty-first Street, San Francisco
VAlencia 4766

Vice Grand.................C. W. English, P. G.
1541 California Street, San Francisco
Telephone GRaystone 3880

Treasurer ....N. Angus, P. G.
238 Point Lobos Avenue, San Francisco
SKyline 2949

Recording Secretary..........F. Jackson, P. G.
471 Rolph Street, San Francisco
Telephone RAndolph 3981

Financial Secretary......Samuel Burton, P. G.
575 Eighteenth Avenue, San Francisco
BAyview 9146

Entertainment Committee
C. W. English, P. G.
A. Raissle, P. G.   R. E. Briggs, P. G.
H. F. Byrne, P. G.   O. E. Buchecker

Finance Committee
M. Abrahams, P. G.
O. E. Buchecker   J. A. Madsen, P. G.

Good and Welfare
Samuel Burton, P. G.
R. Scott, P. G.   F. Jackson, P. G.
N. Angus, P. G.   H. E. Nott, P. G.

CALIFORNIA LODGE
No. 1, I. O. O. F.
MAY - 1937
Meets every Monday Evening
Welcome Hall - Odd Fellows' Temple
26 Seventh Street, San Francisco

OFFICERS AND COMMITTEES
For Term Ending June 30,
1937

Noble Grand...................F. R. MacCubbin
3332 Twenty-first Street, San Francisco
VAlencia 4766

Vice Grand.................C. W. English, P. G.
1541 California Street, San Francisco
Telephone GRaystone 3880

Treasurer ....N. Angus, P. G.
238 Point Lobos Avenue, San Francisco
SKyline 2949

Recording Secretary..........F. Jackson, P. G.
471 Rolph Street, San Francisco
Telephone RAndolph 3981

Financial Secretary......Samuel Burton, P. G.
575 Eighteenth Avenue, San Francisco
BAyview 9146

Entertainment Committee
C. W. English, P. G.
A. Raissle, P. G.   R. E. Briggs, P. G.
H. F. Byrne, P. G.   O. E. Buchecker

Finance Committee
M. Abrahams, P. G.
O. E. Buchecker   J. A. Madsen, P. G.

Good and Welfare
Samuel Burton, P. G.
R. Scott, P. G.   F. Jackson, P. G.
N. Angus, P. G.   H. E. Nott, P. G.

Program

CALIFORNIA
LODGE
No. 1, I.O.O.F.

JULY, 1937

Meets every Monday
evening

WELCOME HALL
ODD FELLOWS TEMPLE
26 SEVENTH ST.
SAN FRANCISCO, CAL.

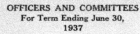

Various Programs for semi-annual installations of officers. California Lodge No. 1.

OFFICERS AND COMMITTEES
For Term Ending June 30,
1937

Noble Grand................F. R. MacCubbin
3332 Twenty-first Street, San Francisco
VAlencia 4766

Vice Grand................C. W. English, P. G.
1541 California Street, San Francisco
Telephone GRaystone 3880

Treasurer ....N. Angus, P. G.
238 Point Lobos Avenue, San Francisco
SKyline 2949

Recording Secretary.........F. Jackson, P. G.
471 Rolph Street, San Francisco
Telephone RAndolph 3981

Financial Secretary......Samuel Burton, P. G.
575 Eighteenth Avenue, San Francisco
BAyview 9146

Entertainment Committee
C. W. English, P. G.
A. Raissle, P. G.   R. E. Briggs, P. G.
H. F. Byrne, P. G.   O. E. Buchecker

Finance Committee
M. Abrahams, P. G.
O. E. Buchecker   J. A. Madsen, P. G.

Good and Welfare
Samuel Burton, P. G.
R. Scott, P. G.   F. Jackson, P. G.
N. Angus, P. G.   H. E. Nott, P. G.

CALIFORNIA LODGE
No. 1
I. O. O. F.

APRIL - 1937

*Meets Every Monday
Evening*

WELCOME HALL
ODD FELLOWS TEMPLE
26 SEVENTH ST.   SAN FRANCISCO

Various Programs for semi-annual installations of officers. California Lodge No. 1.

An 1800's photo of Morrison Point, Russian River, where many of the San Francisco Odd Fellows Lodges frequented for picnics.

ODD FELLOWS RECREATION CLUB
ON THE RUSSIAN RIVER

GUERNEVILLE
CALIFORNIA

7TH & MARKET STS.
SAN FRANCISCO

Directors:
ALBERT BALLMER
FRED BOEKEN
C. A. CORBIN
C. B. JESSEN
A. C. LINDGREN
A. D. KETTERLIN
E. Z. RICHARDSON
W. C. THOMAS

An Odd Fellows playground
of 217 acres with over one
mile of river frontage where
members and their families
may enjoy, amid the scenic
splendors, swimming, hiking,
boating and other recreations
in the redwoods.

C. B. JESSEN, President
224 Washington St.
Box 690   Petaluma, Calif.

C. A. CORBIN, Sec'y
Box 505   Petaluma, Calif.

CLUB GROUNDS   Phone Forestville 29-F-2

October 26, 1937.

Magnolia Lodge Nᵛ. 29,
I.O.O.F.,
San Francisco, Calif.

Dear Brothers:-

        We are enclosing information relative to
our 4% Bonds now available only to Odd Fellows,
Rebekahs, I.O.O.F. lodges and the other branches of
the order.

        We believe this to be an attractive issue
due to our set-up and plan of retiring these bonds.

        Should you desire further information,
kindly let us know.

        We trust we may receive your application
for some of those bonds. They will draw interest from
the date we receive payment for same.

                    Sincerely yours,

                    ODD FELLOWS RECREATION CLUB

                    C. B. Jessen.

Enc.   C. B. Jessen, President.

Odd Fellows Recreation Club correspondence, 1937. Today, the Odd Fellows still use the Russian River facilities.

What was probably the grandest event of the Order happened in September of 1869. The Grand Sire Elias Driggs Farnsworth, along with a delegation of 122 representatives and others, traveled to California by train. This had never been done before in the history of the Order. Both the Union Pacific and Central Pacific Railroads brought

Elias Driggs Farnsworth, Past Grand Sire. Born in
Hartford, Connecticut, December 16, 1818; died in
San Francisco, California, March 29, 1893.

this party to California on different legs of the journey. This was the
first time this Grand Body ever met west of the Missouri River.

In fact, in 1869, the Grand Lodge of the United States achieved the
distinction of being the first organized body to cross the continent "by
rail" from one seaboard to the other, when it held its session in San
Francisco. Most of these dignitaries had originated from the East Coast.

It goes without saying that this would not have been possible if
the railroad was not completed on time. Not only did the railroad have
to be completely constructed in time, but financial backing needed to
be guaranteed for the transportation of the delegation from Omaha to
Sacramento, which was done.

A generous free passage proposal by Templar Lodge No. 17, of
San Francisco, to the Grand Sire and his officers took care of the

problem. The sum of $10,000 was underwritten by the president of California Bank, William Chapman Ralston, who was also a member of Templar Lodge.

This visitation by the Grand Lodge of the United States was made almost immediately after the last spike—the Golden Spike—was pounded into the last piling (on May 10, 1869) at Promontory Summit, in Promontory, Utah, completing the first transcontinental railroad.

The large delegation arrived in San Francisco on September 16, 1869, via Sacramento, where the Grand Sire had previously laid the cornerstone for the new Sacramento Temple.

When the delegation reached the California Theatre in San Francisco, the Grand Master of California John Brown Harmon spoke to an excited audience. Then, the Grand Sire spoke. A jubilant crowd roaring with the expectation of hearing from James L. Ridgely shouted, "Ridgely, Ridgely, Ridgely." Someone in the audience then shouted "Light—a thousand dollars for light!" At that moment, every gas light in the theatre came on. This was a moment none in the audience would ever forget.

Ridgely was one of the most prominent Odd Fellows in the history of the Order in America, and he visited San Francisco. The Secretary of the Grand Lodge of the United States, the beloved James L. Ridgely, had been welcomed by thousands of Odd Fellows as he departed a boat coming from Alameda after an earlier visit. The procession that greeted him at the docks included a "platoon of police and a regiment of the National Guard, followed by thousands of Odd Fellows in full regalia to the Great California Theatre." The California theater was located on Bush Street.

All the visitors were transported by carriages to the theater. The cheers were deafening and only stopped when Ridgely spoke. He was humbled by the welcome. Years before, he had been credited with reviving the values of the Odd Fellows by changing the old image of a "bunch of drinkers" to an honorable band of brothers.

The visiting members enjoyed their time in San Francisco. On Friday afternoon, September 24, 1869, the Grand Lodge of the United States

James L. Ridgely. Born in Baltimore, the birthplace of American Odd Fellowship, January 27, 1807. He is "conceded to be the benefactor of American Odd Fellowship". Noted for writing the Past Grand's charge in the Odd Fellows Ritual.

"in full regalia, by invitation visited the Seventh Industrial Exhibition of the Mechanic's Institute." The delegation was never still as it was invited to many events. The event concluded on September 25, 1869.

Some individuals credit the continued expansion of the West with this particular event. According to the *Fifty Years of Odd Fellowship in California* (1899), the visit did more for California as a state than it did for the Order in the state.

"All that our visiting brethren saw was a new revelation to them and to the millions of people among whom they lived in their far Eastern homes, and those of them who still survive have not yet ceased talking of what they saw, singing the praises of California. Their reports of the visit and what they saw and learned on that trip, made in their Eastern lodges and on public occasions at their respective homes, added many thousands to the population of California and the great but hitherto unknown West."

On December 11, 1890, the Women's Educational and Industrial Union held a benefit event which showcased many performances. The Odd Fellows Building was the venue for this wonderful event. It was a smashing success. The king of Hawaii, King Kalakaua, even came to see the show.

The Odd Fellows Building housed one of the most important musical events of the nineteenth century in December of 1890. Vladimir de Pachmann, considered the greatest pianist of his time, performed four times in the building, emphasizing the music of Chopin.

In the Hall Association report of 1897, an interesting report by its president was submitted which contained a story as follows: "In August last [1896] the officers of the library and other tenants of this building complained of being disturbed by the Socialist Labor Party, which frequently congregated on Seventh Street, near Market, for the purpose of holding 'open air' political meetings. It was represented to them that their exhortations disturbed the lodge's meeting in the building and were annoying to those in the reading rooms of the library. They were respectfully asked to discontinue their meetings at that particular place, which they positively refused to do." Eventually, the speakers were arrested and prosecuted, thereby ending the problem.

On May 22, 1898, soldiers, many of whom were members of the Order on their way to Manila to fight in the insurrection, were welcomed into the building. They were sent to battle with full stomachs and with "Godspeed" and primed by several motivating speeches. After the conclusion of the war, the soldiers were again welcomed home and again shown a wonderful feast and given many thankful speeches. In return, the Idaho Regiment presented its host, Bay City Lodge No. 71, a gavel made of wood from a Spanish garrote, and a silver badge of the Odd Fellows' Association of Manila.

In 1904, the Odd Fellows had welcomed its Sovereign Grand Lodge to the city of San Francisco. In its honor, the organization held a celebration that was called the "Odd Fellows' Celebration—Illuminations

Volunteers returning from the Philippines. In 1898, fighting men had been given a proper send-off by the Odd Fellows of San Francisco, and greeted upon their return. Bay City.

The U.S.S. Hancock. This ship served its troops in the Philippine war.

Fourth of July procession in 1899, also celebrating the return of the troops.

On Market Street," where thousands of lights lit up Market Street from the Ferry Building to the City Hall. Hundreds of thousands of lights were used in the event and the result was nothing short of spectacular. The decorations included lighted symbols representative of and unique to Odd Fellowship: the all-seeing eye, the three links of friendship, love, and truth; and much more. Thousands of people enjoyed the display.

On September 19, 1904, at 8:00 p.m., the officers of the Sovereign Grand Lodge were treated to an evening of entertainment at the Mechanics' Pavilion on Larkin Street. There were several musical events presented during the evening. The orchestra, under direction of Professor Carl Sawvell, played a "Welcome" to the honored guests. The Knickerbocker Quartette also performed, following performances by Susie A. Pracy and H. S. Stedman, a pianist and an organist respectively. Soloists Lulu Purlenky, a contralto, and Robert W. Jones, a baritone, each gave the audience their best renditions of "Let Me Love Thee" ("Arditi") and "Queen of the Earth" ("Penseti").

It is of particular interest that for many years in the early days of California Odd Fellowship, whenever a Sovereign Grand Master, or

Images from Odd Fellows light show on Market
Street, in 1904.

Odd Fellows light show on Market Street, in 1904.

Odd Fellows light show on Market Street, in 1904.

"Grand Sire" as the title was later changed, was visiting the state, he would normally be greeted by the governor.

In 1905, the Grand Master challenged the membership in California to reach a level of 40,000 members by the end of his term. The Order reached 40,000 that year and had a statewide celebration aptly named "California's 40,000 Night," and was celebrated at each lodge throughout the state. This was called "the grandest conception ever recorded in the history of our Order."

For any organization to have reached a membership of 40,000 in a state was phenomenal at that time. To reach that number in less than 57 years is amazing. For the next 20 years, that number would only grow.

The Odd Fellows and all of its Grand Bodies participated in the 1915 Panama–Pacific International Exposition in San Francisco as did

Apollo Lodge No. 123, with other members of the order, at the 1915 Panama Pacific International Exposition.

Odd Fellows participating in parade. September 20, 1904.

Executive Committee for Reception of the Sovereign Grand Lodge
I. O. O. F., SAN FRANCISCO, CAL., SEPTEMBER 20-25, 1915

Fac-simile of Badge

OFFICERS AND COMMITTEES

Jas. W. Harris, Grand Treasurer, President
H. D. Richardson, Grand Secretary, Secretary
C. E. Benedict, Grand Treas., Grand Encpt. Treasurer
U. S. G. Clifford, Asst. Grand Secy., Asst. Secretary
Mary E. Donoho, Sec. Rebekah Assembly, Asst. Secretary
J. K. Ritter, Maj.-Gen. Dept. Cal., Patriarchs Militant
John Glasson, P. G. M.—Badge
Wm. H. Barnes, Grand Scribe Grand Encpt.—Prizes
John Hazlett, Trustee Odd Fellows Home—Hotels
Geo. F. Hudson, P. G. M.—Music
H. D. Richardson, Grand Secretary—Printing
Henry Jacks, P. G.—Finance
T. B. W. Leland, P. G.—Parade, Grand Marshal

VICE PRESIDENTS

Frank D. Macbeth, Grand Master
Wm. P. Schlosser, Deputy Grand Master
C. H. Connick, Grand Warden
John Glasson, P. G. M., P. G. R., Grand Trustee
W. W. Phelps, P. G. M., Grand Representative
W. W. Watson, P. G. M., P. G. R.
T. H. Selvage, P. G. M., P. G. R.
A. P. Johnson, Jr., P. G. M., Grand Representative
E. H. Black, P. G. P., Grand Representative
Geo. F. Ward, P. G. P., Grand Representative
Geo. E. Davis, P. G. P., P. G. R.
W. M. Avis, Grand Patriarch
Adele Stockwell, President Rebekah Assembly
Page Desda Ritter, Vice President Rebekah Assembly
Emily M. Knoph, Warden Rebekah Assembly
Fannie M. Lacy, Past President Rebekah Assembly
Tillie Craig, Trustee I. O. O. F. Orphans Home
D. A. Sinclair, Trustee Odd Fellows Home

ODD FELLOWS BUILDING
Seventh and Market Streets

SAN FRANCISCO, CALIFORNIA
AUGUST 6, 1915

Special Parade Circular

PARADE COMMITTEE
T. B. W. LELAND,
Chairman
J. B. OUTLAND
FRANK D. WORTH
H. W. OSTHOFF
A. W. BENEDICT
M. H. LUDLOW
L. LORENZEN
W. H. WHIMS
THEO. TREYER
FRANK ROTHING
O. H. HARDGROVE

To Subordinate Lodges, Encampments, Rebekah Lodges and Patriarch Militants, I. O. O. F., of California. Greetings:

The Annual Session of the Sovereign Grand Lodge, I. O. O. F., will be held in San Francisco from September 20 to 25, 1915.

On Wednesday, September 22nd, at 10 a. m. will be held a Grand Parade. As this occasion will mark the presentation of our Order before the citizens of San Francisco and the visiting public, we must see to it that this public appearance will be made in a manner most creditable to our Order.

Your Parade Committee, therefore, invite your most loyal, earnest and enthusiastic cooperation in accomplishing this laudable object.

The time is short, but let us at once put our shoulders to the wheel and with prompt, active work we will have a parade, of which we will all be proud.

Just a few suggestions: The attractiveness of a parade depends largely upon its music, special original features, color schemes, etc. Bring music as much as you can afford.

If not uniform get up some original feature. If you can afford to do so, have a float.

Communicate with our Float Committee, of which Brother H. W. Osthoff, 522 Jessie street, San Francisco, is chairman, in regard to floats, size, prices, etc.

We will also depend especially upon the Rebekah Lodges for original color effects in decorated automobiles, floats or other features.

Remember, especially if you bring a band or drum corps, it will be your band or drum corps and will not be separated from you.

If your attendance will be too small to participate as an individual lodge, join in and come as a district; but come anyhow. Bring your flags and banners.

Special dispensation will be granted for wearing regalias in public on this occasion.

In order that your committee may at once take up the parade formation, etc., please fill out enclosed card and forward promptly with such other information as you may consider to be of assistance to the Parade Committee.

The Parade will enter the Panama-Pacific International Exposition Grounds and appropriate exercises will be held in the California State Building.

By authority of the Grand Lodge, I. O. O. F.
FRANK D. MACBETH, Grand Master
H. D. RICHARDSON, Grand Secretary.

T. B. W. LELAND, Chairman
JAS. W. HARRIS, President

I.O.O.F. circular offering information on the 1915 Panama Pacific International Exposition.

91st Session of the Sovereign Grand Lodge. The souvenir badge of this session, held September, 1915.

nearly anyone who resided or visited San Francisco in 1915. However, the presence of the Odd Fellows had to be noticed by everyone as they displayed probably the largest parade during the Expo. William Barnes, Grand Scribe of the Grand Encampment, describes the scene:

"Reaching from the Ferry Building to the entrance of the Exposition Grounds (a distance of four miles) was a solid phalanx of floats, banners, uniformed Patriarchs, marching brethren and sisters, bands and decorations galore. While many parades of many descriptions have occurred in this city during 1915, this procession was unique from the fact that it was composed exclusively of members of the Order, with the exception of a single platoon of police at its head, and was pronounced by thousands of spectators who lined the streets, as well as by the press of the city, to have been equal, if not superior, to any similar parade.

"At the California Building, a plaque was presented by the Exposition officials, who also provided a number of extra features, illuminations, emblematic fireworks, etc."

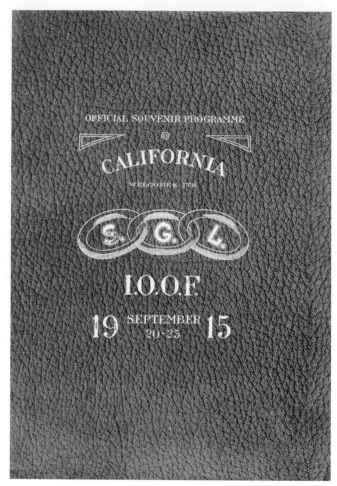

Official Souvenir Program of the Odd Fellows, made for the 1915 Panama-Pacific Exposition.

The Odd Fellows lodges with the largest turnouts for the parade received cash awards from the Grand Lodge. Apollo Lodge No. 123 received $100 for having the most members marching in the parade.

In 1919, Grand Master Hugh W. Brunk held a grand event to celebrate the first 100 years of Odd Fellowship in America. "Brother Brunk presided over the Sixty-Seventh Session of the Grand Lodge, which was held at the San Francisco Civic Auditorium on May 13, 1919. The following day the one hundredth anniversary of the institution of Odd Fellowship in America was celebrated.

Apollo Lodge No. 123 was dressed for the occasion at the 1915 Panama Pacific International Exposition, in San Francisco. This picture is in front of the Palace of Fine Arts.

"The Anniversary Parade consisted of many divisions of Odd Fellows, Rebekahs, Cantons [militant group of the Odd Fellows], Encampment, and many members of the Order in the uniform of U.S. Army, Navy, and Marine Corps." There were several emblematic floats and several marching bands. The float leading the procession held Grand Master Brunk, Grand Treasurer James W. Harris, and San Francisco Mayor James Rolph Jr., who was a long time member of Fidelity Odd Fellows Lodge No. 222. Brother Rolph, 'Sunny Jim' as he was known, became the fourth native-born Governor of California in 1931.

"More than 10,000 members gathered for the Grand Ball in the Civic Auditorium in the evening."

On Sunday, April 15, 1934, the Odd Fellows met at the Mt. Olivet Cemetery to rededicate the Dr. John Frederick Morse Memorial

Souvenir Badge, presented to Sovereign Grand Lodge, September, 1915. This Badge is from the Panama-Pacific Exposition of 1915.

Monument. His grave and monument had been moved from the Odd Fellows Cemetery in San Francisco to Colma. Dr. Morse became one of the most notable Odd Fellows in that he had helped plant the seeds of Odd Fellowship, not only in California, but also in Europe as well. Thousands of people attended this worthy event, including the mayor of San Francisco, the Honorable Angelo Rossi; the governor of California, the Honorable James Rolph Jr.; Grand Master of the Odd Fellows, Fred Boeken; and the president of the Pioneers of California, Charles A. Shurtless. Dr. Morse was a very important figurehead in the growth of California.

Hugh Wilson Brunk, the 66th Grand
Master, 1918.

Originally, the Odd Fellows paid tribute to their beloved member, San Franciscan John Frederick Morse, by creating a Morse Memorial Fund to purchase a monument worthy of this great man. In 1875, during the sessions of the California Grand Lodge, it was decided that $5,000 would be the goal targeted to erect a monument on Morse's grave. After 5 years of saving what was a substantial amount of money in that era, a 17-foot monument was purchased and erected for a cost of $3,000. This left enough money for the maintenance of the monument.

As the Odd Fellows supported one another in participating in events, the membership also supported other organizations. One of these included the support of "Blindcraft," an organization established in 1917 to support the blind. The organization primarily sold brooms to "housewives" in order to raise money for its cause, but it sold other items as well, many of which were made by the blind. The Odd Fellows were regularly asked to support "Blindcraft Week" (October) by asking

Odd Fellows enjoying a social in the Odd Fellows Building at Seventh & Market Streets, prior to 1906.

the membership to buy their products. Blindcraft was located at 1097 Howard Street, San Francisco.

ARABIAN NIGHTS EVENT

The Kings' Daughters' Home for Incurables Association held a 4-day festival at the Odd Fellows Building in January of 1891. As stated in the *Evening Post,* "The object of the association is the founding of a home and hospital for incurables, irrespective of sex and denomination, and it is intended to commence building the same as sufficient funds are on hand to warrant it." The *Post* added that, " . . . several members of the Olympic Club will give exhibitions of wrestling and other feats, and Miss Nellie Bowlin will execute several fancy dances." The event also included *Arabian Nights,* which portrayed the story of Sinbad. The *Caravan* as it was called, included many characters in the

San Francisco Canton No. 5, posing in Regalia.

play: "Sinbad the Sailor, Ali Baba, Blue Beard, Maronf (the henpecked husband), Joudar with his enchanted saddle bags, Ganem and other characters well-known to all readers of the 'Arabian Nights' tales." The event was headed by Mrs. Ella Sterling Cummins.

The events that occurred at the Odd Fellows Building, or by the Odd Fellows in the city, are too numerous to list in this documentary.

THE ODD FELLOWS GOLDEN JUBILEE CELEBRATION

In 1899, a grand celebration was held in the city of San Francisco to honor the first 50 years of Odd Fellowship in the state. This event was a spectacle to be viewed by all San Franciscans. Of course, numerous committees were formed to ensure the success of the entire event. Money was supplied by lodges throughout the state, for they were seeking the "most successful celebration of any secret Order ever held on

San Francisco Canton No. 5, 1936.

this Coast." There were special badges made specifically for the event. Ten thousand books were printed and literally hundreds of local San Francisco businesses placed ads in a limited edition 344-page book which sold for only twenty-five cents. Only 7 years later, most of those hundreds of businesses would fall victim to the Great Quake and Fire.

The official medal of the Jubilee was designed by Odd Fellow Horatio Stockton Winn, who also chaired the Committee on Souvenir Badges. Brother Winn was born May 24, 1824, in Nashua, New Hampshire. In February 1852, he departed Boston and traveled to California. The steamer he was sailing on, the *North America,* was wrecked off the coast of Mexico. His trip to California continued to be accident-prone as he and other survivors of the wreck made a 90-mile journey by mule to Acapulco, where they found another vessel to take them to San Francisco. It was not until July that he finally arrived in San Francisco. After settling in Sacramento, he opened a bakery where he eventually retired as a wealthy man.

Charles L. Patton, an attorney, located at
1011-1012 in the Claus Spreckels Building in
San Francisco, expressed his interest in the Odd
Fellows by sending a short note of inquiry, along
with a $25.00 donation toward the 1899 Jubilee
Celebration.

The souvenir badge of the 1899 Jubilee was representative of a $50 "slug," or gold piece, used in the early years of California's statehood. Featured are the emblems of the various branches of the Independent Order of Odd Fellows. In the center of the badge was a portrait of Samuel H. Parker, the first Grand Master of the organization in California. Today, there are only a handful of these badges remaining.

Horatio Stockton Winn.

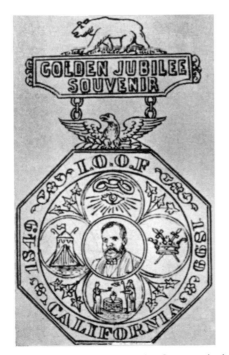 

Image of 1899 Golden Jubilee Souvenir badges designed to have the same shape and size as a $50.00 gold slug. It sold for fifty cents during the celebration of 50 years of Odd Fellowship in California. Its designer was Horatio S. Winn, a long-time member of the order and brother of General Albert M. Winn; also a prominent Odd Fellow.

R. W. GRAND LODGE OF THE UNITED STATES, I. O. O. F., ASSEMBLED AT SAN FRANCISCO, CALIFORNIA, SEPTEMBER 20, 1869.

Photographed by BRADLEY & RULOFSON, 429 Montgomery St., cor. Sacramento, San Francisco, Cal.

CHAPTER 9

TRAGEDY STRIKES—
APRIL 1906

The Great Quake struck! Of the forty-five Odd Fellows lodges in San Francisco, only one escaped destruction. Repeat: only *one* escaped destruction! Spartan Lodge No. 125, which was located at Fourteenth & Railroad Avenue was spared.

The conditions were horrible in the city. The organization's leader, Grand Master William Wyler Phelps, stated:

> "Thousands of brothers and sisters, together with their families, were rendered homeless and in many, many instances, penniless as well. Driven from home by earthquake and fire, exposed to the keen winds from off the ocean, wandering through the streets night and day, and in too many instances clothed in scant attire, our brothers, our sisters, our wives, our children struggled and tramped to reach a place supposed to be immune from the ravages of the awful holocaust, only to be driven again and again through the surging mass of humanity in awful strife to reach a place of safety. Husband separated from wife; father and mother from children, perhaps never again to be reunited; all striving with sheer desperation to escape from the wrecked and burning buildings, only to be exposed to the night air for one, two, three, and perhaps four nights with no place to lay their heads but on Mother Earth, with no covering to shield them from cold but the great canopy of heaven. Oh! how they suffered from hunger and thirst during those terrible days of April 18th, 19th, 20th, and 21st."

The great disaster "was by far the most serious in its effect, of any disaster in the history of Odd Fellowship. In loss of life and property, it is the greatest, by far, of any recorded disaster in ancient or modern history."

William Wylar Phelps was the Grand Master of California at the time the Great Quake and fire hit the city of San Francisco in 1906.

In his written report of 1906, Grand Master Phelps mirrored what many historians of the 1906 disaster now agree: "We well know the policy to minimize the loss of life at this time, to keep no record of deaths but those where there was some possibility of identification, but it is useless to conceal the truth, for the historians, who in after-years will write an authentic account of the 'earthquake and fire of 1906,' and will place a figure far and beyond those given to the world today."

Its flagship—its palace—the Odd Fellows Building was completely destroyed. What the earthquake did not destroy, the fire

Fire approaching Odd Fellows Building shortly after earthquake in 1906. (Courtesy of California Historical Society)

Down Market Street, from Eighth Street, shortly after the 1906 earthquake, prior to the Odd Fellows Building being dynamited. The damaged clock tower of the building could still be seen.

certainly destroyed. The building was actually blown up to prevent the fire from spreading. It was a firebreak in a sense, but a great loss. According to the *San Francisco News,* it took 750 pounds of explosives to destroy the Odd Fellows Building; however, in the dynamiting of the building, the blast was so tremendous that it caused $100,000 worth of damage to the post office across the street.

There may have possibly been two separate incidences where the Odd Fellows structure was dynamited following the earthquake. On the photograph by the Pillsbury Picture Company showing the Odd Fellows Building being dynamited, it states "1000 lbs" was used; however, as stated in the previous paragraph by the *San Francisco News,* it took "750 pounds." There are images showing what remained after the initial explosion. In the actual images of the explosion, each appears to look different. It was apparent and plausible that an additional explosion would have been used to bring the rest down at a later date. There are disparities in the reporting of this occurrence.

Years of work, records, and money in the Odd Fellows Building were lost in the matter of moments. However, there was one incident that is worth mentioning: Odd Fellow member Thomas Mann, against the orders of soldiers, raced into the heavily damaged building by

Odd Fellows Building being dynamited after the Great Earthquake and Fire of 1906.

Odd Fellows Building at Seventh & Market being dynamited with 1,000 pounds of explosives. (San Francisco News agencies reported that it took "750 pounds"). Pillsbury Picture Company, No. 253. (Courtesy of California Historical Society)

climbing a fire escape and entering a window, then returning with the original charter of California Lodge No. 1 His actions were seen as heroic by many members, and the incident was reported in the 1906 Proceedings of the Grand Lodge of California.

There were so few records kept on those who perished in the Great Quake, but some deaths did manage to be recorded. A visiting Odd Fellow from Michigan, George M. Lockwood was killed instantly by a falling brick in front of the Wells Building on Clay and Montgomery. He had come from Stockton, California, for the day. When found, his skull had been crushed; in his possession was a letter from his wife in Wisconsin.

Within weeks after the destruction of the Odd Fellows Building, the parent organization (Grand Lodge), which had been located in the ill-fated building, set up its office in the spared Grant Building. Although the Grant Building was severely damaged, it would be quickly repaired, saved, and house the corporate office of the Grand Lodge.

Meanwhile, only by a narrow vote held on July 25, 1906, did the Odd Fellows decide to keep the property at Seventh & Market streets. With the decision to keep this property, the Odd Fellows guaranteed their continued existence in San Francisco.

The annual Odd Fellows Convention had been scheduled to be held in the city of San Francisco in May. It had to be relocated to Santa

Visible damage to Odd Fellows Building. Southeast on Leavenworth Street from Golden Gate Avenue, San Francisco, April 18, 1906. James O. Rue, Oakland, photographer. (Courtesy of California Historical Society)

Clean up after the dynamiting of the Odd Fellows
Building at Seventh & Market Streets. 1906. (Courtesy
of California Historical Society)

The remains of Odd Fellows Grotto after the 1906
earthquake. Image by Western Photographic
Company, Los Angeles. (Courtesy of California
Historical Society)

Cruz because there were no rooms or halls left standing that could accommodate a convention of any kind. Due to the extreme physical and mental pressures of having to reorganize the event in such short order and handle nearly all of the logistics, the Grand Secretary George Thomas Shaw, sadly, passed away only 5 days after the conclusion of the Convention. Most members agreed it was the stress involved from having to handle the move and the abrupt change that killed Mr. Shaw.

The Samuel Hale Parker Monument was also extensively damaged by the earthquake.

OFFICE OF THE GRAND SECRETARY

Grand Lodge, J. O. O. F.

of the State of California

GRANT BUILDING, SEVENTH AND MARKET STS.
SAN FRANCISCO, CAL.

REMOVAL NOTICE

On and after Monday, July 1, 1907, the office of the Grand Secretary will be located in the Grant Building, corner of Seventh and Market Streets. Fraternally,

H. D. Richardson

Grand Secretary.

This postcard gives notice of the new location of the Grand Lodge. This move coincides with the reconstruction of the Odd Fellows Building at Seventh & Market Streets.

After the San Francisco Earthquake of 1906, the Grand Lodge set up its temporary office at 458 Duboce Avenue on the second floor. Several of the lodges moved their meetings to the Franklin Hall at the corner of Geary and Steiner streets and to the Auxiliary Hall at 1881 Bush street.

Born in 1832, George Thomas Shaw became a member of Spartan Lodge No. 125. He was elected Grand Secretary and served in that capacity until 1906; just six weeks after the 1906 earthquake. It is said the stress of trying to reorganize the office of the Grand Lodge before the annual convention took his life.

Being the type of organization that it was afforded it the unique opportunity of accessing a city under martial law during the initial stages of the crises and the days that followed the earthquake. The governor permitted the Odd Fellows to put into place the Disaster Relief Society (or Committee). This was one of only a handful of organizations allowed into the city under martial law. It should also be noted that the Odd Fellows "fed 12,000 to 14,000 people daily" in the first days of the disaster.

The Odd Fellows Relief Association was given a pass to enter the restricted areas in the city Of San Francisco during the period of martial law immediately after the earthquake and fire of 1906. The Association was able to provide immediate relief to members and many nonmembers. The Odd Fellows were one of the few groups equipped to handle disaster and met an obligation and need never seen before 1906.

It is remarkable, as widespread as the destruction was throughout the city, William Ralston's Palace Hotel managed to stay intact. His well-planned construction of the hotel, utilizing the concept of steel strapping, could have been useful to the Odd Fellows and their building.

A pass from the Governor's office permitting a member of the Odd Fellows Relief Committee to enter the city while it was still under Martial Law dated April 23, 1906.

Tent set up by the Odd Fellows Relief Committee shortly after 1906 earthquake. The Odd Fellows placed many of these "relief stations" throughout the city. (Courtesy of California Historical Society)

Odd Fellows relief station in the Mission. Members of the Odd Fellows standing in front of a I.O.O.F. Relief Station. This station was set up following the 1906 earthquake. (Photo courtesy of John Freeman)

The Secretary of the Committee may be found at his office, **Room 4, Odd Fellows Hall**, every day (Sundays excepted) between the hours of 10 o'clock a. m and 4 p. m. for the purpose of receiving applications for relief and such new cases as may be presented.

In all cases of sickness reported to the President or Secretary during the week, a committee will be immediately appointed, and it shall be the duty of the delegate numbered 1 to visit the brother within twenty-four hours after being notified of his appointment.

The **Chairman of Sub-Committees** on sick are held responsible for the drawing of sick benefits for cases, and in the event of the absence of the Chairman, the next member of the Committee will stand to that duty.

In new cases the Chairman of the Committee will obtain a **blank physician's certificate** from the Secretary, and shall hand the same to the brother who is under the care of the Committee, who shall have it properly filled in, and which must be submitted to the Committee at the **first regular session after the case is reported.**

In case of any disputes as to benefits, refer the same to the President or Secretary.

Always find out who the other members of the Committee are, as it may be necessary for you to know in an emergency.

The Committee meets every Friday evening, at 7 o'clock sharp, at Odd Fellows Hall.

Delegates may be represented by substitute, appointed by themselves, **such appointment being in writing.**

No substitute can serve more than one meeting consecutively, unless his credentials as substitute shall be approved by the Lodge which the regular delegate represents. (Art. X, Sec. 2, Constitution.)

FINES AND PENALTIES

Absences from meetings, delegates fifty cents, tardiness twenty-five cents, Finance Committee one dollar, officers, one dollar, tardiness fifty cents, failure to visit the sick, fifty cents, non-attendance at funerals, two dollars; only excuse taken is sickness of self or family; substitutes may be appointed.

In changing your residence or business place, immediately notify the Secretary.

Phone UNderhill 1737

I. O. O. F.
GENERAL RELIEF
COMMITTEE

OF

SAN FRANCISCO, CAL.

One Hundred and Sixty-seventh
Semi-Annual Term

FEBRUARY, 1936, TO AUGUST, 1936

OFFICERS

President..............................PETER BEASLEY
Morse Lodge No. 257

Vice-President.....................A. J. PATTERSON
Abou Ben Adhem Lodge No. 112

Secretary.............................H. F. JAMIESON
Fidelity Lodge No. 222

Treasurer.............................R. E. MARKWITH
Pacific Lodge No. 155

STANDING COMMITTEES
FINANCE

C. C. Campbell	Fidelity Lodge No. 222
O. J. DeWall	Spartan Lodge No. 125
Walter Brown	Alta Lodge No. 205
Ray Johnson	Occidental Lodge No. 179
R. A. Nelson	Odin Lodge No. 393

EMPLOYMENT COMMITTEE

G. Malchow	Harmony Lodge No. 13
P. I. Meyer	Yerba Buena Lodge No. 15
S. Weinberg	Excelsior Lodge No. 310

HOSPITAL COMMITTEES
SOUTHERN PACIFIC HOSPITAL

C. C. Campbell	Fidelity Lodge No. 222
A. Bell	Bay City Lodge No. 71
G. Monell	Presidio Lodge No. 334
L. Amorsen	Presidio Lodge No. 334

SAN FRANCISCO HOSPITAL

E. J. Kubish	Golden Gate Lodge No. 204
J. Sorenson	Alta Lodge No. 205

U. C. HOSPITAL

A. N. Ivy	Pacific Lodge No. 155
W. Matisek	Unity Lodge No. 131

STANFORD HOSPITAL

F. Figone	Columbus Lodge No. 394
J. G. Reisner	Abou Ben Adhem Lodge No. 112

ST. LUKE'S HOSPITAL

Walter Brown	Alta Lodge No. 205
D. DeGiorgis	Columbus Lodge No. 394

DELEGATES

California Lodge No. 1—Meets every Monday Eve.
G. McCoy, N. G. ....14 Seventh Street
A. Reissle, V. G. ....370 San Carlos Ave.

Harmony Lodge No. 13—Meets every Tuesday Eve.
G. Malchow, N. G. ....3371 25th Street
L. Klee, P. G. ....25 Vesta Street

Yerba Buena Lodge No 15—Meets every Thurs. Eve.
LeRoy E. Moser, N. G. ....130 Milton Street
Paul I. Meyer, V. G. ....434 18th Ave.

Magnolia Lodge No. 29—Meets every Tuesday Eve.
H. McMullen, N. G. ....745 Cabrillo Street
C. W. Hayden, V. G. ....1396 Pacific Street

Bay City Lodge No. 71—Meets every Tuesday Eve.
A. Rethert, N. G. ....3247 Balboa Street
A. Bell, V. G. ....916 Eddy Street

Abou Ben Adhem Lodge No. 112—Meets every Thursday Eve.
A. J. Patterson, P. G. ....2310 36th Ave.
J. G. Reisner, N. G. ....988 Market Street

Concordia Lodge No. 122—Meets every Monday Eve.
A. Hoffman, P. G. ....1831 Eddy Street
A. Ruppman, V. G. ....195 Lexington Ave.

Apollo Lodge No. 123—Meets every Friday Eve.
W. H. Watson, N. G. ....2522 26th Ave.
M. Kuentsle, V. G. ....479 27th Street

Spartan Lodge No 125—Meets every Wednesday Eve.
(4705 Third Street)
Oscar J. DeWall, P. G. ....Hunters Point Drydocks

Unity Lodge No. 131—Meets every Tuesday Eve.
E. George, N. G. ....2408 California Street
W. Matisek, V. G. ....1931 Oak Street

Pacific Lodge No. 155—Meets every Thursday Eve.
R. E. Markwith, P. G. ....358 21st Ave.
A. N. Ivy, N. G. ....246 Capp Street

Occidental Lodge No. 179—Meets every Friday Eve.
Dr. C. Vogt, N. G. ....520 Castro Street
Ray Johnson, V. G. ....2437 23rd Ave.

Golden Gate Lodge No. 204—Meets every Tuesday Eve.
S. Taback, P. G. ....925 San Bruno Ave.
E. J. Kubish, N. G. ....321 Fulton Street

Alta Lodge No. 205—Meets every Monday Eve.
W. L. Brown, N. G. ....1504 Church Street
J. Sorenson, V. G. ....89 Capistrano Ave.

Franco American Lodge No. 207—Meets 1st and 3rd Thursday Eve.
A. Manoni, N. G. ....3703 16th Street
F. Labory, V. G. ....118 17th Ave.

Fidelity Lodge No. 222—Meets every Monday Eve.
C. C. Campbell, N. G. ....1678 28th Ave.
C. E. Kornbeck, V. G. ....1947 Golden Gate Ave.

Morse Lodge No. 257—Meets every Wednesday Eve.
Peter Beasley, P. G. ....2 Alta Vista Terrace
H. G. Agne, V. G. ....Care of Lette man Hospital

Excelsior Lodge No. 310—Meets every Monday Eve.
(2337 Mission Street)
S. Weinberger, N. G. ....3303 Sacramento Street
M. L. Hale, V. G. ....904 Capp Street

Golden West Lodge No. 322—Meets every Thurs. Eve.
U. S. Grant, Jr., N. G. ....263 Lexington Ave.
J. Colliver, V. G. ....1206 Diamond Street

Presidio Lodge No. 334—Meets every Tuesday Eve.
G. Monell, N. G. ....826 Diamond Street
L. Amorsen, V. G. ....1626 Jennings Street

Odin Lodge No. 393—Meets every Wednesday Eve.
(2174 Market Street)
G. O. Malmquist, N. G. ....1427 32nd Ave.
R. A. Nelson, V. G. ....1602 Anza Street

Columbus Lodge No. 394—Meets 1st and 3rd Thurs.
(1524 Powell Street)
D. DeGiorgis, N. G. ....60 Day Street
F. Figone, V. G. ....123 Kearny Street

Stanford Lodge No. 485—Meets 1st and 3rd Tuesday.
(1606 Stockton Street)
A. Bossi, N. G. ....316 Lincoln Ave., Alameda
D. Quarante, V. G. ....1955 Jefferson Street

---

Card of I.O.O.F. General Relief Committee (Cover, and inside).

OFFICE OF THE GRAND MASTER

Grand Lodge, J. O. O. F.

of the State of California

GRANT BUILDING. COR. 7TH AND MARKET STS.

H. D. RICHARDSON
GRAND SECRETARY

San Francisco, Cal., August 1, 1907.

To all Lodges Subordinate to the Grand Lodge, I. O. O. F., of the State of California, Greeting:

Odd Fellowship is progressing rapidly in point of membership and amount of good it is doing in the cause of humanity. If, perchance, there is a weak Lodge it is urged that you do all in your power to revive the waning spirit of that Lodge. The moment may be a critical one in its history, and a careful handling of the situation by the officers may save it and its members to the ranks of Odd Fellowship. Attend the meetings as frequently as possible, thus giving encouragement and support to those you have placed at the helm and as guiding stars in your Lodge.

It is the aim of the Grand Master to visit all the Lodges as laid down in his Official Visitation District at least once during his term of office. Whenever and wherever a date is assigned for a visitation it is the sincere wish of the Grand Master that the members of the Lodge, as well as visitors, will find it convenient to attend, thus making the meeting an instructive, agreeable and enjoyable one to all alike concerned.

With very best wishes for your future success, continued prosperity, and hope that you will make this the banner year in the ranks of American Odd Fellowship in the State of California.

Sincerely and fraternally yours in Friendship, Love and Truth,

F. B. Ogden

Attest:

Grand Master.

H. D. Richardson

Grand Secretary.

Letter dated August 1, 1907 from the Grand Lodge of California (San Francisco).

CHAPTER 10

THE ODD FELLOWS BUILDING—1909

A cting quickly to preserve the integrity of the Odd Fellows in San Francisco, the Odd Fellows Hall Association of San Francisco met immediately after the destruction of the building to plan for the construction of a new building. Using the insurance money from the destroyed building, selling off a piece of the land the 1884 building used to sit upon, and gaining a majority of support from the organization, a new building would stand in the place of where disaster nearly toppled the Order.

The Odd Fellows Board selected local architect George Andrew Dodge whose office was located at 244 Kearny Street. Victor Hoffman was hired as the builder of the new Odd Fellows Building. Unfortunately, George Andrew Dodge died in an automobile accident a short time after the Odd Fellows Building was built.

One sad incident occurred on August 12, 1909, when "in the course of construction" of the steel-framed Odd Fellows Building, an iron worker by the name of Andrew Smith was killed, leaving a widow, Callie Smith. The 39-year-old Canadian native had been employed by the Ralston Iron Works of San Francisco.

In 1909, upon constructing the new building to replace the one destroyed by the earthquake and fire of 1906, the cornerstone was laid. Just about every dignitary in the California Odd Fellowship, along with the members of San Francisco, witnessed the grand event and celebration. The site of the cornerstone was that of the previous cornerstone. The contents of the copper box (the thin-lined vault) presented by

Laying of the cornerstone ceremony. Sunday, 2pm, October 17th, 1909.

Captain J. B. Outland of Canton No. 5, Patriarchs Militant, which was placed in the cornerstone, contained the following:

Constitution of the Sovereign Grand Lodge
Constitution of the Grand Lodge of California
Proceedings of the Grand Lodge, I.O.O.F.S of California, 1909
Grand Masters Visitation, 1909 to 1912

October 19–23, 1909—Portola Festival celebrates the rebuilding of the city with parades and festivities. Odd Fellows Building in background during construction phase. Many people enjoyed watching the parade from the vantage of the construction site. (Photo courtesy of Darlene Thorne)

Constitution Grand Encampment of California

Proceedings of the Grand Encampment of California, 1908

Proceedings of the Rebekah Assembly, 1909

Constitution and by-laws of the San Francisco lodges

Constitution and by-laws of the San Francisco Encampments and Rebekah lodges General Relief Committee, reports and forms used by the Relief Committee, meetings of Excelsior Degree Lodge No. 2

Autographs of the Directors of the Hall Association, to wit: C. E. Benedict, W. H. Blunden, C. Brind, A. H. Cousins, J. H. Cope, J. Deas, Geo. E. Davis, E. D. Flanders, Geo. H. Freiermuth, T. R. Morse, C. E. Post, A. Pauba, M. J. Plashek, Chris. Roeber, J. B. Russell, H. Stern, Theo. Steiner, E. Thiele, Alfred Fuhrman, C. P. Gibbons, M. Greenbaum, J. W. Harris, J. Hinrichs, Hermann Joost, W. C. Johnson, Frank Krull, Jo. J. de Haven, Fred. Toklas, J. H. Thrane, E. J. Thayer, Jos. Winterburn, F. W. Warren, Frank D. Worth, Geo. H. Wilson, W. J. Wigmore, and F. L. Turpin.

October, 1909 Portola Festival. Rare construction
views of Odd Fellows Building at Seventh & Market
Streets. (Photos courtesy of John Freeman)

Plate containing same name of the Hall Directors, 1884, taken from the
    old cornerstone Program of the day's proceedings
San Francisco *Chronicle* of May 14, 1884
Fifty Years of Odd Fellowship in California (1899), presented by Guy
    Lathrop, P. G. ('Past Grand,' a title)
Gold dollar (from old cornerstone) presented by M. Greenbaum, P. G.
Spanish dollar (contributor unknown)
Souvenir badge and various coins, presented by W. A. Patterson, P. G.
Canadian silver coin, presented by W. A. Curtis, P. G.
Badges of the Hall Association

C. W. CROSS   HENRY NEWBURGH

LAW OFFICES OF
CROSS & NEWBURGH
BALBOA BUILDING
593 MARKET STREET
S. E. COR. SECOND ST.

PHONE KEARNY 4774

SAN FRANCISCO, CAL. July 26, 1910.

Ralston Iron Works, Inc.,

20th and Indiana Sts.,

City.

Gentlemen:-

The undersigned is in receipt of a letter from Messrs.
Sullivan & Sullivan and Theo. J. Roche, representing the widow of
Andrew Smith, a structural iron worker who was killed August 12,
1909, while employed by you or your subcontractor on the building
then in the course of construction for the undersigned at the southwest corner of Market and Seventh Streets in the City and County of
San Francisco. Said Smith was at that time engaged in performing work
on the contract theretofore entered into between you and the undersigned, which contract is dated March 11, 1909.

The undersigned will look to you to save it harmless from
any liability on account of the death of said Smith and to defend it
in case any action be brought by the heirs or representatives of the
said deceased to recover on account of said accident. The undersigned
would suggest that you or your attorney take up this matter with its
attorneys, Messrs. Cross & Newburgh, Balboa Bldg., in this city.

Very truly yours,

A. M. Braud
Secretary

THE ODD FELLOWS HALL ASSOCIATION
of San Francisco

Letter regarding the death of an iron worker, during the construction of the Odd
Fellows Building, July 26, 1910.

San Francisco June 9 1910

We the undersigned, Contractors for the Odd Fellows Building hereby agree to do the hereinafter mentioned items necessary to fully complete the said Odd Fellows Building, and to perform the work promptly and in a proper and workmanlike manner; namely,

Repair broken or defective cement plastering around firewalls above roof, Replace broken glass in windows

Have 5 pieces of marble in vestibule replaced by new pieces, all electric wiring made right as per specifications, refit and hang door in attic to Filter room.

Repair damaged plastering in Corridor of Grand Secretary's Office.

It is understood that the execution of filing of the notice of acceptance of said building by the Owner shall not constitute an acceptance of the foregoing items.

Hoffmann & Bjork
Per Paul. Bjork

Contract agreement from a building Contractor, dated June 9, 1910.

TELEPHONES MARKET 936
HOME J 1731

H. D. RICHARDSON
GRAND SECRETARY

ODD FELLOWS BUILDING
COR. SEVENTH AND MARKET STS.

A. M. Brand Secy
Odd Fellows Hall Association

SAN FRANCISCO, CAL., *June 18, 1910.*

To all Subordinate and Rebekah Lodges of the I. O. O. F., of the State of California,

Greeting:

Brother W. L. Kuykendall, Grand Sire of the Sovereign Grand Lodge, is now on his way to California, and will be in the city of San Francisco on Monday, June 27th, 1910. The Board of Directors of the Odd Fellows Hall Association of San Francisco have decided to dedicate the new Odd Fellows Hall at Seventh and Market Streets, San Francisco, while the Grand Sire is in the City and have invited the Officers of the Grand Lodge to officiate in the dedicatory ceremonies which invitation the Grand Master has accepted, and the dedication will take place at 2 o'clock in the afternoon of Monday, June 27th, 1910.

The dedication of this new temple to its noble purposes will be an epoch in the history of Odd Fellowship in California, therefore all Subordinate and Rebekah Lodges are notified of the occasion.

The offices of the Grand Secretary and Secretary of the Rebekah Assembly are now located in the Odd Fellows Building.

Fraternally yours,

T. W. Duckworth

Grand Master.

H. D. Richardson

Grand Secretary.

A letter indicating that the Grand Sire of the Sovereign Grand Lodge "will be in the city of San Francisco on Monday June 27th, 1910". His honored presence was for the dedication ceremony of the newly rebuilt Odd Fellows Building at Seventh & Market Streets.

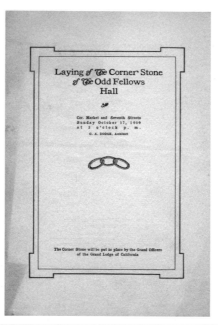

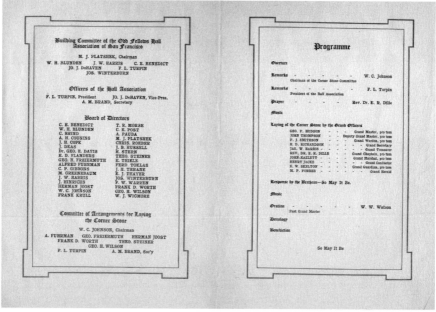

Program for the cornerstone ceremony held on October 17, 1909. (Cover on far left, inside program on right.)

A. HAINES   L. SUMMERFIELD   H. HAINES

SUMMERFIELD & HAINES

Clothing, Furnishing Goods   **Hats and Shoes**

1089=1091 MARKET STREET
Bet. 6th and 7th

San Francisco,   _190_

We hereby agree to take store in
I.O.O.F. Building Corner 7th & Market
37½ ft. on Market and 82 ft on 7th St., the
store to be conducted as a men's
General Clothing store (Mens-Youths &
Boys Clothing-Hats & Furnishings)
Store to be completed
with windows properly backed-
Hardwood floors & electric wired &
Iron posts to be covered with mirrors,
the main entrance to store to be
completed similar to that of Paulsan
& Co. Cor. Sutter & Kearney, and with a
7th st. entrance in rear of store, the
store to be furnished with window awning
casing, toilet & washstand & Electric wired.
Rent to be as follows
from Aug 1st/10 to Dec 31/1912 — 500°° per mo.
from Jan 1/1913 to Dec 31/1915 — 600°° " "

Summerfield & Haines

One of the many tenants the Odd Fellows has had over the years. Rental contract dated 1912.

Program Grand Encampment, sessions at Woodland, 1909
Copies of the *San Francisco Call, Chronicle* and *Examiner* of August 19, 1909

The aforementioned items still remain in the cornerstone of the Odd Fellows Building as far as it is known.

The members of the Odd Fellows not only rebuilt their home in San Francisco, but the decision to rebuild secured a growing future for the organization. The membership in California exploded from 40,974 in 1906, to its peak, an impressive 58,882 in 1928. Once having enjoyed a larger membership than the Masonic Order until the late 1920s, the Odd Fellows fell dramatically over the next several years, allowing the Masons to gain the lead in terms of membership in the state.

The new Odd Fellows building, at Seventh & Market Streets in San Francisco. From left to right, the photos of the building are dated—1915, 1939, and 1940.

CHAPTER 11

THE WARS

As there were hundreds of thousands of men involved in the Civil War between 1861 and 1865, this Order saw many of its own members involved. This was a division that separated the North from the South, the Blue from the Gray, and inadvertently caused the unwanted division and fighting between members of the Odd Fellows. However, there were some incidences between brothers of the Order who recognized each other and expressed little, if any, ill will against their brethren on the opposing sides. There are written recordings of the noble deeds expressed toward members on opposing sides. But this being a war of universal principles, it was larger than any fraternal organization.

The effects of the Civil War involved the Order at what it did—and still does—best. In his report to the members at the sessions of the Grand Lodge of the United States, the Grand Sire, speaking on the status of money given to a fund which had been created to aid the impoverished in the war regions, stated the following: "It is a significant indication of the non-partisan spirit which pervades this great fraternity."

Many members of the Order participated in the Civil War; some lost their lives. In a few instances, those losses were reported during the Grand Lodge sessions. In the California Journal of 1865, the following was reported at the San Francisco Sessions:

"On the 19th [of] September, the Telegraph transmitted the melancholy announcement of the death of P. G., Charles S. Eigenbrodt, of the California Calvary, who was killed instantly on the 2nd of

September, while leading a charge under General Averill, in the Shenandoah Valley. P. G. Eigenbrodt was for many years an active and zealous working member of the R. W. Grand Lodge. In his death the Order has lost one of its most efficient members, whose whole life was a living exemplification of the principles he professed. He will be missed from the familiar post of his accustomed labors, to whose duties the full powers of his active mind were ever devoted. His place will not soon be filled to the complete standard of his moral worth."

And finally at the conclusion of the Civil War, in his Closing Address of the 1865 Grand Lodge Sessions in San Francisco, Grand Master Charles O. Burton stated:

"And now that the scenes of war are passing away, in which our jurisdiction has felt its pangs, in the loss of several noble brothers who have sacrificed their lives in the defense of their country, and while we should be ready at all times to maintain and support our Government in all its trials, and should in no wise countenance or anything that is in opposition thereto, or screen those who have unjustly offended against the law of the land, leaving them to answer to the proper tribunals, I believe we can advance the principles of our Order."

World War I and World War II saw millions of men leave to fight. This also meant many members of the Odd Fellows were compelled to join in these wars. Some members even corresponded with their lodges on a regular basis. Each lodge, in fact, kept blue star—and, God forbid, gold star—flags in the lodge rooms to represent the number of members fighting in the war and even those members that had died, respectively.

An interesting fact is that the Odd Fellows in California kept records of all its members who served in these wars. In the appendix section of the 1919 Proceedings is where these names are found. Because the list is so vast, rather than list all of those names of people who served, only the names of those San Franciscans who were killed, died, or wounded in World War I are listed.

Killed in action: John Mounes, Franco-American Lodge No. 207, May 24, 1916; Karl J. Hagel, Odin Lodge No. 393, October 5, 1918.

Veteran's banner from WWI, representing the number of member veterans serving from Abou Ben Adhem Lodge No. 112. Note the one gold star.

Died of natural death: J. M. Fredline, Abou Ben Adhem Lodge No. 112, December 1, 1918; W. S. Johnson, Abou Ben Adhem Lodge No. 112, April 26, 1918; Ivan Bernhardt, Pacific Lodge No. 155, February 24, 1919; George E. Roche, Fort Point Lodge No. 406, October 2, 1918; Frank W. Winter, Fort Point Lodge No. 406, December 2 1918.

U.S. Cruiser "San Francisco". Circa 1890's.

Transport Sherman, laden with boys from Manila, entering the San Francisco harbor.

Wounded: John G. Teeple, Apollo Lodge No. 123, injured in knee, mine explosion, P. E. Moore, Parker Lodge No. 124, knee injured, recovered; Augustus L. Lawson, Alta Lodge No. 205, right arm permanently disabled, wounds in chest; Fred E. Seike, Fidelity Lodge No. 222, gassed, recovered.

The Order involved itself in the war efforts in both wars. It collected taxes from lodges for support of those efforts. It recognized

9 BREST.—Vue sur le Port de Guerre.—View upon the War Harbour.—LL.

Carte Postale

Correspondance   Adresse

Dear Sir. and Brother.   Brest, France 5/12/19.

Recieved your letter last month, very glad to hear from you. I'm feeling fine think I have seen France thoroughly and am ancious to return home With best wishes to you all I am yours Fred J. Bodiken

Postcards from France. Presidio Lodge No. 334 member, Fred J. Bodiken, sent several cards and letters while serving during WWI.

Postcards from France. Presidio Lodge No. 334 member, Fred J. Bodiken, sent several cards and letters while serving during WWI.

those members that had fallen in war; and it paid tribute to those injured. Members of San Francisco were affected as much as any other city in America.

The impact of World War II on the organization was evident. The Sovereign Grand Lodge did not hold a convention in 1945. In California, the Grand Lodge created many committees related to the war. There was a committee established to urge members to purchase War Bonds and to give blood plasma. Another committee was put into place to assist with the Hospital Project for Disabled War Veterans.

In 1945, Golden West Lodge No. 322 (San Francisco) reported its member Cecil M. Barnes had been killed in action in France. During the 1946 sessions of the Grand Lodge, Grand Secretary Frank D. Mac-Beth requested that all lodges report their members who had served and died in the war. Until then, only scattered reports of deceased members were reported in the lodges. Grand Lodge never received the requested reports.

As late as 1948, the Grand Secretary reported the following: "I have suggested for the last several years that a complete list of all Brothers of California Lodges, who made the Supreme Sacrifice, should be sent to your Grand Lodge and published in our Journal. We have never received a full list. Again, I suggest this." Unfortunately, a listing of those who served, were wounded, or perished in World War II never materialized. Perhaps the lodges were more concerned about holding their membership together and concentrating on membership issues, given this was a pivotal time in the Order's growth and decline. For whatever reason, a listing was never submitted.

After World War II, the Order saw a brief stabilization and even an increase in membership for 3 years in California. But this was most likely caused by veterans seeking camaraderie with others like themselves. But the circumstances that affected the Odd Fellows' decline 2 decades later caught up and the decline continued.

OFFICE OF WAR RELIEF COMMITTEE

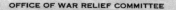

H. D. RICHARDSON
GRAND SECRETARY
ODD FELLOWS BLDG. 7TH AND MARKET STS.
SAN FRANCISCO. CAL.

LYMAN M. KING
GRAND MASTER
REDLANDS. CALIF.

San Francisco, Cal., September 8, 1919.

To all Subordinate Lodges under the Jurisdiction of the Grand Lodge, I. O. O. F., of the State of California:

Dear Sirs and Brothers:

The enclosed blank is to be used in making claim for dues of Brothers now in the Military and Naval service for the period beginning July 1, 1919, and ending September 30, 1919.

This claim should also include 50 cents War Assessment levied at the recent session of the Grand Lodge.

Blanks for sick benefits will be furnished on application.

All claims should be filed promptly.

Please fill out the blanks with typewriter (if practicable) and forward to H. D. Richardson, Grand Secretary, Seventh and Market Streets, San Francisco, in the special envelope enclosed.

Fraternally yours,

Lyman M. King
Grand Master.

H. D. Richardson
Grand Secretary.

H. W. BRUNK, Past Grand Master,
H. D. RICHARDSON, Grand Secretary,
JAS. W. HARRIS, Grand Treasurer,
W. W. WATSON, P. G. M.,
CLIFTON H. CONNICK, P. G. M.,
War Relief Committee.

Lodges were asked to make waivers for dues on members serving in war. At the same time, the organization levied a "50 cents War Assessment" on each member serving. September 8, 1919.

The Sovereign Grand Lodge

OF THE

Independent Order of Odd Fellows

OFFICE OF THE GRAND SIRE

To the Officers and Members of Grand and Subordinate Lodges:

It is not only desirable, but important, that there be furnished, as early as possible, to the Grand Masters of each Jurisdiction, from each Subordinate Lodge, a complete list of those who entered or served in the Army or Navy, also the names of those who died in the service, and a list of those who were wounded, with a statement of the character of the wounds, and if maimed, this also should be stated in the information furnished. When this information is obtained, it is desired that it be tabulated so as to show the number from each Jurisdiction that entered the Army or Navy, with the number of those who lost their lives, the number of those who were injured and incapacitated for service, also the number of those who lost one or both arms or limbs or eyes, and the number of those who are incapacitated for labor by reason of their wounds.

When this information is secured by the Grand Officers of the Grand Jurisdiction, it should be promptly sent to the Grand Secretary, John B. Goodwin, at Baltimore, Maryland. It is not expected that this information can be furnished before July 1, but it is desired that it be furnished as early as possible. The Order should and will make provision for the brethren who were wounded or injured in the service of their country and in need of assistance. Information of the kind indicated will be necessary in order to determine the extent of the demands upon the Order and is necessary to enable the Order to furnish assistance. The Grand Master and Officers of each Jurisdiction should take up this work at the earliest opportunity and advise each Subordinate Lodge what is needed. The task is a large one, but some such method will be needed if we are to do our duty in learning the extent of the demands upon the Order. Until the extent of the demands is known, intelligent action cannot well be taken in the premises.

Done at the City of Amsterdam, New York, this 3d day of February, 1919.

Attest: HENRY V. BORST,
JOHN B. GOODWIN,   Grand Sire.
　　　　Grand Secretary.

The Grand Lodge, I.O.O.F. of the State of California

OFFICE OF THE GRAND MASTER

Odd Fellows' Building, Seventh and Market Streets, San Francisco

Berkeley, Cal., April 10, 1919.

To all Subordinate Lodges under the Jurisdiction of the Grand Lodge, I. O. O. F., of the State of California:

Pursuant to the above request of Brother Henry V. Borst, Grand Sire, I am inclosing herewith blanks to be used by the Subordinate Lodges, giving definite information as to the names of the brothers killed or wounded in either the Military or Naval service of the Government, and, if wounded, the names and kinds of wounds.

As I desire to have this information before the Grand Secretary of the Sovereign Grand Lodge as soon as possible, so that the same may be tabulated, I will thank the brothers for attending to this with the least possible delay. Yours in F., L. and T.,

Attest: H. W. Brunk
                                                                    Grand Master.
　H. D. Richardson
　　　　Grand Secretary.

Letter from Sovereign Grand Lodge and Grand Lodge of California, requesting that all those lodges having members who fought in the war and were either injured or killed to submit each member's name. 1919.

CHAPTER 12

THE END OF THE CEMETERIES IN SAN FRANCISCO

Where the membership flourished, the Odd Fellows Cemetery, along with every cemetery in the city, was being forced to relocate. The Great Quake did not lend itself to the future of the cemetery.

In the late 1890s, officials sought to free up additional land space in the already-growing city. In 1900, the board of supervisors prevented any more burials in the city. This was the beginning of a series of events leading to the end of cemeteries in San Francisco.

The Great Quake only made things worse for the operators of the Odd Fellows Cemetery in 1906. It left many of the stones in ruins. If

Odd Fellows Cemetery, San Francisco, 1906. Note damage to structure. (Courtesy of California Historical Society)

Odd Fellows Cemetery of San Francisco. Damage caused by 1906 earthquake. (Courtesy of California Historical Society)

the stones were not totally destroyed, chances were they were tilted or moved out of place. The monument of Samuel M. Parker, the first Grand Master of the Odd Fellows in California, "was shattered into a thousand pieces." Astonishing, the monument of Charles de Young was not affected. And, the statue of John Morse was an inch from toppling over.

Aside from a crack in the west wing and a few urns moved out of position, the Odd Fellows Columbarium held up quite well.

The cemeteries in San Francisco turned into camping grounds for many people that were displaced after the quake. In years to follow, the cemeteries slipped into an even worse despair. Youths would often vandalize the graves, and looters would rob whatever could be found. This would be the condition of the Odd Fellows Cemetery for the remainder of its existence.

Although the defunct cemeteries stood in poor condition, in the general election of 1914, the people voted not to remove the cemeteries, believing there was a land scheme to remove the cemeteries, as proposed by their beloved Mayor Rolph. And again, in 1924, after sev-

Monument of Dr. John Frederick Morse. This monument, and the remains of Morse were moved from the Odd Fellows Cemetery to Mt. Olivet Cemetery in Colma in 1933, and rededicated on April 15, 1934.

eral ordinances were placed into effect in 1923 by the board of supervisors, ordering the disinterment of all human remains from Calvary, Laurel Hill, Masonic, and the Odd Fellows cemeteries, San Francisco Mayor James Rolph Jr., also a member of the Odd Fellows Fidelity Lodge No. 222, asked the people to fight against the ordinances. The people voted against the removal of the graves.

Despite the legal and political battles to keep the cemeteries in the city, the Odd Fellows removed what graves could be found before any such laws directing such were ever passed. By the mid-1920s, the Odd Fellows had moved all the graves to Colma, the future site for many

Removal of remains from Odd Fellows Cemetery in San Francisco. Nearly all of the remains at this point were relocated to Colma and placed in one mass grave. Circa 1930's. (Courtesy of San Francisco History Center, San Francisco Public Library)

souls still lying in graves in San Francisco. The Odd Fellows moved into Greenlawn Cemetery. Some of the stones on graves that were still salvageable were placed in the new cemetery. If relatives or friends funded removal of a body and headstone, the stone was transferred, to be placed in a single grave with the stone being reset. If not, the headstone would end up being part of the breakwater in areas of the San Francisco Bay or used to build the seawall at the Aquatic Park. For the twenty-eight thousand departed, they were laid under a great monument in one mass grave.

Today, this mass grave sits in a seemingly empty lot, its history or significance forgotten in the memories of those around during the time of the movement of graves. One lone monument marks the location of the graves, which is located in a back lot of the Greenlawn Cemetery. The Odd Fellows have not owned or operated a cemetery business in or near San Francisco since the 1920s.

The Columbarium is the only reminder that an Odd Fellows Cemetery ever existed in San Francisco. The Crematory was demolished after the graves were removed. After it was transferred to the Bay Cities Cemetery Association in 1930, the Columbarium and the five re-

This forgotten lone monument sits near a dump behind the Greenlawn Cemetery in Colma. Beneath it rests the remains of 28,000 people that had been moved from the Odd Fellows Cemetery in San Francisco. Home Depot store is in the background.

maining acres surrounding it were claimed under the Homestead Act. It was under the control of Cypress Abbey until 1980, when the Neptune Society of Northern California took it over. The Society did a fantastic job of rehabilitating an otherwise dilapidated and decaying building. Today, the San Francisco Odd Fellows and the citizens of San Francisco can thank the Neptune Society of Northern California for preserving a piece of its history.

CHAPTER 13

WHAT ONCE WAS . . .

PRIMARY ODD FELLOWS LODGES & OTHER BRANCHES IN SAN FRANCISCO

(Date Instituted & Disposition/Date)

LODGES:

California Lodge No. 1—Instituted on September 9, 1849. After consolidating into Concordia Lodge No. 122 in 1966, Concordia Lodge No. 122 petitioned to take name of California Lodge No. 1 in 1988, which was approved by the Grand Lodge

San Francisco Lodge No. 3—Instituted on July 5, 1851. Consolidated into Morse Lodge No. 257 on November 8, 1918

Harmony Lodge No. 13—(Lodge conducted in German language) Instituted on June 27, 1853. Consolidated into Concordia Lodge No. 122 on November 13, 1963

Yerba Buena Lodge No. 15—Instituted on July 7, 1853

Templar Lodge No. 17—Instituted on October 22, 1853. Consolidated into Presidio Lodge No. 334 on February 1, 1916

Magnolia Lodge No. 29—Instituted on July 12, 1854. Consolidated into Pacific Lodge No. 155 on July 7, 1938

Bay City Lodge No. 71—Instituted on September 4, 1857

Farnsworth Lodge No. 95—Instituted on September 28, 1895. Consolidated into Pacific Lodge No. 155 on June 27, 1918

Abou Ben Adhem Lodge No. 112—Instituted on April 3, 1863. Consolidated into Yerba Buena Lodge No. 15 on October 3, 1940

Germania Lodge No. 116—(Lodge conducted in German language) Instituted on July 1, 1863. Consolidated into Harmony Lodge No. 13 on April 9, 1918

Concordia Lodge No. 122—(Lodge conducted in German language) Instituted on January 29, 1866. Concordia Lodge No. 122 petitioned to take name of California Lodge No. 1 in 1988, which was approved by the Grand Lodge

Apollo Lodge No. 123—Instituted on February 24, 1866

Parker Lodge No. 124—Instituted on July 16, 1866. Consolidated into Templar Lodge No. 17 on April 6, 1903

Spartan Lodge No. 125—Instituted on October 6, 1894. Consolidated into Golden Gate Lodge No. 204 November 28, 1944

Unity Lodge No. 131—Instituted on April 16, 1867. Consolidated into Golden West Lodge No. 322 on September 5, 1946

Hermann Lodge No. 145—(Lodge conducted in German language) Instituted on July 8, 1868. Consolidated into Harmony Lodge No. 13 on January 4, 1916

Pacific Lodge No. 155—Instituted on March 25, 1869. Consolidated into Golden West Lodge No. 322 on July 15, 1965

Ophir Lodge No. 171—Instituted on June 17, 1870. Consolidated into Templar Lodge No. 17 on April 16, 1903

Occidental Lodge No. 179—Instituted on September 16, 1870. Consolidated into Apollo Lodge No. 123 on September 29, 1965

Cosmopolitan Lodge No. 194—Instituted on December 13, 1871. Consolidated into Abou Ben Adhem Lodge No. 112 on June 26, 1913

Golden Gate Lodge No. 204—Instituted on June 28, 1872. Consolidated into Apollo Lodge No. 123 on January 16, 1963

Alta Lodge No. 205—Instituted on June 29, 1872. Consolidated into Golden West Lodge No. 322 on December 9, 1971

Franco-American Lodge No. 207—(Lodge conducted in French language) Instituted on August 16, 1872.

Fidelity Lodge No. 222—Instituted on September 5, 1873. Consolidated into Apollo Lodge No. 123 on January 3, 1967

Morse Lodge No. 257—Instituted on May 7, 1877

Western Addition Lodge No. 285—Instituted on August 20, 1879. Consolidated into Occidental Lodge No. 179 on July 14, 1930

Excelsior Lodge No. 310—Instituted on January 7, 1884. Consolidated into Morse Lodge No. 257 on March 28, 1956

Golden West Lodge No. 322—Instituted on June 4, 1885

Presidio Lodge No. 334—Instituted on October 13, 1887. Consolidated into Yerba Buena Lodge No. 15 on October 3, 1940

Sargent Lodge No. 368—Instituted on May 1, 1891. Consolidated into Golden Gate Lodge No. 204 on December 2, 1913

Odin Lodge No. 393—(Lodge conducted in Swedish language) Instituted in April 29, 1904

Columbus Lodge No. 394—(Lodge conducted in Italian language) Instituted on February 27, 1906. Consolidated into Golden Gate Lodge No. 204 on June 5, 1951

McKinley Lodge No. 396—Instituted on July 1, 1907. Consolidated into Presidio Lodge No. 334 on November, 1912

Fort Point Lodge No. 406—Instituted on January 27, 1909. Consolidated into Morse Lodge No. 257 on December 2, 1925

Stanford Lodge No. 485—Instituted on March 30, 1933. Consolidated into Golden Gate Lodge No. 204 on January 5, 1937

ENCAMPMENTS:

Golden Gate Encampment No. 1—Instituted on February 1, 1853

Walhalla Encampment No. 7—(Encampment conducted in German language) Instituted on March 21, 1856. Consolidated into Golden Gate Encampment No. 1 on March 11, 1985

Wildey Encampment No. 23—Instituted on August 1, 1863. Consolidated into Golden Gate Encampment No. 1 on January 10, 1914

Unity Encampment No. 26—Instituted on March 19, 1867. Consolidated into Golden Gate Encampment No. 1 on February 14, 1955

Oriental Encampment No. 57—Instituted on July 15, 1876. Consolidated into Golden Gate Encampment No. 1 on March 31, 1989

Thor Encampment No. 111—(Encampment conducted in Swedish language) Instituted on September 26, 1915. Consolidated into Oriental Encampment No. 57 on March 2, 1940

REBEKAH LODGES:

California Rebekah Lodge No. 1—Instituted on June 30, 1870. Consolidated into Mission Rebekah Lodge on March 31, 1976, and the new lodge took the name Mission—California Lodge No. 1

Templar Rebekah Lodge No. 19—Consolidated into California Lodge No. 1 on June 21, 1962

Oriental Rebekah Lodge No. 90—As of this writing, this is the only remaining Rebekah Lodge in San Francisco. On May 20, 2006, the lodge took the name and lodge number of California Lodge No. 1.

Walhalla Rebekah Lodge No. 130—(Lodge conducted in German language) Consolidated into Mission—California Lodge No. 1 on November 1, 1978

Amity Rebekah Lodge No. 161—Consolidated into Oriental Lodge No. 90 on October 9, 1974

Loyal Rebekah Lodge No. 215—Consolidated into Mission Lodge No. 225 on December 3, 1975

Mission Rebekah Lodge No. 225—Instituted on May 1, 1897. Surrendered its charter May 24, 2003

Jubilee Rebekah Lodge No. 239—Instituted on December 18, 1909. Consolidated into Presidio Lodge No. 321 on December 19, 1921

Freja Rebekah Lodge No. 284—(Lodge conducted in Swedish language) Instituted on October 18, 1905. Freja Lodge moved from San Francisco to the Odd Fellows/Rebekah Home in 1967

San Francisco Rebekah Lodge No. 302—Instituted on March 11, 1908. Consolidated into Templar Lodge No. 19 on December 30, 1911

Golden City Rebekah Lodge No. 304—Instituted on April 23, 1908. Consolidated into Oriental Lodge No. 90 on March 26, 1941

Bay View Rebekah Lodge No. 317—Instituted on September 14, 1909. Consolidated into Oriental Lodge No. 90 on July 9, 1975

Presidio Rebekah Lodge No. 321—Instituted on May 3, 1910. Consolidated into Templar Lodge No. 19 on November 20, 1914

Of the Rebekah Lodges listed above, only Oriental Lodge No. 90 is still active in San Francisco.

PATRIARCHS MILITANT:

San Francisco Canton No. 5—Closed

In addition to the aforementioned lodges and encampments, there were other Odd Fellows entities in the city which this writer would be remiss not to mention. These included the Veteran Odd Fellows Association, San Francisco Veteran Rebekahs, Ladies Encampment Auxiliary, Ladies Auxiliary Patriarchs Militant, San Francisco Theta Rho Girls Club No. 11, San Francisco Junior Lodge No. 11, and the Excelsior Degree Lodge No. 2.

The Junior Lodge No. 11 was instituted on August 11, 1933, by the Grand Master Fred Boeken at the Odd Fellows Building at Seventh & Market streets in San Francisco. The Junior Lodge was opened to "boys between the ages of 14 and 21 years" (not necessarily the sons of Odd Fellows).

The San Francisco Theta Rho Girls Club was instituted on November 30, 1934, by Sister Mary R. Rewcastle, the Vice President of the Rebekah Assembly of California. The Club closed in the 1970s.

General Edwin Hazen Black was a member of Unity Lodge No. 131 of San Francisco. He was active in all branches of the order; also serving as the Grand Patriarch of the Encampment in 1882. Note the V.O.F. pin on his chest.

Interior of Office of Secretary of the Rebekah Assembly. 1899. Seventh & Market Streets.

San Francisco Junior Odd Fellows Lodge No. 11. February 11, 1937.

San Francisco Junior Odd Fellows Lodge No. 11 in 1947. Photo provided by longtime member Harry Platek (lower right), who is in the photo as an advisor to the Junior Lodge. (As of the writing, Harry Platek has more than 72 years in the order.)

On September 21, 1853, the Excelsior Degree Lodge No. 2 was instituted for the purpose of conferring degrees upon the members of the Order. It is interesting to note that at that time, this lodge also conferred the Rebekah Degree upon brothers. As pointed out in the *First Fifty Years Of Odd Fellowship In California,* "It may readily be seen that the work of conferring the five degrees of the subordinate Lodge and the Rebekah Degree, too, gave the small band of brothers considerable work."

The Veteran Odd Fellows' Association in San Francisco was created April 24, 1877. After a meeting at the office of Nathan Porter, which was located at northeast corner of California and Kearny streets where numerous Odd Fellows attended, the adoption of a constitution was met with overwhelming approval.

The Veteran Odd Fellow had to be a member with at least 21 years in the Order, live west of the Rocky Mountains, and be a member in good standing in an Odd Fellows lodge. Today, this organization is but a faint memory due to the decline in membership.

A. K. Kingsford was a member of Bay City Lodge No. 71 of San Francisco. In 1876 he was elected as Degree Master. For his efforts of conferring the degrees on so many members of the order, he was presented with a "magnificent gold badge studded with diamonds and other precious stones, manufactured by San Francisco's Shreve & Company".

Veteran Odd Fellows' Association
Odd Fellows' Hall, San Francisco

Dear Brother:

The 47th Annual Meeting of this Association will be held in the Odd Fellows Building, Seventh and Market Streets, San Francisco, on Tuesday, May 8th, 1923, at 3 o'clock p. m.

The annual banquet will take place the same evening. You are fraternally invited to be present at these events.

Your dues for the year are ONE DOLLAR. Please remit the same in the enclosed envelope, and also state if you can be present so that proper arrangements can be made.

Any member in good standing who has belonged to the Order for 21 years is eligible for membership.

The admission fee is $1.00, and dues $1.00 per year.

If you have not the V. O. F. Badge, as per design above, and desire one, it can be secured from the Secretary. The price is $2.00.

Hoping to see you present.

Fraternally,

M.H. Ludlow

Secretary.

V.O.F. notice. Meeting to be held at Odd Fellows Building in San Francisco. 1923.

As Friendship, Love, and Truth are principles of the Odd Fellows' lodges and represent three of the first four degrees of Odd Fellowship (an Initiatory Degree takes place prior to the First, Second, and Fourth Degrees), Faith, Hope, and Charity are the principles and degrees of the Encampment. There were additional degrees which were later completely removed or absorbed by the current degrees.

Years ago, after a member attained the title of Past Grand (past presiding officer of a lodge), he was asked to join an Encampment. Today, all members who have received the Third Degree, or the Degree of Truth, are eligible to join the Encampment. It is a level of Odd Fellowship where one can attain not only additional degrees, but also enjoy a fraternal embrace by those seeking principles that embody the strength of those committed to prolonging and enjoying all that the Order has to offer.

"There is no authentic record of the origin of the first Encampment Degree." It has been written the degree was brought from England. Most likely, as stated above, the Encampment was created to allow the teachings of other principles.

The Encampment is best described as follows: " . . . the Encampment branch is to the Order at large what the colleges are to the common schools of our land. The importance of attaining the Encampment degrees should be evident to every member who is desirous of standing upon the highest plane of American Odd Fellowship."

Past Grand Patriarchs, Sonora, California. Several of the members in this photograph are from San Francisco. Note standing 9th from the left is James W. Harris, Grand Treasurer of the Grand Lodge. Second from right is W. H. Barnes, Grand Scribe of the Grand Encampment, considered by many members from this era to be the greatest Odd Fellow. Photography by R. F. Sanford. Circa October, 1912.

The Patriarchs Militant (PM) of the Independent Order of Odd Fellows is a semi-military uniformed branch comprised of Odd Fellows who seek to achieve the highest degree attainable in Odd Fellowship. The principle is based on *Justitia Universalis* (Universal Justice). San Francisco Canton No. 5 was the local unit for the Patriarchs Militant. There are many reasons this degree, or level, of the Odd Fellows was created. But nonetheless, it was adopted on September 24, 1885, without any objections.

The Patriarch's Militant branch of the Independent Order of Odd Fellows has only one degree. The degree is primarily based upon the story of the destruction of Sodom and Gomorrah and saving Abraham's nephew, Lot. Again, this degree teaches the principle of universal justice.

This newly dedicated branch of the Order was headed up by the John C. Underwood, past governor of Kentucky. His title became "General," and he was appointed first Supreme Commander. "The Degree is purely military and for display purposes." The PM enjoyed its own corps of musicians, with a tambour corps, and would usually march together during parades.

Prior to the acceptance of the Patriarchs Militant Degree in 1885, there was a uniformed branch in California, which had also been

General A. R. Stocker, Commanding Patriarch Militant, Canton Lodge (I.O.O.F.).

Major General J. K. Ritter, Commanding Department of California, Patriarchs Militant (I.O.O.F.).

approved by Sovereign Grand Lodge. In 1872, the Patriarchs of California was organized. Their members were comprised of members of the Encampments—another level of Odd Fellowship. The first Battalion was the Golden Gate Battalion, located in San Francisco. The Battalion first performed in Vallejo during a session of the Grand Lodge of California. The practice of uniform drills spread to many areas throughout the state, wherever Odd Fellows could be found. It eventually evolved into what is called the Patriarchs Militant Degree of the Independent Order Of Odd Fellows. In 1886, California officially saw its command of the PM. From its early days in San Francisco, it had grown to "over 1800 members by 1915."

During the Panama Pacific International Exposition of 1915 in San Francisco, specifically on September 22, thousands of Odd Fellows and Rebekahs marched in the parade to the California Building. On the same day, a review of the Patriarchs Militant Army was held at the Marina. A competition of the various Cantons was held in the Civic Auditorium on Grove and Larkin streets.

Today, the Patriarchs Militant branch still exists, but no longer in San Francisco. There is also the Ladies Auxiliary Patriarchs Militant faction which is just as active. The members still wear full uniforms and perform in ceremonial functions of the Order. Although it is not

Odd Fellows Canton No. 5 marching band.

Early image of Patriarch's Militant, San Francisco. (Photo courtesy of John Freeman)

The Rebekahs, near Seventh & Mission Streets (outside of what is now the Appeals Court).

San Francisco Drill Corps of Ladies' Auxiliary (I.O.O.F.).

required to have military experience to join the PM, it is an accepted practice for members to wear and display military ribbons of the U.S. Armed Service which they had earned while serving in the Armed Forces. The PM has the honor of placing a wreath on the Tomb Of The Unknown Soldier each year in Arlington, Virginia, a right granted several decades ago. As in the past, its members strive to compete in drill and become proficient in the manual of the sword. Even this writer has been impressed by the level of commitment and attention that has been placed on the manual of the sword.

June 30, 1870, with the institution of California Rebekah Lodge No. 1 marked the establishment of the Rebekah Assembly, the sister organization of the Odd Fellows, in the state of California.

On Tuesday, May 12, 1891, the Rebekahs elected San Franciscan Mary T. Lyon as their first President in California during their first session of the Degree of Rebekah State Convention. The session was held in the Odd Fellows Building at Seventh and Market streets. This was the first step in establishing the Rebekahs as a significant and important body to the Independent Order of Odd Fellows in California.

Sister Lyon presided for 4 days until a new President was elected and installed on Friday, May 15, 1891. At the time of the session, she was the wife of the Odd Fellows Grand Lodge Secretary Walter B. Lyon (he died 11/4/1893), who most likely gave her some advanced insight as to how a session should be conducted with relationship to the Grand Lodge. Her home Rebekah Lodge was Templar No. 19.

On May 26, 1924, Mary T. Lyon, the first President of the Rebekah Assembly in California, passed away in San Francisco. She was eighty-four years of age.

The Rebekahs' crowning achievement was the creation of the Orphans' Home in the late 1800s at Gilroy, California. In 1896, the Grand Lodge of California granted the Rebekahs authority to establish an Orphans' Home for children of Odd Fellows that had their lost parents. A dedication of the Orphans' Home was held on October 10, 1897.

Today, the home no longer bears the name "Orphans' Home," but is known as "Children's Services" and is one of the nation's foremost institutions offering an array of outreach programs. The Odd Fellows and Rebekahs are proud of this facility.

Rebekah Lodges

California Reb. Lodge, No. 1
1638 Eddy Street

Templar Reb. Lodge, No. 19
1254 Market Street

Oriental Reb. Lodge, No. 90
2121 Market Street

Walhalla Reb. Lodge, No. 130
240 Golden Gate Avenue

Amity Reb. Lodge, No. 161
1254 Market Street

Loyal Reb. Lodge, No. 215
2174 Market Street

Mission Reb. Lodge, No. 225
Schuberts Hall, 16th and Mission

Jubilee Reb. Lodge, No. 239
431 Duboce Avenue

Freja Reb. Lodge, No. 284
2174 Market Street

San Francisco Reb. Lodge, No. 302
159 Church Street

Golden City Reb. Lodge, No. 304
2174 Market Street

I. O. O. F. Directory
San Francisco, Cal.

Grand Lodge, I. O. O. F.
H. D. Richardson Grand Secretary
Grant Building, San Francisco

Grand Encampment
W. H. Barnes Grand Scribe
1999 Post St., San Francisco

Rebekah Assembly
Mary E. Donoho Secretary
Grant Building, San Francisco

S. F. Relief Committee
1254 Market Street
Meets every Sunday at 10 A. M.
A. M. Brand, Secretary

Excelsior Degree Lodge
222 Van Ness Avenue
Meets Second and Fourth
Saturday Evening

Subordinate Lodges

California Lodge, No. 1
1254 Market Street

San Francisco Lodge, No. 3
222 Van Ness Avenue

Harmony Lodge, No. 13
222 Van Ness Avenue

Yerba Buena Lodge, No. 15
1254 Market Street

Templar Lodge, No. 17
134 Fulton Street

Magnolia Lodge, No. 29
1254 Market Street

Bay City Lodge, No. 71
408 Van Ness Avenue

Farnsworth Lodge, No. 95
1254 Market Street

Abou Ben Adhem Lodge, No. 115
222 Van Ness Avenue

Germania Lodge, No. 116
222 Van Ness Avenue

Concordia Lodge, No. 122
Geary and Steiner Streets

Apollo Lodge, No. 123
431 Duboce Avenue

Spartan Lodge, No. 125
14th and Railroad Ave.

Unity Lodge, No. 131
Schubert's Hall, 16th and Mission

Hermann Lodge, No. 145
2121 Market Street

Pacific Lodge, No. 155
321 Devisadero Street

Occidental Lodge, No. 179
1254 Market Street

Cosmopolitan Lodge, No. 194
3345 Seventeenth Street

Golden Gate Lodge, No. 204
1254 Market Street

Subordinate Lodges
CONTINUED

Alta Lodge, No. 205
1254 Market Street

Franco-American Lodge, No. 207
240 Golden Gate Ave.

Fidelity Lodge, No. 222
1254 Market Street

Morse Lodge, No. 257
1254 Market Street

Western Addition Lodge, No. 285
1254 Market Street

Excelsior Lodge, No. 310
2337 Mission Street

Golden West Lodge, No. 322
1254 Market Street

Presidio Lodge, No. 334
134 Fulton Street

Sargent Lodge, No. 368
1254 Market Street

Odin Lodge, No. 393
2174 Market Street

Columbus Lodge, No. 394
1524 Powell Street

McKinley Lodge, No. 396
240 Golden Gate Avenue

Encampments

Golden Gate Encampment, No. 1
1254 Market Street

San Francisco Canton, No. 5
1254 Market Street

Walhalla Encampment, No. 7
1254 Market Street

Wildey Encampment, No. 23
1254 Market Street

Unity Encampment, No. 26
1254 Market Street

Oriental Encampment. No. 57
1254 Market Street

Listing of lodges in San Francisco, along with Committee
assignments (cover on left, and inside on right).

Mary T. Lyon, President Rebekah
Assembly, 1891 (First President).

Group of "Modern Rebekahs", Mission Rebekah Lodge No. 225 in 1899.

Adele Stockwell. President of the Rebekah Assembly in 1915.

I.O.O.F. Orphan's Home in Gilroy, California, at the turn of the century.

I. O. O. F. ORPHANS HOME, MASON CITY, IOWA.

Front and back of a postcard sent to Presidio Lodge No. 334, from a San Francisco member visiting another state.

CHAPTER 14

THE QUOTES

"From personal observation I know this is the fact the City of San Francisco is relieving distressed Odd Fellows, furnishing employment for many, is examining every case with care that the funds of the lodges might judiciously be expended."

Samuel Hale Parker

"Under the most benignant reign of benefits and favors our Order has been gradually and judiciously extending itself throughout the state—our principles and precepts have been rapidly diffusing themselves amongst the masses of society, and our altar-fires, wherever enkindled, have burned with a warmth and brightness that gave the world assurance of an elevated and glorious philanthropy."

Dr. John Frederick Morse

"During the past year the Angel of Death has been busy in our ranks, and some of our noblest members have been stricken down in the pride and vigor of manhood."

James A. Bohen

Grand Master Bohen was reporting on the deaths of various members, including this one of Los Angeles Lodge No. 35. Member H. R. Myles, a Past Grand, had been killed in a steam boiler explosion on the tugboat *Ada Hancock* in the Bay of San Pedro.

"We may restrain our desires, but cannot very easily change our nature; and I, like all other mortals, am not exempt from the common 'ills the flesh is heir to.' It is natural for a man to be pleased with the applause of his fellow men, and although he is always conscious

James A. J. Bohen, the Tenth Grand Master of California in 1862, was also a member of Yerba Buena Lodge No. 15. He died of a sudden illness at the age of 38. Hardly able to speak above a whisper, on his death bed, he uttered these words; "I exhort you, brothers, in your <u>daily</u> works of life to exemplify the beauties of Odd Fellowship—to live moral and religious lives—to be charitable, to be generous, to be just."

of his mortality, and knows full well that he, together with all things, must soon pass into oblivion, yet there is still left a longing desire to write his name upon tablets which will endure longer than his mortal frame; he clings to life and memory, and cannot bear to perish from the minds of men and be forgotten."

James A. Bohen

The Grand Master's response upon receiving special recognition from Past Grand Master John Frederick Morse, on May 9, 1863.

"Although we have escaped the horrors of war in our midst, we have had to struggle very frequently with that terrible enemy—fire."

David Kendall

Grand Master David Kendall, in his annual report of 1864, indicating that the Civil War has not pierced the integrity of the state, but rather that fire has been a worse "enemy."

"We all well know the policy to minimize the loss of life at this time, to keep no record of deaths but those where there was some possibility of identification; but it is useless to conceal the truth, for the

historians, who in after years write an authentic account of the 'earthquake and fire of 1906,' will place a figure far and beyond those given to the world today. How many poor souls were lost in that awful holocaust will never be known. Perhaps it is well it is so."

William Wyler Phelps

"This war presents to Odd Fellowship a greater opportunity than ever before to prove its value to humanity. The very existence of civilization, human liberty, and democracy are threatened. Women and little children are dying by thousands in Europe and Asia from starvation and other causes brought on by this war."

Frank C. Goudy, Grand Sire

"More than two million of our boys were either engaged in active battle on the bloody fields of France, or were in training. But, while the war clouds were hanging low and the hearts and minds of men were keenly anxious that the tremendous struggle going on should soon cease, while the whole world seemed disturbed and somewhat apprehensive as to the future, the principles of our beloved Order shone forth with an ever-increasing lustre." World War I

Hugh W. Brunk

"One year ago today, amid a war-torn world, with victory in sight but not yet achieved, when all attention was directed toward Allied Nations Peace Conference in the City of San Francisco, who were laying the foundation of a hoped for—everlasting peace—a limited session of the Grand Lodge of the Independent Order of Odd Fellows of California was called to order in San Francisco to lay plans for a better fraternal world."

Harry B. Dahlem

"We speak of him as dead because we hear his voice no more. We tell our friends he died in the city of San Francisco, November 29, 1943, and was buried by the officers of this Grand Lodge. But in a very true sense, James W. Harris is not dead."

Eldred Charles, Past Grand Master

James W. Harris was born in Pictou County, Nova Scotia, on December 29, 1854. At the age of 17, he traveled to the United States, residing in Rhode Island, Massachusetts, and Illinois. He returned to Nova Scotia in December of 1874 and joined the Odd Fellows. In 1875, he moved to San Francisco, California, transferring his membership in the Odd Fellows to Alta Lodge No. 205, later joining Templar Lodge No. 17. After additional traveling throughout the state, he finally returned to San Francisco and took a more committed role in the Order. He rose through the chairs quickly, eventually becoming a Degree Master, then a District Deputy Grand Master. He joined the Encampment branch (Oriental Encampment No. 56), also remaining equally active, rising to the office of Grand Patriarch in California. In 1888, Harris was elected Grand Treasurer of the Grand Lodge of California. He was also a member of the Patriarchs Militant. He was described in the following: "He is a man of strong individuality, extremely practical, a thorough judge, of width, breadth, and thickness, quiet and dignified in his bearing; an excellent judge of men. Brother Harris has a host of friends. As a speaker he is terse, going directly to the point; expressing himself clearly, logically and with force." He also served as Chairman of the Special Relief Committee to oversee the needs of the lodges after the heavy damage and toll cause by the 1906 earthquake and fire. He remained Grand Treasurer until his death in 1943. Harris died at 88 years 11 months of age. He was active in all branches of the Order.

James W. Harris served as Grand Treasurer for California for 55 years, until his death.

During the research of this book, James W. Harris was chosen randomly as a study subject. Not only were multiple photos of him available, but various references were made of him in the journals of Odd Fellowship. There were scores of members of this organization that could have been chosen as focal points, as all have unique and interesting histories. In this regard, this project has not been an exhaustive research. There are so many stories, events, and individuals that the direction could have been different and voluminous. However, one fact did repeat itself time and time again—that Odd Fellowship was the strongest, largest, and most influential fraternal organization in California until the late 1920s.

> *"I turned to take a last look at those faces on the wall, our Past Grand Masters and Past Grand Patriarchs. Truly it was a sad parting: hardly one among them whom I had not personally known, many of them had for years been warm personal friends, and it was a sad, sad parting indeed. As I left the room for what was to be the last time, I turned to say Good Bye to my predecessors, T. Rodgers Johnson and Walter B. Lyon, and then passing out of the door, a final look at our Grand Master, Samuel H. Parker, whose cheerful smile seemed to say, 'God reigns and all is well.'"*
>
> *George T. Shaw*

In his 1906 report, George T. Shaw, the Grand Secretary, describing his last trip into the Odd Fellows Building to retrieve what he could from the Grand Lodge office after the San Francisco earthquake and fire. He died only 7 weeks later.

An 1899 photo of the Grand Secretary's office, located at Seventh & Market Streets. Note the portraits of all the Past Grand Masters. Standing to the right is the Grand Secretary, George Thomas Shaw.

CHAPTER 15

THE PROGRESSION— THEN AND NOW

The social dynamic of the organization changed as well. When, until 1971, an applicant was required to be a male "of white blood," today everyone is welcome. There is no gender or race barrier. In fact, women have played a big role in promoting the growth of the Order in recent years. People of every background are seen in the lodge room. It should be pointed out that most organizations set the same criteria and standards for admitting applicants. But not all have changed in order to open their doors to everyone. Because San Francisco is generally accepted as being more progressive, it is no wonder why changes are more easily noticeable in this city. Discrimination would not follow the principles of the Odd Fellows.

As noted, one of the Order's previous prerequisites for membership would require an applicant to be a male of "white blood." It is ironic, given at that period of time up to the 1960s, the reference of "white blood" would have also excluded people of Italian decent, because of the commonality of this group traditionally being associated with the Catholic faith. Catholics were commonly kept out of the Order in rural areas.

Catholics were prevented from joining many organizations. Seemingly, San Francisco Odd Fellowship has always been on the cutting edge of progressivism, allowing "foreigners" to pervade its fraternal ranks. Columbus Lodge No. 394 was instituted February 27, 1906, in San Francisco. Thirty-one Italian Americans were initiated to form the new Italian-speaking lodge. The following residents of San Francisco are listed as charter members: Cyril Alexander Guglielmoni

A membership application to Alta Lodge No. 205, submitted by George Washington Ross in 1943. Notice one of the requirements for membership: "I am of full white blood" (A physician's certificate included in the application was required for all applicants).

(the lodge's first representative to Grand Lodge in 1907), Luigi Guinasso, Frederick Figoni, Stephen J. Rossi, Frank Sperlari, John Fiscalini, Eduardo Effisimo, Joseph Palmieri, Angelo Devencenzi, Erennio Melogli, Joseph Figone, Angelo Lagomarsino, Pietro Ramazini, Angelo Ramazini, Angelo Moreschi, Paul Arata, Guiseppe Frediana, Arturo Biaga, Giovanni Farrari, Andrea Simoni, Felice Chifenti, Guiseppe Pellegrini, Giovani Gambarini, Marco Stassi, Andre Ferrari, Niclas Grilich, Antonio D'Andrea, John Ferrari, Luigi Chaippe, Armanini, Rocci Matteucci, and Louis Ferrari.

By the 1920s, the Columbus Lodge reached a membership of over three hundred. However, with the overall decline in Odd Fellowship, by 1949, the Columbus Lodge membership had slipped to just twenty-one members. The lodge met at Seventh & Market streets until June 5, 1951, when it gave up its charter.

Franco-American Lodge No. 207, a French-speaking lodge, was instituted August 16, 1872. Today, this lodge is still active—and continues to conduct its meeting in French. Its charter members included: Phillippi Theas (the lodge's first Noble Grand and first representative to Grand Lodge in 1873), Meyer Ruef, Auguste Derre, Norbert Landry, Joseph Lenormand, Francois Paul Masson, Henri Latroadee, Auguste Casamajon, Eugene Robinet, Emile Henri Cardinet, Guiseppe Cadenasso, Jean Renault, Victor J. LeBert, and Orsein Lemaitre.

In the year 2000, the Independent Order of Odd Fellows in America allowed women into its ranks. It is noted this organization was not forced to accept women, but did so to take advantage of an opportunity to create new growth and keep in step with a modern society. In the past few years, women have added greatly to the Order. By 2007, of the eight Odd Fellows lodges in San Francisco, Yerba Buena Lodge No. 15, Bay City Lodge No. 71, Apollo Lodge No. 123, and Golden West Lodge No. 322 will have had women as presiding officers (Noble Grands). All eight lodges have seen success because of the disappearance of the gender barrier.

Today, the Rebekahs confer the Rebekah Degree upon their members. Men have always been allowed to receive the Rebekah Degree since its inception. However, these men were required to first become members of an Odd Fellows lodge. Rebekahs, in the beginning, were wives of Odd Fellows. The Rebekah membership was then opened to the daughters of Odd Fellows. Not any woman could join! As the years passed, the rules were relaxed and most women were allowed to apply for membership in the Rebekahs. Still, Odd Fellows could join the Rebekah Lodge, but women were not allowed to join the lodges of the men.

In the early days, even until the 1960s, there were some churches that opposed the Odd Fellows because they thought the organization was undermining the church, trying to usurp its authority. However, this was—and still is—not correct. It is not a religious institution, nor has it ever claimed to be. Its principles of Friendship, Love, and Truth are based on Christianity ideals because the predominate and "accepted" institution in America at the time Odd Fellows' degrees were created was Christianity. The members of that period identified with this faith.

Today, we find members of all faiths: Muslim, Christian, Jewish, Buddhist, etc. The Order does not take the place of any person's religion, nor does it seek to religiously satisfy a person's needs. One does not need to be religious to become an Odd Fellow. But a person with religious ideals in his heart and mind may fit that character of an Odd Fellow.

The main tenet of Odd Fellowship is to *"relieve the distressed, bury the dead, and educate the orphan."* Of course, the Order must adapt in today's ever evolving society. How many fraternal organizations can actually afford to bury all of their deceased members? The costs of burials are expensive. The closest thing to an "orphans' home" is the Rebekah Children's Services in Gilroy, California. This is 75 miles south of San Francisco. To *relieve the distressed* seems to be all that lodges can do to meet their goals.

In recent years, the Order has defined itself, *"to improve the character of mankind"* by employing its main principles of *Friendship, Love, and Truth*. Today, the Order struggles to answer the this question: Can an organization continue when all it has to offer is Friendship, Love, and Truth? Most lodges have very little assets to make an impact in one geographical location. Also, with so few members, what message may be sent to any given community? To survive, the Odd Fellows must show to the world it can "improve the character of mankind through friendship, love, and truth."

The Odd Fellows organization grew for years after the 1906 disaster; however, the Order was not immune to the affects of the economic turmoil that fell upon the nation in the late 1920s. The Great Depression hit the Odd Fellows every bit as hard as it did the country.

As the depression worsened, membership plummeted. In 1928, the membership reached its height of 58,882. In 1932, the membership had declined to 41,926. Of course, people chose to eat and use every means possible to support their families as opposed to giving up valuable dollars for dues in the Odd Fellows, or any organization for that matter.

President Roosevelt's New Deal changed the way Americans would sustain themselves in future years. His administration created Social Security benefits to aid disabled, elderly, and other needy persons. The altering of roles in who or what entity provided the social benefits greatly affected the need of a beneficial society like the Odd Fellows. It is ironic a member of the Odd Fellows would be the instrument in providing assistance to an entire country.

It was in line with those teachings of the Odd Fellows that President Roosevelt sought to relieve those in distress. In a letter to the members of the Odd Fellows, dated February 26, 1936, he stated, "We have incorporated in our good works, education, establishment of homes for the aged, the indigent, the widow and the orphan, so that it is our proud boast that every Grand Lodge in the United States has one or more of these institutions or has taken steps toward their establishment." It was no wonder this country saw those policies so closely aligned with the principles of Odd Fellowship within the New Deal once he took the presidency.

Social programs were established on a federal level, thus affecting some of the social organizations like the Odd Fellows. Membership continued to fall. In 1939, the membership in the state of California had plummeted to 28,302. The Order had lost over twenty thousand members in 10 short years. With World War II, there was a very slight increase in membership, and it is assumed during those years that veterans sought a continued brotherhood and shared companionship upon completion of their service.

Another one of the most damaging changes to the I.O.O.F. occurred in 1925. After years of promoting a stipulated sick benefit—at one time the Order's most "distinguishing characteristic"—the Sovereign Grand Lodge eliminated the compulsory requirement that subordinate lodges pay sick benefits. The reason behind this pivotal decision was the mannerism in which sick benefits were being paid; it had devolved incidences of less frequent payments, non-consistent payments, and a lack of desire by many lodges to pay such benefits. Thus, an added factor to the decline of membership occurred. Three years later, the Odd Fellows would feel the affects and membership would slip decade after decade.

From 1947, and every year thereafter, and for the next half a century, the Independent Order of Odd Fellows in California would see a

An 1899 ad depicting the German Hospital on 360 Geary Street. Notice at the bottom of the ad; the rates for Odd Fellows have been reduced.

decline. By the end of 2005, membership had reached a low not seen since 1862, of 5,680. But, there has been a resurgence and brief stabilization recently.

San Francisco lodges still boast the largest Odd Fellows lodges in the world. Since 1849, the Order has persevered in San Francisco. How many organizations can say they have been around in one city for such a long duration? Not many!

It should also be pointed out that the decline in membership is not due to the ideological or the philosophical principles that still define the organization, but rather, the changing of governmental laws preventing members to benefit by their own nonprofit organizations.

Whereas the Odd Fellows was once a beneficial society, assisting and aiding one another exclusively, its members may no longer receive

An ad for Odd Fellow Daniel Norcross' business, circa 1860's.

T. RODGERS JOHNSON,
MANUFACTURER OF
Regalia, Banners, Costumes, Military Embroidery, Etc.,
ODD FELLOWS HALL,
NO. 184 MONTGOMERY STREET, (SECOND STORY,)
SAN FRANCISCO.

☞ Regalia for Lodges and Encampments; Jewels, Seals, Masonic and Odd Fellow' Books, together with a general assortment of P. G.'s R. Purple, Royal Arch and other Regalia, embroidered in a superior style, at Eastern prices.

An advertisement for the T. Rodgers Johnson business from the 1850's. Business was at the Odd Fellows Building on Montgomery Street. T. Rodgers Johnson was a member of San Francisco Lodge No. 3, and served as the order's first Grand Secretary from 1853 until 1875—a year before his death. His last words being: "Oh, how pleasant."

such personal benefits. Changing from a beneficial society on a nation-wide level has caused a need for the Odd Fellows to redefine itself. For the past several decades, the Order has been searching for its identity and its reason for being. It has embraced many programs, from the Arthritis Foundation, Visual Research Foundation (John Hopkins University), United Nations Pilgrimage for Youth Program, to placing a float in the annual Rose Parade in Pasadena, and supporting the I.O.O.F. S.O.S. Children's Village in Cambodia.

Finding the one program that all of the members will accept and embrace has been challenging. However, the evidence still proves the Odd Fellows are doing a wealth of good in every locality, including San Francisco, in which they reside.

In 2007, the Odd Fellows in San Francisco are proud to hold the distinction of having the largest contingency of members throughout the world. There are nearly one thousand members belonging to lodges within the city. In recent years, there has been a resurgence in membership as well. Some of the contributing factors may be the less conservative approach to attracting members. Activities have changed. Lodges in the city tend to have golf tournaments, art shows, overnight tours, and trips to parks, museums, and much, much more. However, if the Order is to survive, it must learn to adapt and integrate within its constantly changing communities, reflecting the social norms of sur-

J. PORCHER, Hatter

1109 Market Street

NEAR SEVENTH

ODD FELLOWS' BUILDING

Patronize Tenants in Building

LATEST STYLES   **LOWEST PRICES**

Ad from the 1899 Fifty Years of Odd Fellowship in the
California book, depicting the J. Porcher Hatter
business at the Odd Fellows building.

roundings. In other words, it should keep evolving, reeducating its membership, and not become recalcitrant.

Segments of the Order in certain geographical—or isolated areas—regions remain archaic or outdated and have not evolved toward modernization. Some are not yet "politically correct" and have not yet embraced acceptable social norms. But changes are occurring. In San Francisco, the Odd Fellows, have progressed and reached socially accepted standards.

The historical aspect of the organization and how it relates to the growth of San Francisco is significant. The most prominent members of society, as well as the average person, made up the membership. This was not an elitist society, but a group of individuals truly believing in the concept of its principles: "Friendship, Love, and Truth." These were San Franciscans! These were members whose characters added to the rich culture this city now enjoys. The Odd Fellows were there when gold was to be found, when railroads were to be built, when buildings were to be constructed, when final resting places needed to be made, when libraries were needed, when people needed relief from disaster, when wars were fought, when jobs were in demand, and when grand affairs and expositions needed participants to promote the growth of the city. In a sense, San Francisco owes its successes and its expansion to the Independent Order of Odd Fellows.

"San Francisco Spirit of Odd Fellowship #1"

Since 1849, the Odd Fellows have made San Francisco its home. It has faced tough decisions and even tragedy, but the Order still has a presence in the City-by-the-Bay. In the future, what becomes of the Odd Fellows organization is anyone's guess. But, the history left behind by this fraternity has been significant to San Francisco.

"San Francisco Spirit of Odd Fellowship #2"

BIBLIOGRAPHY

Barnes, William H. *1915 Official Souvenir Programme.* San Francisco: Marshall Press, 516 Mission Street, San Francisco, 1915.

Bronson, William. *The Earth Shook, The Sky Burned.* New York: Doubleday, 1959.

Christy, Frank S. *California Odd Fellowship. 1849–1988 Early History of Odd Fellowship In California.* CA: Linden Publications, 1988.

Close, Barbara Rose. *San Francisco California I.O.O.F. Crematory Records.* Oakland, California: California Genealogical Society, 2001.

Cremation. Odd Fellows' Cemetery Association. San Francisco, CA: Joseph Winterburn & Company, Printers and Electrotypers, 417 Clay Street, San Francisco, 1899.

Executive Committee Golden Jubilee Celebration, I.O.O.F. of California. *Fifty Years of Odd Fellowship in California.* San Francisco: H. S. Crocker Company, 1899.

Hascall, Lee Chaflin. *Official History of Odd Fellowship: The Three-Link Fraternity.* Edited by Henry Leonard Stillson (revised). Boston, Mass.: The Fraternity Publishing Company, 1910.

Hewins, Caroline Maria. *Boys and Girls' Reading.* Library Journal, 1982: 182.

Johnson, Kenneth M. *San Francisco As It Is.* Georgetown, California: The Talisman Press, 1964.

Official History of Odd Fellowship: The Three-Link Fraternity. Boston, Mass.: The Fraternity Publishing Company, 1898.

Phillips, David L. *Letters from California. Its Mountains, Valleys, Plains, Lakes, Rivers, Climate, and Productions. Also its Railroads, Cities, Towns, and People, as Seen in 1876.* Springfield, Illinois State Journal Co., 1877.

Proceedings of the Sixty-first Annual Sessions of the Grand Encampment, I.O.O.F. of California. San Francisco: The Marshall Press, 1918.

Proceedings of the R. W. Grand Lodge of the State of California, Independent Order of Odd Fellows, From its Organization, May 17, 1853, to May 7, 1859, Inclusive. Vol. I, San Francisco: Frank Eastman, Printer, Franklin Office, III Washington Street, San Francisco.

Proceedings of the R. W. Grand Lodge of the State of California, Independent Order of Odd Fellows, May 1860–May 1864. Vol. II. Sacramento: H. S. Crocker & Co., Third Street, Sacramento.

Proceedings of the R. W. Grand Lodge of the State of California, Independent Order of Odd Fellows, May 1865–May 1868. San Francisco: Joseph Winterburn & Company, Printers and Electrotypers, 417 Clay Street, San Francisco.

Proceedings of the California Grand Lodge of the Independent Order of Odd Fellows of the State of California. San Francisco: Joseph Winterburn Company, Printers and Electrotypers, 417 Clay Street, San Francisco, 1875.

Proceedings of the California Grand Lodge of the Independent Order of Odd Fellows of the State of California. San Francisco: Joseph Winterburn Company, Printers and Electrotypers, 417 Clay Street, San Francisco, 1880.

Proceedings of the California Grand Lodge of the Independent Order of Odd Fellows of the State of California. San Francisco: Joseph Winterburn Company, Printers and Electrotypers, 417 Clay Street, San Francisco, 1906.

Proceedings of the California Grand Lodge of the Independent Order of Odd Fellows of the State of California. San Francisco: The Marshall Press, 516 Mission Street, San Francisco, 1918.

Proceedings of the California Grand Lodge of the Independent Order of Odd Fellows of the State of California. San Francisco: The Marshall Press, 516 Mission Street, San Francisco, 1919.

Proceedings of the California Grand Lodge of the Independent Order of Odd Fellows of the State of California. San Francisco: Borden Printing Company, 249–253 Minna Street, San Francisco, 1928.

Proceedings of the California Grand Lodge of the Independent Order of Odd Fellows of the State of California. San Francisco: Borden Printing Company, Inc., 329 Minna Street, San Francisco, 1944.

Proceedings of the California Grand Lodge of the Independent Order of Odd Fellows of the State of California. Sacramento: Sanderson's Print Shop, 731 O Street, Sacramento, 1946.

Proceedings of the California Grand Lodge of the Independent Order of Odd Fellows of the State of California. San Francisco: Golden Gate Press, Inc., 117 Golden Gate Avenue, San Francisco, 1948.

Proceedings of the California Grand Lodge of the Independent Order of Odd Fellows of the State of California. San Francisco: Golden Gate Press, Inc., 117 Golden Gate Avenue, San Francisco, 1951.

Proceedings of the California Grand Lodge of the Independent Order of Odd Fellows of the State of California. Santa Clara: Progressive Solutions, 2006.

Schmidt, Alvin J. *Fraternal Organizations.* Westport, Conn: Greenwood Press, 1980.

Stellman, Louis J. *Sam Brannan, Builder of San Francisco.* New York: Exhibition Press, 1953.

Ungaretti, Lorri. *Images of America: San Francisco's Richmond District.* Arcadia Publishing, 2003.

Fifth Annual Report of the Officers & Directors. Odd Fellows Hall Association of San Francisco, Incorporated. San Francisco: Joseph Winterburn Company, Printers and Electrotypers. San Francisco, 1885.

Seventh Annual Report of the Officers & Directors. Odd Fellows Hall Association of San Francisco, Incorporated. San Francisco: Joseph Winterburn Company, Printers and Electrotypers. San Francisco, 1887.

Eight Annual Report of the Officers & Directors. Odd Fellows Hall Association of San Francisco, Incorporated. San Francisco: Joseph Winterburn Company, Printers and Electrotypers. San Francisco, 1888.

Twelfth Annual Report of the Officers & Directors. Odd Fellows Hall Association of San Francisco, Incorporated. San Francisco: Joseph Winterburn Company, Printers and Electrotypers, 417 Clay Street. San Francisco, 1892.

Seventeenth Annual Report of the Officers & Directors. Odd Fellows Hall Association of San Francisco, Incorporated. San Francisco: Joseph Winterburn Company, Winterburn, 1897.

Nineteenth Annual Report of the Officers & Directors. Odd Fellows Hall Association of San Francisco, Incorporated. San Francisco: Joseph Winterburn Company, Printers and Electrotypers, 417 Clay Street, San Francisco, 1899.

1904 Official Souvenir Program of the 80th Annual Session Sovereign Grand Lodge, Independent Order of Odd Fellows. Programme Committee, San Francisco, 1904.

Magazine

"Welcome Odd Fellows," *WASP,* 1904. Vol. LII, 13:228. WASP Publishing Company, 502–6 Mission St., San Francisco. (September 24, 1904): 228.

Newspapers

"Fraternal Fellowship," *The Daily Alta,* (December 15, 1890): 8.

"The Grand Lodge," *The Daily Alta,* (May 13, 1891): 8.

"Society," *San Francisco Evening Post,* (January 1, 1891): 4.

"Advancement of Women," *San Francisco Examiner,* (December 12, 1890): 4.

Miscellaneous

Letter to all lodges in San Francisco from Alva R. Young, Junior Lodge Committee. July 15, 1933.

Bulletin of the Excelsior Lodge No., I.O.O.F. Honolulu, Hawaii. July, 1936.

Odd Fellows Hall Association of San Francisco, Incorporated. Minutes of Corporation, 1906.

Fraternal Societies. J. C. Herbert Emery, Department of Economics, University of Calgary. EH.Net, August 2000.

"Radio Address On Samuel Brannan," by Louise E. Tabor. KYA. September 6, 1934.

Note: In order for the reader to appreciate the historical significance related to the publishers of that era, the bibliography contains the complete addresses for many of the publishers.

INDEX

Come an' Get It

THE STORY OF THE OLD COWBOY COOK

With drawings by Nick Eggenhofer

NORMAN

Come an' Get It

THE STORY OF THE OLD COWBOY COOK

By Ramon F. Adams

UNIVERSITY OF OKLAHOMA PRESS

By RAMON F. ADAMS

Come an' Get It: The Story of the Old Cowboy Cook
    (Norman, 1952)
Charles M. Russell, the Cowboy Artist (with Homer E.
    Britzman) (Pasadena, 1948)
Western Words: A Dictionary of the Range, Cow Camp,
    and Trail (Norman, 1944)
Cowboy Lingo (Boston, 1936)

Dedicated to Elman and Margaret
and to the memory of all the old hard-boiled
but ever faithful cooks of the cow range

Foreword

"COME AN' GET IT!" This familiar and welcome call
of the old range and trail is dimming with the years. The
man who issued the summons—the old range cook—has
been too long overlooked by writers of Western fact and
fiction. Scattered and meager mention of him has been
made, but as yet there has been no complete record of his
life, his character, or his importance in the development
of the West, except in the memories of the men who came
under his direct influence.

To enlighten the younger generation and to keep his
memory alive, I would like to place between permanent
covers the story of this unusual character, his functions,
the food he served, and his manner of preparing it. No less
interesting is the wagon he commanded, its evolution, and
the influence it exercised in the growth of the West's great
cattle industry, as well as its place in the hearts of the men
who called it home. Although there are still a few chuck
wagons in operation upon the larger ranches today, they

have become so scarce that one is rarely seen except in a museum or in a rodeo parade.

You will note that this little book is written in the past tense. There is a reason for that. I am trying to tell you of the old-time cook and his wagon during the days he was in his glory. His kind have since followed the buffalo and the dodo bird. And though to write about him now is but an epitaph to his memory, I do not want his passing to go unnoticed and unhonored.

It is fitting, no matter how incomplete and inadequate the effort, that a recording should be made of his place and influence upon our Western civilization. Without him there would likely have been no cattle industry—certainly not the big business into which it developed.

It was the cowboy who cleared the frontier of the savage Indian and opened the land for the farmer who later came with his plow to create the Dust Bowl. But without the cook and his commissary the cowboy's work would have been limited. There would have been no trail drives to rescue Texas from bankruptcy and spread the cattle business to the states and territories to the north and west; there would have been no roundups so necessary to the development of the growing industry.

As an army marches on its mess-kitchen, so the cowboy worked with his chuck wagon. The strenuous outdoor work he did required lots of fuel to keep the engine going full steam, and he looked to the cook to furnish this fuel in large quantities three times daily.

The cook well knew his responsibilities. As a hotel

chef required to prepare fancy-named dishes, he would take no prizes. He had no butter and eggs for delicate pastries, but he understood his business of preparing good substantial grub for ravenous appetites—grub both satisfying and strengthening. As long as he could prepare sizzling steaks, concoct a stew, cook the beans so they wouldn't rattle in the tin plates, build sourdough biscuits, and boil coffee until it was plenty strong, he could qualify as a cook.

No man ever worked under greater difficulties or with fewer conveniences and yet was so successful in his calling. Hard of visage, rough of speech, and often with a twisted outlook upon life, the cook was nevertheless loyal and possessed many talents.

If, with clemency, we overlook his crankiness and ill temper to see his more worthy side, we find him to be a man of immeasurable value. Not only did he perform a necessary duty, but his life and traditions furnish us with a most unique character, the likes of which we will perhaps never see again.

There are still cooks upon the cow range, for men have to be fed. But they are of a younger generation and, like the cowboy, have been tamed. There are no more trail drives, nor open-range roundups; the color of the wagon cook's calling has faded with the advancement of modern progress. If, in trying to keep his memory green, I tell you something of his life, his character, his work, and its importance, I will feel that the labor of gathering this material has been justified.

I wish to thank such old-time personal friends as the late Jack Potter, J. Evetts Haley, the late John M. Hendrix, and Frank King for the stories and information they have furnished; and Oren Arnold, W. C. Holden, Con Price, and other authors quoted, as well as their publishers, for kind permission to repeat some of their stories. All persons mentioned in footnotes have been most co-operative. My thanks also to Agnes Wright Spring, a friend of long standing, for furnishing me with many of the recipes; to Mrs. Florence Franklin and Bob Kennon, of Montana, Mrs. Julia Michener and Alexander Melton, of the Panhandle of Texas, for information they have furnished; and to Shorty Roberts, of Tucson, Arizona, a former wagon cook for the famous John Slaughter outfit. A goodly portion of my thanks and appreciation is reserved for Mrs. Vivien Keatley and Orville McPherson, both of Tucson, for their reading of the manuscript and their constructive criticism. My gratitude to Henry Biederman, editor of *The Cattleman* magazine, of Fort Worth, Texas, for graciously giving special permission to use the stories by John M. Hendrix. I am especially indebted to Carter ("Tex") Taylor for writing his "Down My Way" rhyming prose jingles expressly for this book. This acknowledgment of my indebtedness to them all is but a feeble attempt to express my deep gratitude.

RAMON F. ADAMS

Dallas, Texas
August 1, 1952

Contents

Come an' Get It

THE STORY OF THE OLD COWBOY COOK

PART I
The Wagon and the Cook

The wagon is headquarters and old Cookie runs the show; four dun mules to pull it, crack the whip and let 'er go. The wagon is a good one with bows and tarp on top, and a coonie underneath it, carries ever'thing we've got. The wagon bed is full of rolls, duffle bags, and feed, an' hangin' all around the bed is ever'thing we need. On the front of this here wagon is a spring seat and a box, where the boys kin keep their hobbles and a lot of other stuff.

On the back end of this wagon there's a box plumb full but neat; it's got tools fer us an' Cookie an' a heap of grub to eat. There's sugar, salt an' pepper, knives an' forks an' spoons; a great big box of soda an' some apricots an' prunes. There's a can of bakin' powder, box of matches, sourdough yeast, cans of milk, Arbuckles coffee, liniment for man an' beast. There's a sack of flour an' cornmeal, can of lick, soap an' lard. Flour sacks hangin' in the sun an' Cookie standin' guard.

Tex Taylor

CHAPTER 1 *The Wagon*

*"The wheel that creaks the
loudest gets the grease."*

ONE OF THE TRAGEDIES accompanying the breaking up
of the big ranches was the passing of the chuck wagon and
its cook. The coming of wire fences and small pastures
crowded out this glamorous phase of ranch life until now
it is but a memory—a memory which brings moisture to the
eyes of old-time cowmen when those good old days are
mentioned. For on the old open range and in the big pastures the chuck wagon and its cook were an institution, the
indispensable nerve center of any outfit. If ever there was
an uncrowned king on the cow range, it was the wagon
cook. He was monarch of all he surveyed, the supreme
sovereign of his jurisdiction. "As techy as a wagon cook"
has long been a common cow-country comparison fully
justified by the mold of his despotic disposition.

As a rule range cooks were a homely lot, possessing
hair-trigger tempers, many of them being as quick with a
gun as they were with a pothook. But the cook's word was
law. The chuck wagon—and sixty feet around it—was under

5

his absolute control. The roundup boss was careful to use diplomacy when giving orders around the wagon, and even the owner of the cattle walked softly there.

Although the chuck wagon's chief duty was to furnish food, it performed many other functions and was responsible for the most pleasant memories of the cowboy's life. It was his bed as well as his board; it was his wardrobe, his social center, his hospital, his recreational rendezvous, and his home. To it he was always loyal. By throwing his bedroll into it, he pledged his allegiance to the brand for which it rolled. Even if he were dissatisfied with the whole outfit and "cussed" the cook for his crankiness or lack of ability, he allowed no outsider to do so as long as he was on the pay roll.

The brand burned upon the sides of the wagon was his address, and though it was seldom long in one place, he usually knew where to find it. If he did become lost, he threw the reins loose on his horse's neck and gave the wise animal its head. Guided by instinct, the horse found the wagon without hesitation because he knew it was the place where he would be relieved of his burden and get time to graze and rest.

The wagon, on roundup, wherever it camped, was the place where the herds were brought to be worked. It was at the wagon that the cowboy got his meals, his rest, and his fresh horse. Here, after his day's work was done, he did his washing and his mending.

Perhaps after a hard day's riding some of the romp and playfulness had been taken out of him. Then he might prefer to loll and smoke, talk and sing until his healthy body had thrown off its fatigue and it was time to crawl into his blankets to snatch what sleep he could before being called for guard duty. Long days, short nights, hard work, little sleep—such was the life of a cowboy in spite of the romantic stuff written about him. Yet many men grew old in following the wagon and would have no other life by choice.

The roundup on the open range developed as the cattle business increased and extended. Like everything else in a moving world, it broadened in scope on demand, and its growth influenced the evolution of its commissary. The "big roundup" arose as a necessity when ranches and herds became more numerous. Ranges began to overlap their borders; neighboring herds intermingled. Stockmen had to adopt co-operative methods by which they could work one another's range to gather up and sort out all the cattle in one operation. As roundups grew in size and extent, the larger outfits sent chuck wagons. At these gatherings each cook vied with his fellow cooks in trying for the best meals and the choicest location in the new section to be worked.

Ordinarily the word *wagon* denotes a means of transportation, for wood, freight, feed, or water. A ranch might possess many kinds of wagons, such as the freight wagon, the calf wagon, and the wood wagon, the cake wagon, and the bed wagon. Each always bore its proper prefix and was never mentioned without it.

But when a cowman talked about *the wagon,* he meant the chuck wagon. No descriptive prefix was needed. The magic of these two words meant home, food, the warmth of a crackling fire, dry clothes, and good fellowship. It was the magnet which drew men together.

"Which way's the wagon?" was the usual inquiry of a stranger when he approached a roundup crew or trail outfit. There he knew he would be welcome; there he could find food, information, and medicine if he were ill.

The chuck wagon, as we know it today, came with the great organized roundups when the cattle industry hit the open country after the Civil War. As this colorful and uniquely American occupation, gathering cattle on the range, developed, its most important adjunct, the commissary, went through a series of evolutions.

The primitive forerunner of the roundup consisted of neighboring stockmen getting together to look over each other's herds for strays. Such neighborly gatherings were called by the various names of "cow hunts," "cow works," "works," "cow drives," or were spoken of as "runnin' cattle."[1] Each man "packed" his own food in a saddle pocket or a flour sack tied behind the cantle of his saddle.

Food, in those days, was simple and scanty. Each man carried a small supply of roasted coffee, salt, and cold corn bread or hard biscuit. Sometimes, if the bread supply ran short, a man would be sent to a neighboring ranch to request the "lady of the ranch" to bake some biscuits. These he usually brought back to camp in a flour sack. Some men augmented the menu with salt pork, and if the crowd was

[1] J. Frank Dobie, *Vaquero of the Brush Country* (Dallas, Southwest Press, 1929), 13.

8

large enough, a beef would be killed. Each man brewed his own coffee to suit his individual taste, and there was no "cussin' the cook," a privilege enjoyed by later-day cow-hands.

If the hunt was to cover distant territory, supplies were pooled and packed upon the back of a mule with a regular pack saddle and alforkas. Before the Civil War when there was a sizable company, a Negro slave would be taken along to do the cooking, or a Mexican hired hand would be used. These primitive commissaries served their purpose in furnishing rib-sticking food sufficient for hard riding, and had the advantage of breaking camp quickly with no loading of a chuck wagon or searching for a lost one. After chuck wagon days were introduced, an outfit which persisted in packing its food supply in a sack on mule-back, as was sometimes done in the rough country, was called a "greasy-sack outfit," and the mule for such duty was referred to as a "long-eared chuck wagon."

The opening of the Northern markets after the Civil War spurred trail driving on its way to becoming a big business, and with this new phase of the cattle industry came the next evolution of the chuck wagon. The trailing of cattle required men, and men required food. Pack mules served the purpose as long as an outfit stayed close to home where supplies could be replenished without too much loss of time. But traveling on a trail for months at a time with a bunch of hired hands, through an unpopulated country, called for a conveyance which would hold sufficient pro-visions for long stretches between supply points.

9

Thus the heavy, two-wheeled cart—commonly called "camp cart"—was brought into service. This cumbersome vehicle, drawn by two or more yoke of oxen, served for a while. It was equipped with bows to be covered with a tarpaulin in rainy weather, and a water barrel with a tight-fitting lid that would stay on as the vehicle clacked and cried its way over the rough trails.

With the increasing demand for beef in the Northern markets and the competition of trail drivers trying to get their herds to shipping points, the old two-wheeled ox-cart became too slow. When a herd traveled at an average speed of ten miles a day, it would seem no haste was necessary. But the plodding work-oxen made even poorer time, and it was sometimes essential to have the grub wagon ahead to ford a river and establish a camp on the other side before the arrival of the herd for watering and crossing. Then, too, it was often necessary to send the wagon off to pick up supplies at some town not on the line of march. The speed of the commissary department set the pace of the entire

outfit. The crew had to hold up the herd and wait for the grub wagon to catch up if they wanted to eat—and they were always hungry.

To gain speed, the next evolution of the chuck wagon was a four-wheeled vehicle drawn by horses or mules, usually four. It is claimed by some that Charles Goodnight invented the chuck wagon as we know it today. He bought a government wagon, took its running gear over to a woodworker, and had it rebuilt of bois d'arc to his own specifications.[2]

Heretofore the axles of the carts had been made of wood and greased with tar. Colonel Goodnight had axles made of iron and greased with tallow, which was used from that time on until the invention of axle grease. He also added a chuck box at the rear of his wagon, and there has been little change in it to this day.

Any good wagon could serve as a chuck wagon, but some outfits had wagons specifically made to withstand the terrific strains of a rough country. The chuck wagon had to be sturdy, not too long-coupled, and be equipped with fairly wide tires. The narrow-tired wagon of the farmer (called a "butcher-knife wagon" because of the narrow rut its wheels cut into the soil) did not have the wheel strength or the proper traction for the rough usage the chuck wagon experienced.

Soon the Bain, the Studebaker, and the Schutler wagons became the standard. Most of these were from three-

[2] J. Evetts Haley, *Charles Goodnight: Cowman and Plainsman* (Boston, Houghton Mifflin Co., 1936), 121.

to three-and-one-half-inch wagons, this being the diameter of the axle where it entered the hub of the wheel.

The wagons were equipped with a bed consisting of a bottom, and side-boards, and generally supplied with bows over which a wagon sheet could be stretched for protection from rain or sun. Most of them carried extra side-boards for added capacity for the outfit's bedding and duffle.

The invention of the chuck box at the rear of the wagon never received the dignity of a patent, but its use spread over the range and it became standard equipment. The endgate of the wagon bed was removed and this convenient, substantial cupboard was built of strong lumber at the end of the wagon. It was usually two or three feet in depth and its perpendicular front wall was about four feet in height, the whole held firmly in place to the side-boards by wagon rods extending through it. Its rear wall sloped outward from top to bottom and was hinged at the bottom so that it could be swung down at right angles to form a working table. It was supported at this angle by ropes or chains, or, more commonly, by a single heavy prop to the ground, this leg being fastened to the outer edge by rawhide hinges so that it could be folded flat against the outside when the box was closed.

The inside of the box was fitted with partitions, shelves, and drawers. Indeed, here was the original kitchen cabinet. Usually two doors folded snugly over the partitions to hold everything in place while the wagon was on the move. Each item had its place. The larger divisions were for the sourdough jar or keg, the partly used sack of flour, and the bulky utensils. There were convenient drawers for tin plates, cups, spoons, knives, and forks, the "eatin' irons." Within easy reach were the coffee, sugar, beans, lard, rice, dried fruit, and "lick." Another section held salt, pepper, soda, baking powder, and the less bulky commodities, each in tins with close-fitting lids to keep them from spilling out when being jostled over rough country.

Every cook reserved a drawer for a few simple remedies such as quinine, calomel, pills, black draught, and horse liniment, the latter to be used on man or beast. Reserved for the cook's private use in case of "snake bite" or his own "private misery" was a bottle of whiskey, the only whiskey allowed with the wagon. Some ranchmen even forbade this.

The lid of the chuck box, when let down, was the cook's private work bench, and no trespassing was tolerated. Any greenhorn who tried to use it for a dining table would be called names that would peel the hide off a Gila monster. Occasionally this privilege would be granted the wrangler when he ate after the others had finished and the cook was washing up the dishes. Even then he had to "stand in" with the cook. The dining table at the wagon was anywhere on the surrounding prairie, wherever the individual puncher found a place to "set, squat, or hunker." He was privileged to use the ground, his lap, or his bedroll as a table for his plate.

The major part of the heavy supplies, such as flour, bacon, molasses, coffee, beans, and canned goods were carried in the bed of the wagon. Here also the beef was kept.

There were some things carried in the chuck wagon

that would break or leak or shake out, and most cooks were particular about tying these down to stay. No man liked molasses on his pet rope or bedroll, or axle grease on his dried apples.

A supply of grain was carried under the seat of the wagon for the work teams. The spring seat itself was usually much lower on the right side where the driver had weakened that spring and worn the green paint off the seat from long hours of driving.

Attached to the bottom of the wagon bed and beneath the chuck box was sometimes another smaller box with a hinged door. It contained the heavier cooking utensils such as Dutch ovens, pots, and skillets. On one side of the wagon was fastened a water barrel, usually fitted with a wooden spigot and often wrapped in a wet gunny sack or canvas to keep the contents cool. On the other side of the wagon was a tool box. Some wagons carried a jockey box, commonly called the "jewelry chest," outside in front of the bed beneath the foot-board, in which were stored hobbles, a horseshoeing outfit, and anything else that might be needed quickly in case of an emergency.

Beneath the wagon bed was sometimes fastened a *cuña*, Spanish for "cradle." More often it was called the "coonie," "possum belly," or "bitch." This was a rawhide stretched, while green, to the running gear of the wagon. The head and forelegs were fastened to the front of the wagon, the sides to the sides of the bed, and the hind legs to the rear axle. It was filled with rocks while drying to stretch the hide to greater carrying capacity. It was the duty of the wrangler to keep this filled with cow chips ("prairie coal") or wood to be used as emergency fuel in case the next camp was devoid of this commodity.

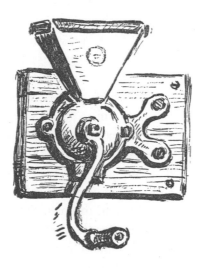

The smaller outfits used only one wagon, which was a carryall for everything—chuck, beds, ax, shovel, and branding irons. The bigger outfits with larger crews had a second wagon, called the "bed wagon" or "hoodlum wagon," which relieved the chuck wagon of the bedrolls, spare saddles, and some of the more unwieldy tools. It was usually driven by the night wrangler, or "night hawk," who, while on this duty, was called the "hood." Some outfits carried an extra wagon to haul fuel, especially when working a timberless section. This vehicle was known as the "chip wagon"

or "hooligan wagon," not to be confused with the "hood-lum."

In later days a "fly" was also included in the cook's equipment. This was a canvas sheet which could be stretched at the end of the chuck wagon to make shade and shelter for the cook. Also a necessary implement for the cook was his "gouch hook" or "pothook," an iron hook used to lift the heavy lids of his cooking utensils. There was also a supply of "fire hooks," short iron rods crooked at each end in opposite directions, from which the cooking vessels were hung over the fire. There were iron stakes to be stuck in the ground vertically and an iron rod to be placed horizontally across them, so that the fire hooks could be hung from it.

With every wagon went one or two large pans or tubs called "wreck pans" or "roundup pans." These were placed in convenient places to receive the dirty dishes after a meal, and woe unto the man who failed to place his dishes therein. Some cooks used a large can for scraps. It was called the "squirrel can," and when anything was lost—whether it be a saddle blanket or a spur—someone would jokingly suggest looking for it in the "squirrel can."

Somewhere in the bed of the wagon or fastened to the side was an ax for chopping wood and a shovel or spade for digging the fire trenches. And, of course, there was the cook's precious sourdough keg. But that sourdough "kag" is another story. More will be told about it in a later chapter.

A writer in the Prescott (Arizona) *Courier* who signed his articles with the initials F.A.G. facetiously described

16

the chuck wagon as a "vehicle used to haul chuck and the cowboy's beds (though I never rightly figured why we brung 'em). The chuck is mainly beans, dried prunes, rice, syrup, biscuits, coffee, and lots o' salt pork. Some outfits even furnish sugar and beef; but the boss sez these all went broke."

The boss, he kin figger an' write in a book, but he shore has to have a chuck wagon cook. The wagon is loaded an' rigged up complete, but without our ole Cookie there's nothin' to eat. This gent's a stemwinder an' knows where he stands, with the boss an' the wrangler an' all the cowhands. He's the king of the wagon and shore loves his throne, an' while he's at work better leave 'im alone.

There are cooks that kin cook; there are cooks that cannot, an' it's a lucky outfit that knows when it's got for its wagon a cook that kin cook up a stew, some biscuits of sourdough, an' frijoles too. Now when our ole Cookie gits through with his cookin' he yells, "Come an' git it," an' sits back a-lookin'. He's techy by now, don't make no remarks, jes' fall to an' eat it like starved medder larks.

Tex Taylor

18

CHAPTER 2 *Sultan of the Skillets*

*"Only a fool argues with a skunk,
a mule, or a cook."*

THE COOK was the most important person in any ranch outfit, for he could keep men working competently more than any other one individual. Cowhands might like everything else about the outfit—the boss, their wages, their mounts—but if the chuck was inferior, scanty, or poorly prepared, they became a discontented and balky lot.

To work efficiently, men must be satisfied; to be satisfied, they must be well fed. The experienced cowman knew that nothing indicated the good or bad management of an outfit like a well-supplied chuck wagon and a good cook. Some outfits were widely known for the thorough manner in which they equipped their wagons. Their contented cowboys spread the news over a wide territory.

But no matter how well supplied the wagon, if the cook was a sorry one, it was sure to be reflected in the work and morale of the men of the outfit. As happens in the case of all malcontents, they became careless and inefficient. On the other hand, if the cook was cheerful and

19

willing and produced eatable food, you would find an outfit striving to work their best. Indeed, he didn't even have
to be cheerful—and few cooks were. The old-time range
cook developed a universal reputation for crankiness. It is
said that if a wagon cook was not hard-boiled, it was because he hadn't cooked long enough.

Originally, perhaps, the range cook's crankiness ema-
nated from the fact that he worked under such adverse conditions. Battling wind, sand, and rains with limited supplies and equipment, trying to prepare a meal for fifteen
to twenty savage appetites, doubtless contributed to his
ill temper. Besides, if he had been raised to the cow business, he was usually past his riding days, and this soured
his disposition.

Although grouchiness became characteristic of the
roundup cook, he had plenty of excuse for it. His work, like
that of a good housewife, was never done. He had scarcely
fallen asleep when it was time to get up again. Duty called
him several hours before the cowhands crawled out of their
soogans. Half the time he was short of fuel. Often it was
wet. Some animal was always kicking dust into the food,
or a colony of insects invaded his sourdough keg. Everything seemingly contrived to test his temper.

Eventually the wagon cook took pride in this reputation for crankiness and did his best to live up to it. He felt
that he had a tradition to uphold. Rarely was a cowboy,
even the most reckless, rash enough to "fool with the cook."
This lord of pots and pans was not a better man physically,
but he had methods of reprisal denied the cowhand. The

coffee might suddenly become weak. The sourdoughs had a way of becoming scorched or yellow with soda. The steaks might be saltless, and there would be no pies to fill a sweet tooth. "Accidents" could happen to create a grub shortage, or the gravel could be left in the beans. Some offender of his rules might learn, too, that all his talents did not run to cooking. At swearing he was an artist whose cuss words could take the frost out of the morning chill and make a mule-skinner jealous.

There was no one particular type in wagon cooks, except that very few were young men. They ran the full gamut of culinary ability from marvelous efficiency to criminal incompetence. One might be a Negro, a Mexican, or a white man from the dregs of the city, whose only knowledge of cow was that it was "dished up in a stew." Many were broken-down punchers whose riding days were over, but who could not endure life away from cattle and horses, and thus took up cooking to follow the chuck wagon. Most all cowboys, of necessity, could cook a little.

Some cooks have been known to divide their time between horse stealing and cooking, following the latter pursuit to give themselves the appearance of respectability. One old fellow, when tired of cooking in Texas, would ride over into Mexico and serve as a general in the army of the rebels. Every time he lost a battle he would drop back to Texas to cook awhile—needed more seasoning, the boys said. They used to call him General Nuisance—behind his back—and told him if he wanted to kill off the enemy, all he had to do was feed them some of his sourdoughs.

Most bosses preferred a native white cook, both at the ranch and at the wagon. Some Negroes were good cooks, but were usually lazy, and, too, white cowboys refused to take orders from them. The Mexican wanted to flavor all the food with chili peppers—a diet which became monotonous to the white man. Foreign-born cooks, such as Germans and Swedes, did not exercise the common "horse sense" with which the cowmen were endowed.

"There was a Swede cook at the Quarter Circle Block," wrote W. P. Rickett. "One evening after supper the cowboys, while sitting around in front of the kitchen, saw a skunk come in the back door and look around. When the cook saw him, he was all excited. Someone said, 'Let him alone and he will go out.'

"But the cook said, 'Me scald him, me scald him.'

"Seizing a teakettle, the cook proceeded to carry out his threat. Every time the hot water fell on him the aroma flew, around and around the Swede and the skunk went. That kitchen wasn't used any more that summer."[1]

Necessary at all times during range work, on trail drives and roundups the wagon cook was even more indispensable. Men at this time needed plenty of food, for the work was exhausting. Since they were away from town or headquarters for perhaps months at a time while on roundup, much depended upon their being well fed and satisfied. No wagon boss with a crew of hungry men on his hands wanted a cook to quit miles from town, where he would be forced

[1] W. P. Rickett, *Fifty Years in the Saddle* (Sheridan, Wyoming, Starr Publishing Co., 1942), 16–17.

22

to ride to hire another. Consequently, a good cook was a jewel and humored in his every whim to keep him at work and his temperament sweet.

The supply of good cooks was always low and the demand keen. Frequently they were hired long before the wagon started out for the spring work. To hold a good cook, he was often paid his wages for a month or two before he was to report to work. Cowhands could gripe and josh each other, but they were warned to let the cook alone or "roll their tails for home." Cowhands were plentiful, but cooks hard to find.

The cooking profession, even in the early days, was sufficiently recognized to demand a standard wage scale. As a rule a cook received from ten to fifteen dollars above the wage paid the cowhand, and a good one was worth it. Some cooks, by reason of their higher pay and the fact that they were essential to the operation of the outfit, felt that they were above the common riders. The cowboys held the opposite view, though few of them had the courage to express such an opinion within the cook's hearing.

The cook rarely condescended to acknowledge a favor audibly. A nod of the head was as far as he went. Yet he was not unappreciative. Though his dignity forbade direct demonstration, the author of the favor might receive an extra helping of food or a cup of coffee after hours. Perhaps there would be a pie for supper which otherwise would not have been made. Consequently, even the most reckless and independent punchers would cheerfully "snake in" wood or gather "bull chips" for his fires, hold slickers over

23

his cooking vessels on rainy mornings, or hook up his teams.

The wagon cook's greatest weakness, like that of most kings, was his love of power, held by virtue of his indispensability. He made his own rules and saw that they were obeyed. He tolerated no cowboy's rummaging around in the wagon to disarrange his orderly placement of the supplies. One part was reserved for their hobbles, and these were all they were allowed to touch, except, perhaps, when some cowboy wanted to help himself to a can of tomatoes to quench his thirst.

The wagon was the cook's royal chamber on wheels. While the cowboys slept upon the prairie rolled in their blankets in fair weather or foul, the cook could take refuge from storms in his canvas-covered chamber, a place he closed to all others. For fear some cowhand might crawl under his sacred wagon for a noonday snooze while waiting for the wrangler to drive in the saddle band, more than one old-time cook has thrown his dishwater under it to make such a bed uninviting.

He allowed no horse to be tied to a wagon wheel or picketed too close to camp. He issued standing orders that riders approaching camp watch the direction of the wind so that no dust be raised to blow into the food he was preparing. Disobedience to this law really brought forth his wrath. Some cooks forbade cowboys wearing leggin's in their domain because of the dust they stir up.

The intrusion of animals into the sanctity of the cook's royal realm always brought forth a display of temper.

"Over in Foard County Dick Hill cooked for an outfit until he was looked upon as one of the family," wrote my old cowboy friend John Hendrix. "One summer the outfit was split up to brand calves and receive small bunches of yearlings that were being bought up from nesters and 'little men.' To serve both crews, the wagon was camped in the Blue Hole country. A long-aged brindle yearling took up with the wagon, using it for shade and salting himself by chewing on the work team's collar pads. No amount of scaring or liberal applications of hot water could persuade him to stay away from the wagon. One afternoon when the dishes were washed up, Dick walked down along the creek to return to the wagon with a half-dried beef hide, a dozen empty tomato cans, and a ten-pound lard bucket half-filled with smooth washed gravel. With awl and stay wire he fringed the hide with cans, placing a little gravel in each and squeezing the tops together to prevent it from losing out.

"From the supply of mule feed in the front end of the wagon he poured a generous portion near the right front wheel and invited the yearling to eat, at the same time tying the loose end of a stake rope around his neck and securing it to a wagon spoke. As he ate, Dick, with the aid of more wire, attached the can fringed hide to the yearling's tail, not loosely, but wired firmly in the burr-infested bush. While the yearling was enjoying the last of his feed Dick reached into the tool box on the front end gate to bring forth a pint bottle of turpentine and a long red cob. As the yearling finished, Dick applied the turpentine-soaked cob —with pressure—where it would be most effective, slipped

25

the stake rope off, and headed the brindle yearling out across the flats.

"A couple of miles out the yearling ran through the day's branding which was being loose herded until cows and calves got together. These he scattered to the four winds, and passed on over the ridge to the beef pasture, where a thousand or more prime steers awaited the few days when the market would steady and they would be sent to town. The brindle made an opening in the fence where he struck it and began to slow down with the idea of joining his fellow creatures. He was a Pariah among them. They fled at his approach. Not only did they flee before him that night, but for days and nights they circled the beef pasture, stopping neither for food nor drink lest the rattling terror overtake them.

"The *Old Man* came out to ride through the beef and estimate his profits. These he found badly shrunken, due to the brindle. It took a day to work the beef pasture and get the remainder of the hide and cans off the yearling and another three to get the nervous steers back to eating. The day the job was finished, the *Old Man* rode in to the wagon early with the idea of administering, privately, a mild rebuke to the cook. Easing around where the latter was working his dough, he began, 'Dick, that prank you played with that brindle yearling—You hadn't oughta done that—It's cost me four days' time—I'll bet them beef steers have run off four or five dollars apiece—Wouldn't be surprised if that danged foolishness didn't cost me five thousand dollars.' Dick said nothing. His eyes strayed toward the out-

26

stretched wagon tongue where four new yellow collar pads hung in good array, then swopt the sacred circle around the wagon to find no sign of recent bovine occupancy. Between thumb and forefinger he pulverized the one small lump that his unerring fingers found in the otherwise faultless batch of dough. As he dissolved this, he observed—not to the *Old Man,* but to the world in general—'By God, it was wuth it to me.' "[2]

"I was workin' for the LU outfit and Bilious Bill was our cook," said Bob Kennon, in telling me another story of animals breaking the cook's laws of the chuck wagon. "The outfit had an old mule they had worked to the chuck wagon for years, but they had put him on the retired list. He was like a well-trained fire hoss, and we couldn't break 'im of the habit of follerin' the wagon from range to range.

"A number of outfits were camped close together on roundup, among them the 79. Vinegar Jim was their cook, and he was an expert at makin' pies. Outfits up in Montana used tents a lot for their cook kitchen.

"One day when things got slack between meals, Vinegar strolled over to chin with Bilious Bill, who was settin' in the shade. The 79 outfit had bought a case o' canned pumpkin and Vinegar had jes' baked a lotta pumpkin pies which he had set on a table in the tent to cool. When he left to talk with Bilious, he took the flap off the mess tent so the air could blow through.

2 John M. Hendrix, "Chuck Wagon Pets and Pests," *The Cattleman,* Vol. XXVI, No. 1 (June, 1939), 5. Used by special permission of *The Cattleman,* Fort Worth, Texas, and the author, John M. Hendrix.

"He'd jes' settled himself beside Bilious and was rollin' a cigarette when he jumped up and let out a string o' cuss words that'd sizzle bacon. That ole mule was comin' outta Vinegar's mess tent and strollin' toward them and he had pumpkin pie smeared all over his face. Those pies had been the pride of Jim's heart and he had baked 'em for the boys' supper. He blamed it all on Bill for lettin' that mule follow his wagon 'round. Bill got more bilious and Jim got even more of a vinegar disposition as they pawed up the sand. This broke up a friendship of long standin' and goes to prove that animals ain't got no business around the mess-wagon."

Quite often some salt-hungry animal might come to the wagon and, unnoticed by the cook, chew up a sweat-soaked saddle blanket. A rider might spoil his pet horse by feeding him sourdough biscuits and bits of sweets. These "pie-biters," as the cowboy called horses with such acquired tastes, made nuisances of themselves around the wagon. If some such horse made his way close to the pots muzzling the ground in search of scraps, the cook was quick to send a piece of firewood his way, emphasized with a string of oaths. But no matter how he was scared away, his quick-turning getaway threw dirt and dust over the food and cooking utensils.

Nothing so upset the cook's smooth-running kitchen or made his life more miserable than these wagon pests. One cook set his sourdough to rise and went to the creek for a bucket of fresh water for the coffee. When he got back, he found one of the spoiled work horses with his mouth and lips full of the gummy dough. The sight of this finish of the sourdoughs he had made with such painstaking care sent him into a rage. Pulling his hat to a fighting angle, he seized a pothook, and with language hot enough to singe his tail off he chased that dough-eating pest until he ran out of both wind and words.

To jar the decorum of the cook's kitchen in any way was to cast discredit upon his profession. It was at such times that he practiced the tyranny with which his office endowed him. In order that all might not have to suffer for the mistakes of one, the group became the cook's ally to punish the offender—perhaps with a chapping.

Some of those old cranks also had a twisted sense of humor, like the one Con Price described when he wrote:

"The boss put two of us night-herding the cattle. We moved camp every day and they put new cattle in the herd every day that they gathered and the nights were long and cold—so we had a hard job.

"We had a good cook that year—but like most good cooks he was sure cranky. . . . We called him 'Big Nose George' and he was so mean I think he hated himself. I have seen him drop something out of his hands when he was cooking and would jump on it and stamp it in the ground.

"After we had night-herded about a month we had about a thousand head in the bunch—and the nights got long. We used to get hungry during the night. One day I asked George for a lunch to take with us. My partner spoke up and said, 'How about a pie, George?' He looked at us like a grizzly and said, 'Yeh, I will give you fellows a pie.'

"That night we started for the herd we talked about it and decided George wasn't such a bad fellow after all. That was a tough night and the cattle drifted about three miles. We couldn't carry the pie very handy, so set it down by a cut bank where we thought we could find it if the cattle settled down, but we didn't get back to where we left it, which proved to be a good thing for us.

"When the day-herders came out at daylight, they began kidding us about the pie. They thought we had tried to eat it. George had told them the joke he had played on us. So we went back and hunted up the pie to see what the joke was. We found it was made out of potato skins, onion peelings, and clay, and other filth around the camp, with a cover on it in a pie tin and nicely baked.

"So we held a council of war to decide what to do about it. My partner wanted to take it to camp and hit him over the head with it. I suggested we make him eat it. He said that was a fine idea. Now I told him, 'He is a big guy. Let's double up on him.' So we planned our attack right there, and George not expecting it, we had him at a disadvantage. We unsaddled—walked into the cook tent.

"He said, 'How did you like your pie, boys?' We said, 'Fine—but we brought part of it to camp so you could enjoy it with us.' I had the pie in my hand and he knew what was coming. He said, 'The hell with you,' and started for a butcher knife—but my partner met him head on and they clinched. I nailed him from behind and we brought him to the ground with both of us on top of him. I got the pie in his mouth but he wouldn't open, so I used the pie tin for an opener (not very gently), and got his teeth apart. I don't think he swallowed any, but he at least got a good taste of it—and any other dirty things I could reach. When the pie-eating contest was over and had worked out to the mess-wagon tongue, and when we let George up, the first thing his hand found was the neck-yoke which was about four feet long, and a bad weapon just at that time, and George was sure going to clean up on us. But my partner had a forty-five Colts stuck in his chaps that George didn't see, and before he could get the neck-yoke into action, the gun was right against his stomach—full cock. He throwed the neck-yoke over his head and both hands in the air and said, 'Don't kill me.' Then we gave him some not too kind advice what his actions should be toward us in the future, and I will say George was a pretty good dog from that time on."[3]

[3] Con Price, *Memories of Old Montana* (Hollywood, Highland Press, 1945), 58–60.

Although Charlie Russell, the famous cowboy artist, was friendly with all men, both good and bad, there was one old wagon cook whom he could never forgive. Charlie was young and just breaking into the business of being a cowboy as a night-herder. One night the herd was nervous and difficult to control. While he was riding around the cattle just before daylight, his horse stepped into a badger hole, throwing Charlie into a cactus patch.

He was filled so full of stickers he couldn't sit his saddle, so he led his horse and walked back to camp. The cook, a tough old hombre, was just starting breakfast. By the light of the lantern in the cook tent Charlie undressed and had started picking the thorns from his anatomy before the cook discovered him.

"What the hell y'u think this is, a hosspital?" he yelled.

Here was a young upstart invading the sanctity of his premises. He had a butcher knife in his hand as he threw Charlie's clothes outside and told the young cowboy to "Git to hell outta here." In later years Charlie said that when he met a stranger and learned that he was a roundup cook, there was always some doubt in his mind about his being a human being.

Many of the old cooks were fighters, their speed of action often surprisingly breathtaking. Charles J. Steedman described such a cook in the following story:

"Our new cook was a character. Bob was the only name I knew him by. . . . He was the best cook we ever had and the hardest man to keep out of a fight. He did not weigh more than a hundred and twenty-five pounds, but

32

was willing to tackle any man, no matter what his size. . . . Brown was the first one to step on the tail of his coat, and a more disillusioned man than the foreman after the clouds rolled by, it never was my pleasure to meet. It all happened the next morning.

"Bob took charge of the kitchen as soon as he got his blanket unstrapped from his horse the night he got in, as Foss [the old cook] was a novice and glad to surrender the job. I saw from the way he took hold that we had a chef. He had his breakfast ready right on time, and everything was hot and savory. Mr. Brown, in his capacity as foreman, undertook to take a stroll about that time, just to let people know he could walk, I suppose. At all events, although in sight of camp and having been summoned several times, he did not come in until all hands were through and our new cook had begun to clean up. Bob had left a frying pan with some meat in it, however, near the fire, and the coffee pot.

"Mr. Brown finally came in and allowed that things were not hot and must be heated again. In about two seconds the air was full of fried beef, coffee, and swear words, and Brown was apparently getting his brains beaten out with the frying pan and coffee pot swung alternately like Indian clubs by the little cook. Brown stampeded, jumped his horse, and with threats of six-shooters, etc., lit out for the herd. The subject was an embarrassing one, and it was dropped, but little Bob was in charge of his department from that time until he left us."[4]

[4] Charles J. Steedman, *Bucking the Sagebrush* (New York, G. P. Putnam's Sons, 1904), 126–27.

33

Yet wagon cooks seldom carried their powers to this point, and rarely was a cowboy forced to take physical retaliation.

In spite of their tyranny, most cooks were regular fellows in a pinch. As a rule, they liked to talk, even if only to grumble. They led a lonesome life. There was not the camaraderie that existed between the riders. During the meal the cook might "hunker down" against the rear wheel of the wagon, and as he rolled the last of the sticking dough from his hands, he would try to be heard above the rattle of tin dishes and the loud noises of coffee-cooling as he expressed his opinions on ornery horse wranglers or the hardships of his own life. The subjects of his conversation might be anything from the weather to women, or from politics to the fine points of poker. Few paid him any mind. If he was a good cook, they were too busy eating his food to interrupt him. Besides, his opinions did not interest them at this time.

When away from the wagon, cooks could be as congenial as anyone else. And as long as they were with a wagon, they were loyal to the company and its riders to the last. In an emergency, a cook cheerfully did his best. In case of an accident he was the doctor and the first to tear up his dress-up shirt for bandages.

Most of the old cooks were good-natured deep down, even if they did try to hide it in upholding the tradition of their profession. Too much praise cannot be given them because they did more than any other one person to keep the work going smoothly. On the other hand, there was an occasional one ill tempered and mean by nature. Though he be an artist as a cook, he could bring about a mass discontent that would ruin the morale of the whole camp.

One cowman, speaking of wagon cooks, grudgingly observed that they, "although belonging to an independent, drunken, disagreeable tribe, usually had more than average intelligence."

To quote again F.A.G. in the *Prescott Courier:* "A roundup cook is a sort of human that was kicked in the head by a brindle cow or a cross-grained mule when very young. This leaves him queer and accounts for the line of work he does. Nobody with good sense could be a roundup cook, and nobody, unless they is queer, kin do it. Takes a special talent to wrangle Dutch ovens and feed fifteen or twenty men that eat like walruses all hours of the day or night, rite through wind and dirt, snow, cold, rain, and mud, an' git the job done. They're temperamental as wimmin too; an' like the bosses, don't need no sleep neither. Also, they is very cranky. The breed is fast dyin' out; they can't stand domesticatin'."

When it comes to gittin' ready to start the wagon out, ole Cookie
is a busy man, of that there's no doubt. It had gathered dust
all winter, was a sort of chicken roost, an' the pots an' pans was
rusty an' the spokes was sorta loose. So with the help of Bill
an' Slim he rolls it from the shed an' starts right in to clean it up,
for it's his home an' bed. Lye soap an' good hot water, with a
touch of ash an' sand soon made the wagon good an' clean, the
pride of ever' hand. He checks the mules an' harness, makes a
few miles practice run, oh I tell y'u he's a teamster an' the boys
all whoop 'im on. 'Bout then's when he gits reckless an' bogs up
in the sand, the boys all cod an' josh 'im but lend a helpin' hand.

Ole Cookie does a lot of things besides the chuck he fixes;
he kin make a good dung poultice or mend yore torn-up britches.
He keeps the harness in repair, kin fix the wagon too, kin cut
yore hair or shave y'u or patch yore boot or shoe. He's a doctor
an' a dentist, an' at times a shinin' light; he'll hold the bets an'
referee a foot race or a fight. There's a lots o' things that Cookie
is an' a few things that he ain't; one thing for shore I'll tell y'u,
he ain't no holy saint.

Tex Taylor

36

CHAPTER 3 *A Man of Many Talents*

"Crossin' a range cook's as risky as brandin' a mule's tail."

NOT EVERY COOK could qualify as a wagon cook. It was essential that the latter be a man of many achievements. To execute the varied duties he was called upon to perform, he had to be unusually resourceful. First, of course, he had to be able to cook. If he couldn't do this to the satisfaction of the men, he wouldn't last long. But he had to be more than a cook. He drove his own teams, and thus it was essential that he be an expert teamster. No respectable cook would deign to "hook up" his own teams, so a couple of punchers were ordered to this duty by the wagon boss. When ready for the moving of camp, the cook crawled upon his well-worn wagon seat, kicked the brake free, and "jes' throwed the lines away an' herded his hosses across the country." Although seeing a wagon outfit pull out in the morning was something like watching the start of a cyclone, no one ever accused the cook of inability to drive.

Often his teams were raw broncs and hard to control. If they had a habit of running away, he rough-locked his wheels with chains and let the devils use up their energy dragging the heavy wagon. Sometimes there was a trail to the next camping spot, but not always. Now he left one of his own, broad, deep parallels where the heavy wheels had cut. Trail or not, the cook usually took the shortest route. He had to be at the next appointed camp to set up and have a hot meal ready on time. Perhaps there were long stretches of sand or mud, or rocks which made the wagon careen dangerously and threatened to splinter wagon spokes; or perhaps unbridged streams of uncertain depth and steep banks had to be crossed. He has been known to get stuck in such places, but he was never discouraged. If he was not within sight of the riders who could come to his aid by "tyin' on" with their ropes, he just "set" there until he was missed. He knew that sooner or later they would come searching for him. As he kept one eye on his chosen route, a line instinctively picked as offering the least resistance to sagebrush, mesquite, or a network of washouts and ridges, he kept another anxious eye on his pan of bread for fear it would need his attention before arriving at the next location.

Some of the larger outfits used "pilots," men familiar with the country, to gallop before the mess wagon and choose the route to get it safely to camp. But no cook was ever satisfied with his pilot, especially when the trail grew rough. A pilot might think himself an expert when it came to taking the visual measurements of a cut-bank; he might pride himself on his estimate of how much the wagon could stand without turning over; but the man on horseback did

38

not get the same view of these obstacles as the man on a high seat behind four "shorty" horses. Small wonder this unwelcome guide came in for much of the cook's profanity.

There were occasions when the wagon had to cross a dry, barren section where the feathery dust, buoyant as mist, enveloped it, settling softly on the cook and his provisions like yellow snow. Or again he might have to detour toward the shoulder of a hill to avoid a treacherous and boggy flat whose crusted top was but a deceiving trap for the mirey bog beneath.

While on the trail between camps, if he feared a scarcity of fuel at the future camp, he kept his eyes open for dry sticks and bits of wood. If enough of this material was close together to justify a stop, he halted to pick it up and

throw it into the possum belly under the wagon bed. And so he went, through dust or mud, his wagon crying loudly in complaint of its load.

Added to his strenuous duties as cook and teamster, he served in many other capacities. He was expected to keep the harness mended and his wagon in repair. Although he might not have more than one or two bottles of medicine in his chuck box, he was called upon to create a dosage good for any ailment of both man and beast, from bellyache to boils, from bruises to broken bones. Not infrequently he was required to act as dentist. As was sometimes the case, when some sick cowboy was beyond the help of his concoctions and no bona fide doctor could be reached, he listened to the patient's last words as a kind of father confessor. Always in case of tragedy he was the first to grab a shovel. His experience in digging fire trenches made him the man for this job. Besides, the cowhands had their traditions, too. Few of them would think of being "caught on the blister end of no damned shovel."

Often the cook served as banker. Even though the cowhand on roundup was not usually burdened with ready cash, there was some occasional small change which the owner did not care to lose in the rough work he was doing. The cook was also the custodian of a fiddle or guitar with which a musical puncher was wont to entertain his fellows around the campfire at night.

He was the stakeholder of bets and acted as referee in any disturbance which might arise. He was the mediator forced to listen to the complaints of the cowboys about the boss's slave-driving tactics, and the boss's grumblings about the small amount of work being accomplished.

Although the working cowboy cared little about haircuts while out on the range, sometimes his hair grew so long it started down his back or clogged his ears. Then the versatile cook acted as barber. He might take no blue ribbons as a tonsorial artist, but he managed to do a passable job with the shears.

If not too cranky, he could occasionally be persuaded to sew on a missing button or even do a little laundry work when a cowhand he liked expected to ride over in the evening to call upon a nester gal for an hour's visit. The kid of the outfit, too, might get help in fixing his saddle.

The boys of the outfit could be rough in their good-natured kidding of the cook and might cuss him plenty, but an outsider had better not try it. It was their privilege alone to show their appreciation and affection. They considered the cook their friend, and to them, if he was a good cook, he was the "best damned cook that ever throwed dishwater under a chuck wagon." And the cook, if he was not too hard-boiled took pride in "his boys."

Unless cooks were exceptionally scarce during the season, a rancher hesitated to hire a man of slovenly appearance for fear his personal habits might cause dissension in camp.

"One day," wrote W. P. Ricketts, "a long-haired man came to the roundup looking for a cooking job. He interviewed seven or eight foremen and none wanted him. As a last resort he accosted John Snodgrass, foreman of the

Quarter Circle Block ranch. John sized him up and re-
marked, 'When I want a woman I'll hire one, but I don't
want a long-haired man.' "[1]

No one ever accused the cowboy of having an appetite
which could be called dainty. He rarely complained about
a little dirt, which he expected from open-air cooking. It
was when the cook became extremely careless in his personal habits that the cowhand let it be known he was no
different from other men in wanting his food as clean as
possible. There have been a few dirty cooks on the range,
but they didn't last long. Their reputation soon spread to
other ranges and it became difficult for them to get a job.

The average cowboy could better tolerate a few worms
in the dried apples and ashes in the coffee than he could the
lack of personal cleanliness in the cook. When the latter
became "considerably whiffy on the lee side," or allowed his
clothes to become so stiff with dough and beef blood "they'd
have to be chopped off," or kept his jowls "full o' Climax"
and "wasn't particular where he unloaded it," then the cowboy "pulled on the halter."

A Texas puncher, who had a reputation of being a bad
man to fool with, was working on the Flying Circle in Wyoming. Toughy Jones was cooking for the outfit. One afternoon the boys were sitting around outside the cook tent
waiting for the call to chuck. Tex was sitting with his head
against the tent canvas. Supper was late and he was loud
in his condemnation of the cook. After expressing his opinion of the cook's slowness and other faults, he finished by

[1] Ricketts, *Fifty Years in the Saddle*, 17.

saying, "That damned cook's gittin' so greasy we oughta take 'im down to the creek an' roll the sonofabitch in sand."

Toughy had not earned that nickname for nothing. He heard Tex's remark, and seeing his head outlined against the tent, he picked up a heavy iron skillet and knocked him out cold.

"That'll learn 'im to keep his opinions under his hair," muttered Toughy as he continued with his supper preparations. Some of those old cooks might be careless in their personal habits, but they were boss of their domain.

Not all wagon cooks have been masters of their craft. Some have been hired because no other cook was available; some have been known to take a job of cooking as a matter of convenience. Even had these latter been acquainted with the art of cooking, their meals would have been ill prepared because they kept their attention on the horizon as if they were expecting a sheriff to "bulge up on 'em." More than one of them "wasn't on speakin' terms with the law."

Any cowhand would hesitate to complain of the poor quality of the food if he saw the cook making every effort to be clean with his cooking. If he took time occasionally to scour his Dutch ovens and pots with sand and wood ashes, if he cleaned the dirt and dough from beneath his fingernails, if he kept his aprons clean and was careful to sort the gravel from the frijoles—all these things overcame his lack of cooking talent.

Although they worked under many disadvantages in preparing meals, the majority of cooks vied with each other

43

for a reputation for clean, well-cooked food. Some of them were as particular as an old maid about personal spoons and forks being used in public dishes. This was a good sign as far as cleanliness was concerned. More than one such cook has built a reputation which caused cowhands to fight for the privilege of "signin' on" with his particular outfit.

Such a cook started his campaign against dirt when the wagon was rolled from under the shed in the spring. While a slovenly, careless cook would putter around in his attempt at cleanliness by giving the chuck box a lick here and a promise there, the conscientious and sincere one would do the job thoroughly and systematically.

Like a man preparing for a hog killing, he built a fire under washpots and tubs for a plentiful supply of hot water. Perhaps a few early arrivals who had signed on for the spring work were busy oiling saddles or getting their ropes into working order. These the cook conscripted as assistants, and, knowing his authority and means of "gittin' even" for disobedience, they promptly dropped whatever occupation engaged them at the moment to lend a hand.

After the wagon was rolled out into the sunlight, the cook examined its "innards" with a critical eye. The sight which greeted him was usually discouraging, to say the least. The cooking vessels which had been coated with a layer of grease to prevent rust, had now accumulated an additional coating of winter dust, particles of hay, and other refuse. The shelves and compartments of his cupboard showed signs of where the rats and mice had wintered.

Calling for boiling water and lye soap, he went to

work with a will. He allowed his helpers to clean out the worst of the mess, but with the actual final cleansing he trusted no man but himself. He scrubbed his "let-down" table and all interior woodwork until it was clean and bright; he proceeded with a knife to scrape out all cracks, corners, and even around the nailheads which held the box together, to remove any accumulation of dirt and grease which the water had failed to get out.

Dashing on more water as a rinse, he swabbed the box dry. As he mopped the sweat from his brow, his critical eye gave a final inspection. While his helpers cleaned the harness, the exterior of the wagon, got the bows and the wagon sheet ready, and greased the axles, he busied himself with the pots, pans, and skillets, scrubbing each vessel with lye soap and sand to remove all grease, both burned and unburned. Knives, forks, spoons, tin cups, and plates all came in for a like treatment.

The water barrel received a thorough cleaning, later being filled with clean water to swell its seams closed that it would not leak while doing duty away from its supply. There would then follow a day in the sun so that its bare interior would become clean and sweet. The sourdough keg or jar received similar treatment, except that if it were a jar, it needed no soaking for swelling staves.

The drawers of his chuck box were now ready to receive the "eatin' irons," the various compartments his supply of seasonings, such as salt, pepper, soda, baking powder, and perhaps a portion of cinnamon, nutmeg, and extracts. The ovens and pots were stowed in their proper places, but the heavy supplies such as sacked beans and flour and the cases of canned goods, along with the slabs of sowbelly, were not loaded until just before time to pull out.

By the time his helpers were through, the cook went into the kitchen to unravel a supply of empty flour sacks to be used as aprons and dish towels. These he wanted in goodly supply because it was not every day he would be close enough to water for laundry work. During his absence his assistants viewed his handiwork with pleasure. They knew he would live up to his reputation for cleanliness, and though their work might make them miss a meal or so, they had no fear of dirt when they did eat. Here was a man who would use water and towel instead of the biscuit dough to cleanse his hands.

A good cook liked to make out his own list of supplies, and although many ranchmen did not relish turning their purse strings over to some one else, the better the cook the more apt he was to get his wishes.

"In those days," wrote Con Price, "the cow outfits didn't feed very good and I think the RL outfit was the worst of them all—mostly Arbuckle's coffee and beans. In fact the other outfits called us the RL bean eaters. One spring Jim went into Custer Junction (fifty miles) to hire a cook and he got one of the best roundup cooks in that country by the name of Lin Coates. We all knew of him and were tickled to death. He could make what we called son-of-a-bitch-in-a-sack that would melt in your mouth. But Lin was a terrible crank and woe be unto the cowboys that got in his way or touched the mess box without his permission.

"We got the chuck wagon and mess outfit out and spent two days cleaning things up ready to start the roundup. Usually the cook made out the grub list, but old Jim [the foreman] didn't want any luxuries so he made it out himself. That didn't set well with Lin. The morning we were ready to start on the roundup Lin climbed up on the mess wagon and looked the grub over. Right away he jumped down and said to Cox, 'Hell, this outfit don't need a cook. All you need is a teamster. You ain't got nothin' to eat.' He grabbed his coat (which was all he had) and beat it across the prairie fifty miles to town."[2]

[2] Con Price, *Trails I Rode* (Pasadena, Trail's End Publishing Co., 1947), 44–45.

When the weather's nice an' balmy an' the moon an' stars is bright, Cookie rises good an' early, seems the middle of the nite. The racket made by pots an' pans an' Cookie stirrin' 'round, soon has the riders wide awake an' risin' from the ground. The wrangler an' the nite hawk both give a helpin' hand an' ever'- body's happy; best coffee in the land.

But when the weather changes, an' it's mean an' cold an' wet, Cookie rises jes' as early, but he's techy y'u kin bet. The ole "round browns" don't burn so good, the firewood's gettin' low, go search the prairie, cowboy, an' snake in a chunk or so. In times like these the ole boy needs good help an' some kind words, from cowpokes standin' 'round the fire like wet an' hun- gry birds. But whether weather's good or bad, be it nite or early morn, Ole Cookie stays right on the job, as shore as y'u are born.

Tex Taylor

CHAPTER 4 *Helps and Handicaps*

"Bacon in the pan,
Coffee in the pot;
Get up an' get it—
Get it while it's hot."

COOKING OVER A CAMPFIRE for a large number of men is an art. No man cooking in the open worked under the best conditions. Fickle Nature, with her changing moods, was constantly testing his patience. Stooping over a hot fire with a blazing sun baking his back and shoulders, or being soaked by a cold rain which sent horses to humping backs and turning tail and men into their slickers, might make the cook "cuss" the life, but it didn't weaken his determination. In spite of handicaps not easily overcome, some of the old wagon cooks left behind reputations remembered to this day.

Cold, wet weather made it all the more imperative that the men be properly fed. Cooking in the rain with a scanty supply of fuel, or in the wind when the heat of his fire was directed everywhere except where it should be and at the same time covering his efforts with sand, were not conducive to good humor. But in spite of the weather and his

49

limited equipment, speed was essential. The men had to be fed on time.

A wagon cook never seemed to be in a hurry, and rarely did he appear frustrated. To a close observer every movement seemed to accomplish something without lost motion. Practice made him an expert in his profession. In spite of all maledictions heaped on the old wagon cook, he was never accused of failure to have his meals on time. True, there were occasions when his wagon might be mired hub-deep in a mud hole or the calamity of a breakdown might overtake him, but he seemed to have a habit of announcing his meals with uncanny promptness.

Some cooks carried no timepiece, yet through years of experience and from the position of the sun they rarely missed schedule. If they had no alarm clock or the men going on last guard did not wake them, instinct seemed to come to their aid. The cowboys would have been glad had this seemingly sleepless human alarm clock overslept. They would have welcomed an extra hour's rest.

Many of the later-day cooks carried alarm clocks and when moving camp packed them away with loving care. Invariably they practiced the disturbing habit of placing them on the bottom of an upturned tin bucket or pan when they set them to go off. They seemed to be envious of letting their subjects sleep a few moments longer than themselves and wanted their alarm to be as disturbing as possible. Though no cook slept far from his wagon, the cowboys were well scattered over the prairie far removed from camp, hence the use of this "soundin' board."

Some cooks considered an alarm clock to be a vital part of their equipment. Many years ago Montague Stevens, an Englishman turned rancher in New Mexico, wrote for a magazine the story of his experience with one of his cooks. Among other things, this cook had the following to say about clocks:

"There ain't many men that thinks as much of a clock as I do, or takes as much care o' one as I does. Now I have had this yer clock for many a year and she's never gone wrong. O' course I allus wraps her up careful when we move camps, 'cause I would be afeared, if I didn't, that the jostlin' o' the waggin over them rough roads might discomplicate her innards, but she has never gone back on me so fur. Now I used to pack a watch, but in my business of cookin', a watch ain't much use compared with a clock. Ye see, a man's hands is often covered with dough makin' bread, or wet and greasy washin' dishes, or all bloody handlin' meat, so he kan't be a-fumblin' in his pocket for his watch to see the time, but you take a clock and she's allus a-talkin' to you all the time. Whenever I looks at my clock she's allus a-sayin' somethin', maybe it's 'Dick, are yer buckets full o' water, or' (here he glanced at the clock) 'why she's tellin' me to grind the corfy right now.'"

And Dick was not the only cook who relied upon a nickle-plated alarm clock to remind him of his duties and get him up on time in the morning. Often it gave such messages as, "It's half-past time for them beans to be a-bilin'" and he'd pile on more fuel to make them "hump themselves."

Whether awakened by an alarm clock, instinct, or habit, the wagon cook's day began about three o'clock in the morning. He usually managed to have breakfast ready to serve so the men could eat and be at work by the time the sky began to redden in the east. Figuring his time to a nicety, he gave a warning call so that "the boys" could dress, wash the sleep from their eyes, and be ready to eat by the time the meat was done and the sourdoughs brown.

A cook might call his crew to meals by simply shouting "Come an' get it!"—the most common of all calls. There were other cooks, however, with individual talents who chose calls to suit their particular virtuosities. They might claim a call as their own; but even if it was uncommon, it made little difference to the cowboys, for however original the call, they soon learned what it meant and readily responded.

Some cooks used the simple "Chuck" or "Grubpile" because the words were short and easy to shout. Others stuck to the common "Come an' get it." The more windy ones used such calls as "Grub pile, come a-runnin' fellers," "It's a-l-l-right with me," "Grab a plate an' growl," "B-o-n-e-h-e-a-d-s, b-o-n-e-h-e-a-d-s, take it away," "Grab 'er boys or I'll throw 'er out," or "Grab it now, or I'll spit in the skillet." The summons to breakfast might differ with such calls as "R-o-l-l-o-u-t, r-o-l-l-o-u-t, while she's hot," or "Wake up snakes an' bite a biscuit."

The poetic cook might break forth with:
   "Bacon in the pan,
   Coffee in the pot;

Get up an' get it—
Get it while it's hot."

Or

"Wake up Jacob!
Day's a-breakin',
Beans in the pot,
An' sourdoughs a-bakin'!"

Perhaps some old cooks were religiously inclined, and they put some of this sentiment into their calls. To quote James Cook, "A cheery voice ringing out about daybreak, shouting 'Roll out there fellers, an' hear the little birdies sing their praises to God,' or "Arise an' shine an' give God the glory!' would make the most crusty waddie grin as he crawled out to partake of his morning meal—even when he was extremely short on sleep."[1]

If he happened to be working for some skinflint outfit and the supply of grub was slim, the cook might express his humiliation with, "Here's hell, fellers," or "Shut yo' eyes an' paw 'er over." A scanty meal and food of poor quality was called "cut straw an' molasses."

For some reason the majority of cooks, when back at the ranch, seemed to try to act a little more civilized. Here they referred to the various meals as "breakfast," "dinner," and "supper," and used a more polite manner in announcing the meal such as, "Sit in gents, she's on," "the banquet awaits, my lords," or "the beans are on." But when they

[1] James Cook, *Fifty Years on the Old Frontier* (New Haven, Yale University Press, 1923), 39.

got away from the kitchen and out into the brush to cook in the open, they became somewhat more savage and the rougher calls seemed to fit into their vocabulary better.

But no matter what his lusty call, it was well understood and brought sudden action. Wagon rules permitted no lagging. No man had to be called twice. The cook was unforgiving to the breaker of this rule. For that matter, a second call was unnecessary. The bracing oxygen of the crisp, high air and the possession of a naturally keen appetite made a man eager to crawl out and eat. One city boy, anxious to be a cowboy but too accustomed to the ease of luxury, slept right through the morning's noise and activity of one roundup camp. The whole outfit drove off and left him to his dreams. The long walk to the next camp broke him of oversleeping.

Nicknames for the cook were legion. Some punchers who did not like the quality of his bread might give him the name of "Soggy," or a cook who was inclined to be parsimonious with the food might be christened "Lean Skillet." One old cook in Montana was called "Cold Bread Joe" because he baked his sourdoughs in big batches, then fed them to the boys cold so they would not eat so many. An old cook on the Box T was called "Old Pud" because he always announced "Boys, there's goin' to be an old pud tonight." There was no limit to such nicknames, each created by its own circumstance.

Many were the slang titles for the cook also. Although his most common title was simply "Cookie," he was called by many others such as "Coosie," from the Spanish *cocinero*, meaning cook; "bean master," "belly cheater," "biscuit roller," "dinero," "dough belly," "dough boxer," "dough puncher," "dough roller," "dough wrangler," "greasy belly," "grub spoiler," "grub worm," "gut robber," "pot hooks," "pot rustler," "sheffi," "sop an' 'taters," "sourdough," "Sallie," "Old woman," or "Old lady"—though the language he used could never be attributed to a lady. Many of the uncomplimentary names above were never used to his face, but spoken behind his back. Sometimes a Chinese cook was employed at the ranch. Usually he was merely called "John," or "Joe," but more often referred to as "that damned Chink."

One thing could be said in favor of the majority of the old-time cooks. They were loyal. No matter how hard the weather, how poor and scarce the water, how short the grub, the cook never deserted in the time of trial. Yet when the crisis had passed, he might fool you by his unexpected decisions, and arguing to make him change his mind was a waste of time. There is an old saying, "Only a fool argues with a skunk, a mule, or a cook."

Illustrating the unpredictable whims of a wagon cook, a good many years ago Vincent Fortune wrote in *Outing Magazine:* "There was Sorrel Top, who presided over the commissary of an Oregon outfit that had brought in two train loads of cattle to be delivered to the Indians on the Blackfoot Reservation in Montana. The stock were unloaded at Cascade and held up to rest before starting the long drive across country. That very night a rain came on that lasted three days. It washed miles of railroad out of the country; the lowlands became small seas, and substantial houses left their moorings and floated about. Big four-year-old steers died of exhaustion, and the boys holding the herd were about all in, when the storm abated.

"All during this time, Sorrel Top prepared his three hot meals a day and hot coffee at all hours, with only Dutch ovens, and no suggestion of shelter. The boys insisted afterwards that he sang all day long and far into the night as cheerfully as though he had not a care in the world.

"When the storm cleared and the bright sun burst forth again, one of the owners went out to view the wreck. The first person he encountered was Sorrel Top, who, without any introductory formality of any sort, insisted in the wildest and most villainous language that he immediately be given his pay, as he was going to quit then. Not at some future date, when all was agreeable, but then!

"He was just a moving bunch of alkali and 'dobe from leaky boots to the longest, most indignant yellow hair that stood menacing right at the apex of his weatherbeaten dome, and he sure presented a queer appearance, besides being vexed.

"The owner tried to reason with him; told him that the storm was over and that nice weather was due for a long time. There was no changing the fiery determination to quit. He swore upon good information, so he stated, that that particular outfit was the most undesirable layout that ever hooked to a mess-wagon; that the owners, singly and together, arose from a questionable race, and that so far as he was concerned they were privileged to start at once upon a journey from which no one has yet returned."

56

As a rule, such characters, after receiving their pay and packing their few belongings, made their way to the nearest town to drown their troubles in drink. After sobering up, they were usually back on the job. Such must have been the case, too, with Sorrel Top for the writer continues:

"The owner was so overcome by the complimentary things said about himself and partner by the eloquent Sorrel Top that he could scarcely wait to accede to the demands made. In admiration for this well-cultured talent, he took Sorrel Top back to town with him, and bought him a lot of drinks and some dry clothes. Seven years later, I found the belligerent cooking for the same company."

The range cook was not without his quick humor and keen repartee. True, his humor ran largely to sarcasm, perhaps because of his outlook on life. When he became vicious in his wit, his ridicule paralyzed the defenses of most cowboys, leaving them too bewildered for a good comeback.

When one cowboy saw the cook throw out a kettle of stewed raisins, his vision of a pie went glimmering.

"Hey, Cookie," he yelled, "what's matter with them pie stuffin's?"

The cook, feeling that this upstart was prying into his business, answered with biting sarcasm: "Well, son, they got tangled up with one o' them damned whirligigs an' assay 'bout 80 per cent sand. I ought to feed 'em to y'u rannies though; y'u'd have more grit in yore bellies than y'u got in yore craws."

Another puncher thought to poke a little fun at the cook's biscuits.

"Cookie," he said, "y'u needn't flavor these washers with leather no more."

He was silenced with the cook's quick retort: "Well, why don't you pay Ole Man Moore for yore saddle an' y'u wouldn't have to hide it in my dough barrel ever'time he passes camp."

Again a would-be wit had the laugh turned on him when he said, "Cut down on the sody in them biscuits—I'm gettin' plumb yeller inside."

"Y'u always was yeller—don't blame it on the biscuits," retorted the cook.

One cowhand came to the wagon and asked, "What's that cookin'—coffee or sheepdip?"

"It's sheepdip this time. The boss says y'u *lambs* have all got the scab," answered the unruffled cook.

Once when several of the boys came in from the herd a little early, they got to camp before the cook had his meal ready.

"Stick yore spurs in, Cookie, I'm plumb starved to death," called one of them.

"How'd I know y'u was sneakin' in on me early like this?" answered the cook.

"Looks like y'u'd a-heard our empty bellies a-rattlin' 'fore we got here."

"I did hear a rattlin'," grinned the cook, "but I thought it was yore empty heads."

The cook's helper was the wrangler. He was usually a youngster, but not always. Sometimes he was a man older than the cook himself. A youngster would serve his apprenticeship to the cowboy profession, a goal to which he had set his ambitions, by working as a wrangler. Of the two, the day and night wranglers, the "night hawk" had the toughest job. He was the boy said to have "swapped his bed for a lantern." He spent a lonely night in the saddle circling the horse herd, broken only perhaps by an occasional ride into camp to snatch a cup of coffee. If he was late bringing in the horses at daylight or let any of them get away, he was sure to "ketch hell" from the wagon boss.

After breakfast he turned the saddle band over to the day wrangler, gulped a hasty meal, and proceeded to help the cook break camp. If the outfit carried a bed wagon or hoodlum wagon, he drove it to the next camp, where he helped the cook unload and set up his equipment. It was only then that he could crawl into his wagon to snatch a little necessary sleep.

Besides the wrangler, who also acted as the cook's "swamper," sometimes a kid who wanted to become a cowboy hired out and became the cook's "louse." Both he and the wrangler were usually the butt of the riders' rough jokes and pranks. If they became too rough in their horseplay, however, the cook usually came to the rescue.

In addition to helping the cook load and unload the wagon, the swamper and louse assisted with the dishes, ground the coffee, cut the firewood, or when that was not to be found, took a gunny sack and searched the prairie for cow chips. When sending the swamper out on such a forage, the cook admonished him to bring back nothing but the "round browns" and to leave the "flat whites" alone. The "round browns" were good solid chips which burned fairly well, but the "flat whites" were the result of scours and were used only as a last resort.

Of great concern to the cook was the procuring of fuel. He was responsible for its acquisition, even though the wrangler or the "louse" did the actual gathering. When leaving a timbered belt, he would see that the "coonie" was well filled.

Most cooks were cranks about their firewood, some wanting nothing but hardwood because it gave more heat, burned a longer time, and made better coals. But why they should be so choosey in a land of little timber is beyond comprehension. Some were like the "Mr. Jones" Ross Santee

told about who quit his job rather than cook with juniper, though there was no other kind of fuel within fifteen miles.[2]

Though aware of his authority, a cook rarely asked a top rider to do menial work. Yet the cowboy knew the importance of the fuel supply, for it affected his own comfort. Therefore, when he ran across a piece of down timber or a fallen limb and he could secure it without dismounting, he would "snake" it to camp at the end of his rope. Perhaps the cook would not even look up from his work, but this cowboy knew his act was not unnoticed or unappreciated.

Cooks working in a timberless country had to resort to cow chips for fuel. In the early days some outfits carried an extra cart, called the "chip wagon," to haul this fuel. These cow chips were called by the various names of "compressed hay," "cow wood," "prairie coal," "prairie pancakes," "surface coal," and "squaw wood," though strictly speaking, squaw wood was the tiny branches of a tree such as were usually used by Indian women for cooking. In sections of the Texas Panhandle these chips were called "Babcock's coal."

Amos Babcock, a man who knew nothing of cattle or the cattle country, was one of the four original holders of the contract to build the capitol at Austin in exchange for three million acres of state land. His partners, the Farwell brothers of Chicago, and Abner Taylor sent him to Texas to inspect the land and establish what was to become the famous XIT Ranch.

[2] Ross Santee, *Men and Horses* (New York, The Century Co., 1926), 253.

Being a fastidious man, Babcock brought a trunk of foodstuff along for his own use. After some days, though, he was advised to conserve his food for a "rainy day" and to eat with the group. As they were in the plains country, the wood supply was soon exhausted, and Felix, the Mexican cook, fell back on the native fuel of cow chips. When Babcock saw what this was and got a whiff of its smoke, he raised such a howl that the incident became the joke of the country for many years afterwards, and cow chips are still called "Babcock's coal" in that section. His "rainy day" had arrived, and refusing to eat any food prepared with a cow-chip fire, he had to fall back on the contents of his trunk.

While cow chips produced an unpleasant odor, the taste of the food was not affected. They made a hot fire in dry weather, but burned so quickly that it took a lot of this fuel to cook a meal. When wet, they would scarcely burn at all. Even by using his hat for a bellows, the cook could barely get enough heat to boil a pot of coffee. One old range cook said that in a single season he "wore out three good hats tryin' to git the damned things to burn." This did not sweeten his temper or add to his efficiency.

Cooks were particular about their fire when cooking outdoors. They built up a big one, but did no cooking upon it until it had burned down to a bed of coals, for a big blaze was useless in cooking.

Andy Adams, in his classic *Log of a Cowboy,* has one of his characters speak the mind of a cow-camp cook when he says:

62

"Honeyman soon had a fire so big that you could not have got near it without a wet blanket on; and when my biscuits were ready for the Dutch oven, Officer threw a bucket of water on the fire, remarking: 'Honeyman, if you was *cusi segundo* under me, and built up such a big fire for your chef, there would be trouble in camp. You may be a good horse wrangler for a through Texas outfit, but when it comes to playing second fiddle to a cook of my accomplishments—well, you simply don't know salt from wild honey. A man might as well try to cook on a burning haystack as on a fire of your building.' "[3]

There have been tall tales told about cooking fires, too, such as when a boastful cook told an eastern lady of his cooking prowess even when there was no wood or chips for fuel. Telling how he set the grass afire, he admitted that the blowing wind kept him plenty busy holding the skillets in its path as he followed the fire, and he declared that by the time his meal was thoroughly done, he was twenty miles from camp.

[3] Andy Adams, *Log of a Cowboy* (Boston, Houghton Mifflin Co., 1903), 333.

PART II
The Chuck

Them words "Arbuckle Brothers" on a sack of coffee beans, saved the West an' all of Texas, from them Injuns an' their schemes. When the wagon left headquarters for the roundup, Spring an' Fall, it was shore to carry with it lots of coffee fer us all. The boys shore liked their coffee ever' mornin', noon an' nite, an' even in between times when the wagon was in sight. The coffee pot there by the fire was full of Cookie's brew, hot an' black an' strong enough to float an ole hoss shoe.

There's another institution that the ole chuck wagon's got, it's a most important item—that sourdough risin' crock. Our ole Cookie shore can make 'em an' they're plenty fit to eat, jes' reach in that Dutch oven son, they're mighty hard to beat.

When the weather's cold an' fallin', y'u kin bet yore bottom dollar, Cookie's got Arbuckle's warmin' an' sourdoughs when y'u holler.

Tex Taylor

CHAPTER 5 *Arbuckles and Sourdoughs*

"Goin' 'round a coffee pot huntin' the handle would cover the extent of some folk's travel."

HIGH on the old-time cowboy's list of necessities was coffee. He regarded it as essential at every meal, and when he could get it between meals, it contributed to his contentment with life. It was said that if there was anything a cowpuncher liked better than having a fiddler in camp it was drinking coffee between meals. The cook who kept the coffeepot over a bed of hot coals during the day and night would find that the boys were "for him."

With trail and roundup outfits, when cattle were held under herd at night, this service was demanded by the hands serving guard duty. Men going out on guard needed a cup of coffee to keep them awake; those being relieved needed a cup when they rode in to warm them up before resuming their interrupted sleep. And no matter how short his sleep, the cowboy wanted another cup immediately upon arising.

He wanted his coffee strong and black. He wanted no sweetened or cream-weakened concoction. Coffee that

67

suited his taste would doubtless be pronounced vile and undrinkable in more refined circles.

"Cookie, pour me a cup o' that condensed panther y'u call coffee," said Joe Beal as we sat at the table of the Swinging L Ranch. "This is the way I like it, plumb barefooted," he continued after gulping a quantity of the boiling hot liquid. "None o' that dehorned stuff y'u git in town cafés for me."

The cowboy's aversion to milk and cream, especially in his coffee, perhaps stemmed from the fear that it might lead to a milking job if its use became general. He might drive, herd, and "cuss" cows day and night, but when it came to milking one, he drew the line. Drinking milk, too, might make his breath smell like a young calf's and he wanted none of that, though he thought nothing of its smelling of whiskey and tobacco. Even after canned milk became available, the cowboy had little use for "canned cow." The old Eagle Brand was occasionally found on the cook's shelf, but as Charlie Russell once said, "I think it came from that bird. It's a cinch it never flowed from any animal with horns."

Later canned milk became more common upon the ranch table. At one time Carnation milk was advertised in the stock papers, and a prize was offered for the best jingle praising the product. There is a story about a ranch woman who tried her talent in this contest. She wrote a little jingle that went:

"Carnation milk, best in the lan',
  Comes to the table in a little red can."

68

Next day a cowboy from a neighboring ranch stopped by on his way to the settlement, and she handed him her literary prize, giving him the address and asking him to buy an envelope and stamp and mail it for her. Several weeks later, she finally heard from the company—that they could not use her poem because it was unfit for print.

She could not understand this point of view, for her poem had seemed innocent enough. Then, knowing the cowboy to whom she had entrusted her literary effort, she became suspicious. When she finally saw him again, she asked him what he had done to her jingle. Reddening under her accusing gaze and greatly embarrassed by the turn of events, he finally stammered, "Well, ma'am, I read yore poem an' figgered it was too short. I wanted to see y'u win that prize, so I figgered I could add a verse an' make it better."

"Well, what in creation did you write to make them send me the letter they did?" asked the bewildered woman.

"Oh, I jes' give it a little more punch by makin' it read:

'Carnation milk, best in the lan',
Comes to the table in a little red can.
'No teats to pull, no hay to pitch,
Jes' punch a hole in the sonofabitch.'"

The early cowman never saw sugar, so he learned to drink his coffee without it. Later, when sugar became more common on the market, a few wagons carried it, but it was hard to keep in usable shape. If the ants were not in it, the rains kept it damp. Most cowhands, if they wanted a little sweetening in their coffee, preferred a small amount of "lick" or molasses which they called "long sweetenin'."

Teddy Blue told a story about a Texas cowboy who was working in Montana. When he rode into a roundup camp at dinner time and they passed him the sugar, he said, "No thanks, I don't take salt in my coffee." He had never seen sugar before—only sorghum syrup.[1]

The cowboy's recipe for making coffee was "take one pound of coffee, wet it good with water, boil it over a fire for thirty minutes, pitch in a horseshoe, and if it sinks, put in some more coffee." He liked his coffee "to kick up in the middle and carry double." Good strong coffee was sometimes called "six-shooter coffee" because it was said to be strong enough to float a six-shooter. All joking aside, the standard formula was about one handful of ground coffee for each cup of water. If the brew was of less strength, there was apt to be grumbling about the cook's ability as a coffee maker. In spite of the fact that the cowhand drank quarts of this strong liquid daily, no one ever heard him complain of sleepless nights.

Frank King has a rich fund of stories about cowboys eating in town. He used to tell one about a cowhand who went into a city café for a cup of coffee. He consumed six cups before his craving was satisfied.

"You like coffee, don't you?" said the sweet little waitress, amazed at his capacity.

"Y'u have to drink a heap o' this watered stuff to get

[1] E. C. Abbott and Helena Huntington Smith, *We Pointed Them North* (New York, Farrar and Rinehart, 1939), 162.

70

any coffee," answered the cowboy. Such coffee was called "belly wash" or "brown gargle" by the cowman.

Always eager to impress the public with his code of Western hospitality, the cowboy was the subject of many stories. Here is one I heard somewhere on the range. It seems that when a train from the East, without a dining car, stopped at an eating station, an Eastern lady rushed from her Pullman to the railroad "swaller-an'-git-out trough." The conductor had notified the passengers that the train was late and consequently would make only a short stop. The lady, fearing to order a meal, merely called for a cup of coffee. When she got it black and boiling hot, she voiced her doubts about being able to drink it before the train pulled out.

A cowboy, a native with lots of time, was sitting next to her at the counter and overheard her remark. Wishing to show her the true Western hospitality natural to his

kind, he shoved her his cup and politely said, "Here's one, lady, that's already saucered and blowed."

A three- to five-gallon pot was considered the standard size for a cow outfit of ten or twelve men. The sight of a wide-bottomed, smoke-blackened coffeepot on the coals, with the brown boiling liquid overflowing bubblingly down its sides, was a picture to warm any man's innards and whet his appetite—especially in the early chill of the morning.

Sometimes a camp kettle or a metal bucket was used for the coffee making. In such a case the cowboy dipped his cup into it, and when helping himself to a second serving, was careful to wipe the bottom of the cup on his pants so that no dirt which the damp cup had gathered from the ground where he had placed it while eating would be deposited in the pot.

After the cook had gotten the rest of the meal well under way, he placed the coffeepot, two-thirds filled with cold water, upon the coals to boil. When the water reached the boiling point he dumped in the correct quantity of ground coffee. After it had boiled sufficiently to gain the necessary strength, he dashed in a little cold water to settle the grounds. From this point he paid the coffee no attention except to keep it hot.

In the old trail days, when the cook was pestered with Indians begging for food, he served them what became known as "Injun coffee." This was merely pouring water upon old grounds and bringing it to a boil. He deemed this concoction good enough for Indians, but wouldn't dare serve it to the "boys."

72

In spite of the care and cleanliness a cook might exercise in his coffee making, accidents occasionally happened, such as the one Rollie Burns recounts:

"After breakfast one morning the cook started to empty the grounds out of the coffeepot, when he noticed a queer-looking insect among the grounds. He called me (I was the only one left in camp) and asked what I thought it was. I told him it was a vinegar-roan.[2] The cook got pale and began to complain of feeling sick. Then he got panicky, and knew that all the boys would die. I figured that his ailment was purely imaginary, so I manufactured a lie for him.

" 'I was working with an outfit one time when the cook found a whole nest of vinegar-roans in the coffee grounds.'

" 'Did the boys die?'

" 'No, it just gave them more pep.'

"That seemed to help the cook, and he was soon feeling better. I told him not to tell the boys, for they might run him out of camp. I also suggested that it would be a good idea to wash the coffeepot after each meal, and keep it covered up. The vinegar-roan juice did not hurt any of the boys. A few days later I told them about the incident. Some of them 'remembered' that they had felt puny that day, but others said they never felt better and told the cook to put a vinegar-roan in the coffee every morning."[3]

[2] A vinegarroon is a large whip scorpion which emits a vinegarlike odor when alarmed.

[3] W. C. Holden, *Rollie Burns* (Dallas, Southwest Press, 1932), 122.

With no running water near camp, if the water barrel was low, the cook might walk to a near-by pond to inspect the water there. If there happened to be any carcasses of dead cattle floating about, as was often the case, he chose the clearest spot as far away as possible, brushed the skimmers aside, dipped his coffeepot full and returned to his fire without comment. He subscribed to the theory that boiling killed the germs, and anyway a cowpuncher's stomach seemed to be made of iron. Pure-food laws were unheard of at that time.

Most cowmen would prefer coffee made with such water than to follow the custom of some of the English outfits and drink tea. The cowboy had no use for tea, or the man who drank it. One cowhand had to go to an English outfit to make inquiries about a stray. When he returned to the home ranch, he told of his astonishment at seeing those Englishmen drinking tea *for breakfast.* "There they sets," he marveled, "at *breakfast,* mind y'u, sippin' tea like it was hot solder."

Although one or two other brands of coffee were used on the range, the Arbuckle brand was so common that most cowmen didn't know there was any other kind. At a meeting of the Chuck Wagon Trailers' Association in Los Angeles, I talked with Jack Culley, former manager of the Bell Ranch in New Mexico and author of *Cattle, Men, and Horses.*

"I don't know who the Arbuckles were," he said during our conversation, "but they should have a monument

74

erected in their honor somewhere on the High Plains. For many years they were the principal standby of the range cow business."

Few people today know what a package of Arbuckle's looked like, and even many of the old cowmen have forgotten its appearance. For that reason it seems fitting to include here some pertinent facts about this once famous beverage.

In the days before and immediately after the Civil War, coffee came packed green. The housewife did her own roasting in oven or skillet. The Arbuckle Brothers, wholesale grocers of Pittsburgh, Pennsylvania, conceived the idea of shipping coffee already roasted. They developed a process of coating the roasted beans with a mixture of sugar and egg whites to seal in the flavor and keep it fresh. The demand for this roasted coffee was so great that the Arbuckles became known as coffee specialists, and cowmen eventually began worrying about what they would do for coffee if the Arbuckles died.

This coffee was shipped in cases of one-pound bags. The ranch owner kept a supply on hand at all times. When the chuck wagon loaded out for the roundup, plenty of coffee was taken along. There was no stinting on this item if the men were to do good work and be contented.

Its gaily colored manila bag was a familiar sight at the chuck wagon. The word "Arbuckle's" was printed in bold letters across the front, beneath which was the picture of a flying angel in long flowing gray skirt, and around her neck a streaming red scarf. This was the trade mark. Beneath the angel were the words "Ariosa Coffee" in black letters on cream background bordered in red.[4]

At the bottom of the package was a coupon which helped this brand of coffee to become so well known. This was the facsimile of the signature "Arbuckle Brothers," printed in red on a white-splotched background and bordered in black. At one time a stick of striped peppermint candy was packed in every sack. If the wrangler happened to be busy and the cook was out of ground coffee, he would merely ask, "Who wants the candy tonight?" and there would be a rush for the coffee grinder fastened to the side of the wagon. Perhaps while two or three men were scuffling to keep each other away from the grinder handle, another would slip past them and grind the coffee.

The wagon cook tried to keep a supply ground ready for use. During a slack period he had either the swamper or the wrangler grind up twenty to thirty packages. After being ground, the coffee was poured back into the bags and tied up for future use. If the cook already had a good alarm clock, a razor, or other items for which the coupons were good, and he felt generous at the time, he would give his helper these coupons and the candy as pay.

One of the most famous of all Western foods was perhaps the sourdough biscuits of the range cook. No one seems to know who first created them, but they became a standard of the ranch country. One will never sink a tooth into

[4] Frank King, *Pioneer Western Empire Builders* (Pasadena, Trail's End Publishing Co., 1946), 125.

better bread, if properly made, and the fame of sourdoughs spread throughout the West. Perhaps some inspired cook experimented until he found a method of making bread without the commercial yeast which was not always available. The West owes him a debt of gratitude.

Every conscientious cook strove for the reputation of turning out the best sourdoughs on the range. All cooks took infinite pride in their baking, many of them with good reason. Some were so jealous of their reputation that they spent many of their waking hours, and some when they should have been sleeping, watching their dough keg, working it down, moving it closer to the fire or away from it, as need be.

The cowboy preferred sourdough bread to any other kind. Baking-powder biscuits he could eat with only a mild complaint; buttermilk biscuits were passable if some pretty little nester girl made them; but none of them measured up to sourdoughs.[5] Baker's bread, which the cowboy called "wasp's nest" or "gun waddin' bread," he did not relish at all.

The cook's most particular job in preparing for the start of the roundup was to secure the proper keg or jar for his sourdough mixture. Once selected and cleaned properly, it never left the outfit as long as the roundup lasted. If anything happened to this precious keg, the outfit was in for a bad time indeed. Most cooks would defend their sourdough kegs with their lives. Some became so attached to them that they carried their own from job to job.

[5] E. E. Dale, "Cowboy Cookery," *Hereford Journal*, Vol. XXXVI, No. 17 (January 1, 1946), 37–38.

No matter how particular its cleaning at the start, only a few weeks passed before the inside was coated with an inch or so of hardened dough and the outside streaked and spattered with dry batter. This caused the keg to look anything but sanitary, but most cooks claimed that this coating made the sourdough better.

A keg holding about five gallons was a good size. Into it the cook placed three or four quarts of flour, added a dash of salt and enough warm water to make a medium-thick batter when stirred with a flat wooden paddle until well mixed. The keg was covered and placed in a warm place, usually in the sun, and its contents allowed to ferment for a day or so. Some cooks added a handful of sugar or molasses or chipped potato, or even a little vinegar, to hasten fermentation, but this was not necessary.

Many cooks used this first batch of batter merely to season the keg. After the fermentation was well started, it was poured out and a new batch mixed. Each day the keg was kept in the sun and each night was wrapped in a blanket to keep the batter warm and working. Often on cold nights, the cook wrapped his keg in a blanket and took it to bed with him. His task was to see that the fermentation never stopped. By the time fermentation was thorough, the contents would double in bulk so that the keg would be full and he saw that it was kept so. Every time he took out enough of the bubbly sourdough for a batch of bread, he put back enough flour, salt, and water to replace it. In this way there was always plenty of dough working.

When ready to prepare his bread, the cook poured

78

flour into a large pan until it was about two-thirds full, made a deep impression in the center, and poured in the proper amount of sourdough batter. Added to this was a teaspoon of soda dissolved in a little warm water. A small amount of salt and lard was next. Bacon grease could be used with equal success. Some cooks added a little sugar to make a browner crust.

As he stirred this batter, the cook gradually worked the dry flour from the sides, being careful that the soda and shortening were distributed thoroughly. As soon as all was worked into a mass of dough, he drenched his work table with flour and proceeded to knead the batch until it was thoroughly mixed.

During this time he had a hot fire going in order to have plenty of red-hot coals burned down for his baking. Leaving his dough on the table for the moment, he took his gouch hook and raked the coals into a nice bed. He next put a generous portion of lard or bacon grease into the Dutch oven to melt. When the oven was placed on the coals the lid also received coals on top so that it too would be thoroughly heated.

Here it might be well to digress for a moment to describe this most important utensil of the cook's equipment— the Dutch oven. It was a very large, deep, thick iron skillet with three legs under the bottom, and a heavy lid with upturned lip fitting the top. Used either as a skillet or an oven, it cooked many items of the chuck on the cowboy's bill-of-fare. Even though this vessel was used especially for baking biscuits, steaks cooked in it were hard to beat.

The range cook had no use for a biscuit cutter. One would certainly become bent, broken, or lost. When the grease had melted, he merely pinched off pieces of the dough somewhat smaller than an egg. These pieces he rolled into balls between his palms, placed them in the grease and turned them so that all sides would receive a coating to prevent their sticking together. As he placed the biscuits in the oven, he jammed each tightly against the other, for the tighter they were, the higher they would rise and the lighter they would be.

The oven full, it was placed near the fire for thirty minutes or so to allow the biscuits to rise while the cook went about other preparations for the meal. If he had not done so before, he took this opportunity to replace what he had taken out of his dough keg. Let him forget to replace the flour and water, and his crew would soon be without bread.

Experience taught him the correct timing for putting his bread on to bake. To be good, sourdoughs had to be served hot. When the other articles of food on his menu were nearly done, he placed his bread ovens on, nestling them down in the coals. Using his gouch hook, he covered them with the hot lids and shoveled more coals on top until the vessels were almost hidden. Bread was better when fewer coals were used at the bottom and plenty above so that the top crust would be good and brown and the center soft and tender.

After turning the steaks on another fire and keeping an eye on the coffeepot, he took an occasional peek at the bread by lifting the lids to see if it was browning properly.

To bake successful sourdoughs, one may follow this procedure: Sift one-half gallon of flour into a pan. Into the hollowed-out center pour two-thirds of the sourdough batter. Dissolve a level teaspoon of salt, one-fourth teaspoon of soda, and a teaspoon of sugar in one-half cup of warm water. Add this to the sponge and gradually work in the flour from the sides; then knead until the dough is smooth. Pinch off in small pieces, roll between the palms into a ball, coat with warm grease melted in the oven, then set in a warm place to rise. When light, bake in a moderately hot oven, being sure plenty of coals are on top.

Adept at giving everything special names, the cowboy had many for sourdoughs, among them "dough gods," and, if the cook happened to be in a good humor, one of his "boys" might refer to them as "sinkers," "hot rocks," or "sourdough bullets." The cook knew this was but a feeble attempt to be humorous, for every cowhand liked sourdough bread. At the ranch the cook might make a baking-powder bread which contained raisins for a change. It was called "hunkydummy."

Most of the cowboys' good-natured kidding of the cook was concerned with his sourdoughs, because he knew this to be a touchy spot. The wise cook took it in good humor because he knew they were merely trying to get his goat.

On occasion, a puncher might point out a buffalo wallow on the prairie and declare that this depression in the earth had been caused by someone's throwing one of the coosie's biscuits away, the soil being unable to withstand

81

the weight of the discarded bread. Another might state that one thrown into the river had sunk like a rock, and it wasn't long until the fish came to the surface, all with broken mouths from trying to eat it; even the water couldn't soak it soft. Still another might ask to borrow the cook's ax so that he could break his biscuit open. There was also the story of the boss who asked the cook how his flour supply was holding out, declaring that the last cook had made four hundred pounds of bread out of a fifty-pound sack of flour. To all this kidding, a good-natured cook might merely smile in toleration, but an ill-tempered one could retaliate with staggering unexpectedness.

Ever' cowhand loves a stew, calf-fries, steaks, an' barbeque, but the stew that's best an' so almighty rich, is called on the range, a sonofabitch.

We kill us a beef an' we take the heart an' then cut it up to get a good start; tallow an' tongue are then cut up too; it's startin' to look more like a good stew. Ole Cookie then stirs it for quite a long while, an' then adds some liver with a taste of the bile. He stirs it an' stirs it an' stirs it, so slow, then with sweetbreads an' brains he makes 'im a dough. With this in the pot it looks sort o' thin so he cuts up some meat an' throws 'er right in. Then he stirs it an' cooks it an' puts in some salt with a lot o' good pepper an' then calls a halt.

There's one little item, the secret of which makes our Cookie so proud of his sonofabitch. Jes' step to one side while he stirs up his stew an' I'll whisper his secret to you an' to you. There's a spot in a beef, be it heifer or steer, an' it's shore hard to find, it might take y'u a year. Y'u think that I'm queer, y'u think I'm a nut? Sonofabitch ain't no good without marrowgut.

Tex Taylor

84

CHAPTER 6 *Steaks and Stews*

*"A lean belly never feeds
a fat brain."*

COWBOYS were meat eaters. It took quite a quantity of beef to satisfy the robust appetite of a roundup crew. According to tradition, no old-time cowman liked the taste of his own beef. It was customary for cowmen to kill one of their neighbor's animals, but as the neighbor, in turn, killed theirs, the score worked out evenly. One of the standing jokes was about the rancher who invited his neighbor over to dinner "so he could see what his own beef tasted like." Such a beef was referred to as "slow elk," or "big antelope." So prejudiced was the old-time rancher against eating his own beef that one ranch woman declared she would just as soon eat one of her own children as one of her own yearlings.

City dwellers demand that their meat be "hung," seasoned and refrigerated before using, but the cowman liked his beef freshly killed. The range man did not "butcher"; he "killed a beef." As soon as the cattle got fat after the coming of grass, a calf was killed. Having spent the winter

85

living on sowbelly and beans, the cowboy usually found his system upset by the first meat of the spring, but he quickly got over it.

After the roundup got well under way, the wagon boss rode out to select an animal for meat. He kept his eyes open for a yearling heifer, and, if he was breeding up the herd, he tried to choose one with poor markings. Having selected the animal, he drove it toward the wagon, and assistants were detailed for the work of slaughter. Some bosses merely had the animal shot in the head, but shooting caused internal bleeding. The more particular man had it roped by the head and hind feet, thrown, and stretched out. Then a blow was delivered on the frontal bone of the head with an ax. A quick knife thrust in its throat and the beast's eyes became glazed in death as a torrent of hot blood gushed over the dust.

After the animal had bled, the carcass was turned on its back with the head under its shoulders to balance it, and the work of skinning commenced. A sharp knife handled by a man who knew his business slit the hide from chin to tail right down the center of the belly. Then the inside of each leg was slit from heel to the split in the belly. The whole was peeled off, leaving it on the ground as a protection against dirt while the meat was being quartered and cut up.

An animal was never killed close to other cattle, especially in the early days when the odor of blood would cause the old-time longhorn to run amuck. It made even the slow-gaited modern animal nervous, and the wagon boss took precautions.

There was no refrigeration on the range, but the killing was done in the late afternoon and the meat hung up to be chilled by the cool night air of the high plains. In the early morning it was wrapped in tarps or slickers and placed in the wagon bed where bedrolls or other trappings would be placed on top to hold its temperature and keep it from the day's heat. This nightly cooling would be repeated as long as the beef lasted, usually only a few days.

Sometimes a forequarter would be sent some near-by granger and swapped for eggs or vegetables, if he was known to raise these commodities. The granger was glad to get the meat to help the family larder. Even if he raised beef himself, his herd was small and he disliked killing his own.

When a beef was killed, especially if it were a calf, the tongue, liver, heart, sweetbreads, marrow gut, and brains were placed in vessels and carried to the cook, who knew what was expected of him. These were the chief ingredients of a famous stew, which will be described later.

Broiled steaks, a favorite with the town man, were not considered good by the cowboy because the juices and flavor were lost. No cowboy worthy of the calling wanted his steaks any way except fried. He never seemed to tire of them. Even when he went to market with a load of cattle, he would wander into a city café, look over a menu full of names he did not "savvy," and order a fried steak. He wanted his steaks done through. Some outdoor men like rare steaks, but not the cowboy. There's an old, old story about the cowhand who went into a Kansas City restaurant and ordered a steak. When the waitress brought it to him rare, he ordered her to take it back and have it cooked done, with the remark, "I've seen cows git well that was hurt worse'n that."

When a cowboy bought a steak in a city restaurant, he wanted a "full-grown" one, not some little *filet mignon*. Once when a cowboy ordered a steak from a city menu, he was brought one "that wouldn't make a meal for a yearlin' tomcat." Later the head waiter came around and politely asked, "How did you find your steak?"

"Well," answered the cowboy, "I jes' lifted up that little piece o' lettuce, an' there she was, cozy as a toad under a cabbage."

On another occasion a hungry cowboy went into a city

88

restaurant, his mind filled with the prospects of a big steak. When the waitress brought it, he looked it over critically.

"It seems to be cooked done 'nough," he said, "but I was figgerin' on a steak 'bout the size of a mule's lip from the ears down. This'n's kinda puny."

"It might be small, but don't worry about its size," she answered. "It'll take you a long time to eat it."

When the range cook started to prepare his meat for the meal, he sliced off a sufficient number of medium thick steaks to feed the men, and cut them into generous slabs. These he tenderized by pounding with a hammer or hacking with a heavy butcher knife or cleaver. He cut a quantity of the suet into small pieces and put a generous handful into the several Dutch ovens he had heating on the coals. Steak was not as good fried in lard or bacon grease as it was fried in the fat suet of the beef itself. When this had melted and the oven was filled to a depth of an inch or so in grease, he fished out the cracklings which were left. The slabs of steak were salted, covered with flour, and dropped into the sizzling fat and the lid put on. If steaks were fried without being floured, it was better to sear them quickly on each side to hold the juices in, then salt just before the meat was done. Otherwise, salt would shrink the fibers and cause the meat to become tough.

When the cook lifted the lid to turn the steaks, the odors escaping would whet the appetite of a dying man. If he wanted to make pan gravy, he stirred a little water into the fat, making a "sop" for the boys. Another cook might put a little flour into the hot grease, stir the mixture until browned, then add water and cook until it thickened. This made a better gravy. In some sections gravy was called by titles which would not look good in print.

If the cook thought the boys were getting tired of fried steaks—which they never did—and he wanted to give them a change, he might make a pot roast by taking a good-sized chunk of beef, salting it, covering it with flour, then putting it into the Dutch oven to bake slowly for four or five hours. If he had any potatoes and onions on hand, he peeled them and added them when the meat was nearly done.

Some cooks made another beef dish which was delicious. Selecting pieces of fat beef, they put them into a pot to simmer over a slow fire until cooked tender. Some biscuit dough, which had been set aside to rise, was then pinched off into small pieces and dropped in with the beef. As they cooked, they became light and puffy. A flour gravy was then made of the juices and the whole became a toothsome dish.

Meat also came in for some of the cowboy's kidding. If it happened to be a little tough, someone might remark, "This beef acts like it was sawed right off the horn of some old range bull. Y'u can't hardly dish the gravy out with a fork."

Rare indeed would be the occasion when the old-time cowman condescended to eat mutton. He called a lamb chop "wool with the handle on," and one old cowman declared that the only time he ever had indigestion was when he ate sheep meat. "Cookin' mutton" to the cowhand meant setting a sheep range afire to destroy sheep, as was sometimes done in the range wars between sheepmen and cowmen.

Son-of-a-bitch stew is the cowboy's own dish. No one knows who originated this widely known, yet mysterious concoction. Perhaps some economically minded cook, trying to salvage the parts of the beef usually thrown away, made the first one, by adding one thing and then another, tasting each as he experimented, until at last he declared it good. It has been said that to make this stew, everything was thrown into the pot except the horns, hoofs, and hide.

Some people claim that the first cook to make such a stew got his idea from the Indians, who ate with relish all the discarded parts of the beef when slaughtering was done in their presence.

The origin of the name is as mysterious and uncertain as the genesis of the concoction itself. Its mystery has become legendary. Possibly the first cowboy who tasted it exclaimed, "Sonofabitch, but that's good!" and the name stuck.

This enigma of its making, and of its name, has, as the years have gone by, created for the cowboy an opportunity to satisfy his love of a joke. He never lets a joke die if he can possibly keep it alive. It was in the presence of the tenderfoot that he went the limit in having his fun with this dish. When he watched some greener picking around in a plate of this mysterious looking stew as if trying to discover its ingredients, he would remark that a stew was no good without plenty of *guts* in it. If the tenderfoot grew pale and pushed the dish aside, his reward was ample.

It became the custom to name this dish after some enemy for whom one held a special grudge. It was like a toast or a pledge to this enemy's downfall, a subtle way of calling him names which one dared not do to his face.

Of course, if delicate ears were present—as when a lady, or group of them, visited the wagon—the stew was spoken of as a "son-of-a-gun" instead of by its fighting name. But the experienced ranch woman knew this was merely an attempt to be polite.

The presence of women at the wagon always more or less handicapped the cowboys in their language. If the visitor happened to be young and good looking, you would notice the boys sneaking away to feel between their soogans for clean pants and shirts. When they came back, if a creek had been handy, their faces would be shining and their hair slicked down, giving them away "like a shirtful o' fleas."

Women around the chuck wagon seemed wholly out of place. Their presence created an embarrassing situation for the woman-shy cowboy, cramping his freedom of both speech and action.

"After the women folks moved to town," said Ab Evans in an interview with John Hendrix, "when we would be in there shipping, the old lady would round up all the other ranch women and drive out to the wagon in their surreys and phaetons.

"I never will forget what happened to the fellow that

was cooking for Ben Haddox when he was runnin' that big outfit down in the Wichitas. They came in to Quanah with a herd to ship and camped the last night out in the edge of the 'Nesterments' and the milk-pen calves ate the cook's clothes up while he was taking a bath in Riley Wheat's tank. The only surplus clothes in the outfit was a pair of chaps that one of the boys had in the wagon. This coosie climbed into them and got his breakfast and dinner O.K., and then pulled into town and camped at the railroad tank near the stock pens and got his fire going and his supper started. He hadn't more than got started good when Mrs. Haddox and a surrey full of women folks drove up to see Ben and eat supper at the wagon. You can imagine how that poor boy felt cookin' a meal of victuals, tending his fires and all without ever turning his back on them women folks."[1]

To get back to our stew, one old story, told with many variations, is about two cowhands riding up to the chuck wagon when the cook was preparing dinner. Sniffing the odors thrown up by the various pots and kettles, one of the visitors said, "I see y'u're goin' to have a sonofabitch for dinner." The cook, already touchy because other visitors had arrived earlier, gave the new arrivals a withering look and answered, "Yeah, a few more drop in an' we'll have a crowd of 'em."

Alexander Melton, an old-time cowboy of the Texas Panhandle, told me of a town barber visiting the chuck

[1] John M. Hendrix, "Salad or Son-of-a-Gun," *The Cattleman*, Vol. XXXI, No. 5 (October, 1944), 15. Used by special permission of *The Cattleman*, Fort Worth, Texas, and the author, John M. Hendrix.

wagon. It seems this barber had tired of his profession and decided he wanted to be a cowboy. When he arrived at the wagon to seek a job the cook was cooking a stew.

"What's that cookin'?" he asked.

"That's a sonofabitch. Did y'u ever eat one?" answered the cook.

"No," replied the barber, "I never et one, but I've shaved a helluva lot of 'em."

This stew was called by many other names, according to the locale or the enemy of the group, but always its implication was obvious. When the law began its westward march and started to clamp down on the government of the cowman's happy, carefree days, the blame for this cramping of liberties was placed upon lawyers. This caused the offended cowmen to feel resentful toward the law, and they soon began calling this dish "District Attorney" as an outlet to their indignation. After the Taylor Grazing Act was passed, the cattlemen and the Forest Service had so many misunderstandings that this stew often took the name of "Forest Ranger."

A cowhand at the wagon might become offended at the congressman from his district over some action or lack of it. When he said, "I believe I'll have another dish of Congressman Blank," the others nodded approval, and the stew was called by that name for a few weeks, or for the season. It has been called "Cleveland" because this president ran the cattlemen out of the Cherokee Strip, and, in later years, "Hoover," on account of the depression which occurred during President Hoover's term of office.

94

The feuding of rival towns also furnished names at various times. A man from a near-by envious town might call it "The Gentleman from Odessa," "The Gentleman from Cheyenne," "The Gentleman from Roswell," or any other. In some sections it frequently went by the name of "Rascal"; others called it by the abbreviated "SOB."

Occasionally the wagon cook named his first stew of the season after some one against whom he had a pet peeve and it retained that name for the rest of the roundup. Cooks have been fired for calling this dish by the boss' name.

Many arguments have developed about the proper way to make this famous stew. Though perhaps no two cooks would make it exactly alike, each might think his way the best. Some made it the easier, safer way by cooking in water, while others claimed that by using only the juices of the meat, a finer flavor would be obtained. Some might add an onion to the mixture; others claimed this merely made a hash of it; some wanted to use chili powder, this ruined it for others. But all agreed that no vegetables, such as corn, peas, or tomatoes, were to spoil the dish. Some liked it thick, some thin, but whatever its consistency, it must be served hot. Also some claimed it was good only when served fresh, others that a warming up the next day made it better, but rarely was there any left to prove this theory.

Aside from the mystery of the title itself, the one thing, as we have said before, which gave this stew a bad name among the uninitiated was the word "marrow gut." Yet, as all cowmen know, this marrow gut was a most necessary ingredient, though only a small portion was used in comparison with the other solids. It gave the stew its distinctive flavor. Another ingredient or two might be omitted, but as one cowman said, "A sonofabitch might not have any brains and no heart, but if he don't have guts, he's not a sonofabitch." Marrow gut is not a gut at all, but a tube connecting the two stomachs of cud-chewing animals. It is good only when the calf is young and living upon milk, as it is then filled with a substance resembling marrow through which the partially digested milk passes. This is why only young calves were selected for a good stew. The marrow-like contents were left in, and they were what gave the stew such a delicious flavor.

To make this stew, a fat calf was killed. While the meat was still warm, the heart, liver, tongue, marrow gut, some pieces of tenderloin, sweetbreads, and the brains were taken to be prepared. First the cook cut the fat into small pieces and put them into a pot. While the fat was being rendered, he cut the heart into small cubes, adding it first because it was tougher than the other ingredients. The tongue was skinned and cubed likewise, then added. This gave the two toughest ingredients longer cooking time. While these were cooking, the cook proceeded to cut the tenderloin, sweetbreads, and liver into similar pieces. The liver was used sparingly, or the stew would become bitter. The marrow gut was cut into small rings and added to the whole. If water was used, it must be warm, the ingredients well covered with it, and more added from time to time. The various ingredients were added a handful at a time, the contents being slowly stirred after each addition. Between stirrings, the cook proceeded to clean the brains of blood and membrane. The brains were cooked separately, some cooks adding a little flour to make them thick. When cooked until they became beady, these were added to the stew. This was the last ingredient added, and it gave the stew a medium of thickening. salt and pepper were then added to taste, and some cooks put in an onion, or "skunk egg" as the cowboy sometimes called this vegetable.

It took several hours to cook the stew, and about the only way you could ruin a good one was to let it scorch. If a cook committed this blunder, he had better be prepared to receive some titles less complimentary than the one given the stew. When it was done, you had something sweet and delicious, and after eating it you would no longer be a skeptic.

While range men have seemed to keep this dish mysterious to the outlander, to an old cowman the only mystery about it was whose calf went into its making.

The pinto bean is hard to beat, with dry salt in the pot. Frijoles? Well it's jes' the same, jes' give me what y'u've got. Now jes' in case yore beans is white, knowed as the navy sort, I'll take a helpin' jes' the same, about half a quart. Or if yore beans is big an' red an' sort of kidney shape, I'll go along besides the fire an' fill my ole tin plate. But a man can't live on beans alone, he's got to have some beef. Now beans for breakfast ain't so good, too much will bring y'u grief. It's a swellin' that they gives y'u, an' at times them whistle-berries, jes' make a man plumb miserable, he'll wish them beans was cherries.

When the wagon camp is by a draw an' weather's warm an' dry, wood an' water handy, our ole Cookie's ridin' high. It's then he'll make them extrys sech as pie an' cobbler too, fluff-duffs, raisin' puddin', some dip that's thick like goo. A good fried pie to top it off, dried peach or apricot, or bear-sign fresh from out the grease, we'll take 'em while they're hot.

Tex Taylor

CHAPTER 7 *Frijoles and Fluff-duffs*

*"You can judge a man by the hoss
he rides; you can judge a cow outfit by the grub it serves."*

N O RANGE COOK would start his roundup wagon without a good supply of dried beans. They have long been a
staple item of food in the cattle country, and are so commonly relied upon that meal time is referred to as "bean
time" on many parts of the range. There are various kinds
of beans, but in the Southwest all are called "frijoles" (free-
hol-es), though in reality, the frijole is a specific kind
of bean.

Most cooks prefer the pinto bean which takes its name
from the brown spots on its surface. Some like the navy
bean, some the red, but any are good if cooked right. The
cowman knew nothing of proteins, minerals, and vitamins,
but he did know that the lowly bean satisfied his hunger,
was easy to keep, easy to cook, and cheap. The sight of a
black iron pot half full of beans cooking, its miniature gey-
sers throwing up little jets of steam with a *plop, plop,* as it
bubbled away over a slow fire would excite any man's
appetite.

99

When the cook expected to cook beans, the first thing he did, if he was a good and conscientious cook, was to pour out about five pounds and pick the gravel out of them. These little rocks had been placed there purposely to add weight to the beans before they were sent to market. But if a cowhand broke his "bridle teeth" on a rock carelessly left in the beans, it would not make his love for the cook any greater.

Next he washed and put them to soak overnight. On the following morning he drained off the water, covered them with more cold water and placed them on a slow fire to cook. A quantity of dry salt pork was cut into pieces and dropped into the pot to give a good seasoning. Since minerals tend to harden beans, water was never added and the salt was withheld until the beans were thoroughly done.

Beans should never be cooked less than five hours, and a full day's cooking is better. The higher the altitude the longer the cooking necessary. They should never be cooked into a muck, yet until so tender they burst open at a touch. The cowman says they taste better when eaten with a spoon.

Some cooks liked the red bean cooked until tender, then added a can of tomatoes, stirring them into the beans; to this mixture he added two or three diced onions, salt, plenty of pepper, a dash of cayenne, and perhaps a little garlic, but garlic and onions were not always with the wagon.

Some cooks preferred the "bean hole" method of cooking. The beans were washed and soaked overnight the same as in any other method of cooking them, but instead of placing them in a pot over a fire, the cook secured an old syrup bucket or any kind of bucket with a tight-fitting lid. The beans were placed in this, the salt pork cut up and added, and the bucket filled to the brim with water.

A hole was dug at the edge of the cooking fire. The lid of the bucket was punctured several times to allow surplus steam to escape, and the bucket was buried, lid deep, in the hole. Hot ashes were raked around its sides from time to time to keep the heat even. If the cook had to be away from his fire for any length of time, the wrangler or some puncher who happened by would see that hot ashes were always in the hole. A stranger passing an unoccupied camp and seeing beans cooking in a hole, even though he had no hope of partaking of them, took the trouble to inspect and replenish the heat. It was one of the courtesies of the land. By supper time, if the beans had been put on at mid-morning, they were tender and delicious, all the flavor being held in the bean. If the cowboy liked beans for breakfast, they were put on after supper and allowed to cook all night. This was rarely done, however, because someone would have to lose sleep to see that the can was always surrounded by hot coals.

Beans received such names as "Mexican strawberries" or "Pecos strawberries" in the Southwest, and "prairie strawberries" and "whistle berries" in other sections. I heard one cowboy call them "deceitful beans—'cause they talk behind yore back."

101

While the cowboy seemed never to tire of fried steaks, he did get "fed up" on beans if they were on the menu too many times a day. There is a story of a cowboy from the plains of Texas who went into a restaurant in St. Louis.

"The menu was chiefly in French and he could not make heads or tails of it.

" 'Waiter,' he said, 'do you have any beans on here?'

" 'Yes,' said the waiter.

" 'Put your finger on the one that's beans.'

"The waiter pointed out the item.

" 'Is that the only one that's beans?'

" 'Yes, that's all.'

" 'Are you sure that none of the rest of them ain't beans?'

" 'I'm sorry,' said the waiter, 'but that is the only bean dish on the menu tonight.'

" 'All right,' said the cowboy, 'bring me everything else.' "[1]

The fruit on the cowboy's menu was of the dried variety—raisins, prunes, and dried apples. Prunes, of course, were stewed, but the raisins appeared both in the "spotted pup" and in pies and puddings, while apples were used mostly for pies. Dried apples had the same swelling qualities as rice, as many a cook discovered on his first attempt to prepare them.

Not all wagons furnished prunes, though they were as cheap as other dried fruits. Some considered them too much

[1] Roy Holt, *Frijoles, Texian Stomping Ground, Publication* of the Texas Folk Lore Society (Austin, 1941), 55.

of a luxury, and there were ranchmen who, like people in other callings, would "skin a flea for his hide an' tallow." Their stinginess made them difficult to work for and they were rarely successful. Jack Culley told of such a man:

"A notable 'character' was old man Wight. Mighty rough-tongued, even for those days. His most widely known characteristic was his tight fistedness. Everyone around Folsom knew his buckskin horse, Hyena, with black mane and tail, which the boys would leave tied up to a hitching post in town so the old man could ride out to the ranch and not have to hire a rig, the times he came in on the train from his home in Trinidad. These visits were pretty frequent, for he could never be brought to put any trust in his men. As familiar as Hyena was the figure of Wight himself crouched on the store steps over a lunch of sardines and crackers that saved buying a twenty-five cent meal at the restaurant. He kept all his hands, cattle and sheep alike, on scanty rations. One time a deputation from his roundup wagon came to see him and tell him the boys would like to have some prunes in camp. 'Prunes!' exploded the old man. 'What the hell do you want with prunes? Don't I kill my own beef for you, and give you white flour and beans and sowbelly? And you ask for prunes! To hell with ye, ye high-headed, cigarette-smokin' sons of bitches!' And the old man got away with it. The boys got no prunes."[2]

If the cook was in an expansive mood and had the time, he would concoct some kind of pie because he knew that

[2] Jack Culley, *Cattle, Horses and Men* (Los Angeles, The Ward Ritchie Press, 1940), 230.

pie was the one delicacy high on the cowboy's list of luxuries. Although he might enclose his fruit in a crust only a wagon cook dare make and only a cowboy could eat, it was devoured with relish. It has been said that the cowboy "would go to hell for a piece o' pie."

Having no eggs, the cook limited himself to closed-top pies. There was no meringue, or "calf slobber," as the cowboy called it, or open-faced, or "boggy top," pies. Like any good housewife, the wagon cook made his pies first. Rolling his plastic dough out with a beer bottle, he placed it in a greased pie pan, put in his stewed fruit, placed the top crust on, trimmed it with a knife, then scalloped it around the edge with a fork to seal the top and bottom crusts together. Instead of fancy cuts on the top crust to allow for escaping steam, he usually cut the company's brand.

He baked his pies in the Dutch oven as he did his bread. Placing the oven on a smooth bed of coals, he put the pie inside and placed the previously heated lid on top, then covered the whole with hot coals. If he had used sufficient shortening to make the crust tender, he had a delicious pie, but most wagon cooks seemed inclined to use biscuit dough for pie crust.

When raisins were enclosed in such dough, the confection was called "nigger in a blanket." But to make a good "nigger in a blanket," the dough should contain quite a bit of shortening and not be rolled quite as thin as for pie crust. It was liberally sprinkled with raisins and beef tallow, cut very fine, then sprinkled with cinnamon and sugar. The dough was then rolled over, and more raisins, tallow, cinna-

104

mon, and sugar added as it was rolled. After being placed in a greased Dutch oven, usually in a half-moon shape, a little water was added and it was allowed to bake slowly.

Some cooks were expert at making vinegar pies, and although the name seems the very antithesis of a pie, the cowboys found them very tasty. To make these, he used about a quarter of a pint of vinegar to a half-pint of water and added enough sugar to taste. Placing a good-sized lump of fat in the skillet to melt, he stirred in a little flour as for gravy. Slowly stirring all the time, he then added his vinegar mixture, letting it boil until it thickened.

Into previously prepared dough-lined pie pans he poured this mixture, placed on a dough top, usually strips

of rolled dough in a criss-cross pattern, and baked until done.

Fried pie was another form of dessert some cooks condescended to make. The fruit and dough were prepared as for any other pie, but the dough was cut into disks about the size of a small plate, a large-sized empty tin can being used for a cutter. The fruit was placed on only half of the rolled dough, the other half being folded over the fruit in a "turn over" shape and the edges sealed with the pressure of a fork. The pie was then dropped into a skillet which contained deep, hot fat and allowed to fry until a golden brown. In an average skillet three or four pies could be fried at the same time. When done, they were taken out and the surplus grease allowed to drain on a paper or flour sack.[3]

Another dessert the cook made of fruit when he wanted to be especially nice to the boys was called "son-of-a-bitch-in-a-sack." It was made by preparing a soft dough of water, flour, sugar, salt, and baking powder. To this mixture was added raisins or dried apples, previously soaked, and suet. The mass was placed in a sack and hung in a big hot-water bucket and placed over the pot-rack to steam until done. Perhaps it got its name from the trouble it took to make it. Some cooks weren't too successful with this dish, and a cowboy might complain that the cook "jes' bogged down a few raisins in dough an' called 'er puddin'." On the trail, if a thicket of wild plums or a berry patch were found, the cook would perhaps make a fruit cobbler.

[3] Dale, "Cowboy Cookery," *Hereford Journal*, Vol. XXXVI, No. 17 (January 1, 1946), 49.

The roundup cook took great pride in his pies, although he had only stewed fruit from which to make them, but his greatest triumph was, perhaps, his suet pudding. Suet pudding was more of a rarity than the pies, even though suet was naturally plentiful where beef was so frequently killed. It was made by mixing together one cup of chopped suet, one-half cup each of raisins and currants, one-half cup of sugar, one cup of flour and one and one-half cups of bread crumbs. Two teaspoons of baking powder and one-half teaspoon of salt were added. These ingredients were mixed into a stiff dough with two cups of water. The dough was then rolled in flour and put in a flour sack, leaving room to "swell." It was then placed in boiling water, covered, and boiled over the campfire for two hours. Served with a plain sauce of water and sugar, thickened with a little flour and flavored with a teaspoon of vanilla or other extract, it was a welcome change from the usual camp fare. The sauce for such puddings was often called "dip."

Another wagon dessert not commonly known was originated by Lum Pagrum, a wagon cook of New Mexico and called by him "houn' ears an' whirlups."[4] It was made from thin sourdough dropped from a spoon into hot grease and fried brown. It usually spread out in the shape of a dog's ear. The "whirlup" was a sauce made with water and sugar and beaten up with flavoring and spice, or dried fruit, if available, could be chopped or mashed and added to the whirlup and poured over the "houn' ears."

[4] Mrs. Julia Michener to R.F.A.

Some folks it seems, jes' lives to eat, an' others eats to live; like hosses an' cow critters, they jes' eats to git their fill. Now round-up hands an' cowpokes is neither folks nor beasts, but somewhere in between them two, they calls good food a feast.

For instance, take tomatters, in a little tin airtight, when y'u're thirsty they is hard to beat, for food they're jes' all right. An' when y'u're tired an' hungry, fancy foods don't mean a thing, jes' give us meat an' biscuits an' black coffee with a sting.

Of course when work is easy an' we're loafin' 'round the wagon, old Cookie really struts his stuff; we eat an' keep on braggin'. It's then we gets them fancy foods, like fruits an' pies an' cake, an' life out on the open range ain't quite so hard to take.

Tex Taylor

CHAPTER 8 *Miscellany*

"*A man that's got teeth in his saddle don't chew grub long with a good outfit.*"

Food at the chuck wagon has always been simple, but in the words of an old Spanish proverb, "*Abuena hambre no hay el pan duro*"—"To good hunger there is no hard bread." In the days of the first cow hunts men were satisfied with meat, bread, and coffee, and they got that fare three times daily.

Although this diet became monotonous, it was sustaining and there was plenty of it. Lack of variety was made up by quantity and healthy appetites. Later, when wagons were introduced, more food could be carried, and hence more variety could be achieved. There has been quite an improvement in the cowman's food since the old days. Beans were added to the menu and later came the novelty of canned goods. Vegetables, as the cowboy came to know "grew in cans"—"airtights" he called them. The green salad served in Eastern society would have been repulsive to him. When one cowboy saw such a salad, he declared that "if the good Lord wanted man to eat grass, He'd a made him into a cow."

The cowman did not seem to relish such vegetables as canned corn, peas, and their like. Canned tomatoes, on the other hand, filled a large place in his cravings. While he knew nothing of the vitamin content advertised today, there was that tangy acidity which his system seemed to demand. And since canned tomatoes were cheap, the boss could afford to keep a good supply on hand.

Tomatoes not only served as a food, but were most satisfying as a thirst quencher, allaying thirst even longer than water. A man going on a dry ride would likely take a can or two of tomatoes along; also a man coming in from such a ride would go to the wagon and open a can of tomatoes to cut the dust and thirst. It became more or less a custom for the cowboy to climb the wagon wheel and help himself to such a treat if he wanted it, this being about the only time he could paw around in the wagon without hearing from the cook.

No cowhand liked to "pack" a lunch, so line riders and fence riders often carried only a can or two of tomatoes rolled in their slickers to serve as both food and drink when they would not get back to camp until evening. If the cowboy was riding in a country with drinking water of poor quality, he preferred the tomatoes to a canteen.

Like the town man who ordered tomato juice to settle his stomach the "mornin' after," the cowboy learned to rely upon this antidote, too. If he could add pepper sauce and salt to it, so much the better.

Tomatoes stewed with a little sugar and some left-over biscuits made a tasty dish. Some enjoyed it as much as they did dessert, and the cook who occasionally furnished this delicacy did not lessen his popularity with the boys. For no earthly reason, this dish was known as "pooch."

If the cowboy saw milk, it was of the canned variety, known as "canned cow." The tenderfoot could never understand why, in a country of cows, there was no milk. Because he *was* a tenderfoot, he didn't know that range cows gave very little milk. In fact, had he tried to milk one of them, he would have found that they didn't *give* at all—you had to *take* it the hard way. The old-time cowboy might steal a slick-ear, but he wouldn't steal milk from a calf. The common cowboy liquid measure is "two gills, one pint; two pints, one quart; four cows, one gallon." It was frequently said of the Old West that it "had more cows and less milk, more rivers and less water, and you could see farther and see less than in any other country in the world."

Besides tomatoes and enough milk for cooking purposes, few canned goods were carried with the wagon. They were bulky and added too much weight.

Salt pork, another standby of the cow country, went by such names as "sow belly," "hog side," "sow bosom," and "pig's vest with buttons." Bacon was often sarcastically referred to as "fried chicken," "chuck wagon chicken," and "Kansas City fish." It was not used to a great extent, because it became rancid in the heat and anyway the cowman preferred fresh meat.

While salt pork was used chiefly for seasoning at most

111

wagons, a few have been known whose owners were so stingy they "wouldn't give a nickel to see an earthquake," and they used it steadily rather than kill a beef. One cowhand who quit such an outfit said he was "fed hog side till he sweated straight leaf lard and his hide got so slick he couldn't keep his clothes on."

There was always a supply of molasses, called "blackstrap," "lick," "larrup," or "long sweetnin'." To satisfy his sweet tooth, the cowboy often ended his meal by sopping up molasses with his biscuits. Several years ago I met a young JA puncher who could neither read nor write. He had seen a waitress in an Amarillo restaurant filling the syrup pitchers from a can of White Swan syrup, had sampled it and liked the taste. One day at the wagon he complained of the thick black "lick" served by the cook.

"Cookie," he said, "why don't y'u buy some o' that white gooses syrups instead of this stuff. It's plumb good."

To him the picture of a white swan on the can looked like a goose. He had never heard of a swan.

I remember another unschooled cowboy of the JA of later years. There was quite a bit of talk about vitamins during the days soon after their discovery. News about them had spread to the ranch country and they were discussed considerably, but still this cowboy didn't know what the talk was all about. During a meal, he poured his plate full of syrup. Ants had gotten into the syrup jug, and he found his plate full of the little black insects.

"Looky," he said as he stirred them about with his

fork, "this larrup's plumb full o' them vitamins y'u been talkin' 'bout!"

"Texas butter" was made from the hot lard in which the steaks had been fried, by putting some flour in the pan and letting it brown, then adding hot water and stirring the whole until it thickened. While it was simply gravy, it often went by the name of "Texas butter" or "immigrant butter."

After rice was introduced to the cow country, it became a frequent dish at the wagon. The first cooks to use this grain were ignorant of its swelling qualities, and when they put on enough (as they thought) to make a meal, they had to call for help to round up all the vessels in camp, and in the end had enough to feed an army.

"We got pretty tired of just having biscuits, meat, and gravy," said Rollie Burns. "One day one of the boys was at Dockum's and decided to buy some rice, on his own hook. None of us knew anything about cooking rice. We put a half-gallon in a Dutch oven and started to boil it. It started swelling up and filled the oven. We put part of it in another oven, and pretty soon we had both ovens full. We put some in a small bucket and still there wasn't enough room. Then we piled some out on the ground. We had to eat all the rice in our bread ovens before we could cook any more biscuits. We had rice for three days and were pretty well caught up on that cereal by the time we finished with the batch."[1]

Boiled rice was called "John Chinaman," "moonshine," or "swamp seed." Some cooks, in an effort to make a fancier

[1] Holden, *Rollie Burns*, 94.

dish, added a liberal quantity of raisins to it. Cinnamon was also used to add flavor. Most of the cowboys liked this better and gave it the names "spotted pup" and "hoss thief special."

Occasionally at branding time, there were "calf fries," or what the cowman more commonly called "mountain oysters" or "prairie oysters," depending upon whether he was in mountainous or prairie country. These were not served with the meals, as the cook seldom prepared them, but were generally roasted on the coals of the branding fire until they popped open. They were salted and eaten there at the fire as a between-meal snack.

As a rule the cowhand dreamed of the fancy food and "throat ticklin' truck" he knew was served in the city, and his palate craved a change from wagon grub. Yet it often happened that when he had the opportunity to test these dishes he was disappointed in them as articles of food. He soon learned that fancy desserts were too fluffy to be filling. Oren Arnold and John P. Hale tell of such a case:

"The menu provided by the cook at one big roundup and branding spree several years ago grew so monotonous that the foreman threatened to kill the cook unless he made a change. The cook left his chuck wagon that night after supper, rode a long way to town, got a grocer out of bed and made a purchase, and rode back in time to prepare breakfast for the boys. As a breakfast dessert he served a new-fangled concoction called Jello. The boys ate it, wearing various expressions of curiosity and contempt. When the meal was over, the cook spoke to the foreman.

" 'Well, how'd you like that Jello, hah?'

" 'Jello be damned!' barked the foreman. 'I'd just as soon put a funnel in my mouth and run against the wind!' "[2]

Only recently I read about a modern cow-camp cook who fed the boys cantaloupe with a hole cut in the end and filled with Jello. The chill of the night hardened the Jello, and the melons were served for breakfast. How times have changed! The old-time cowboy would have been ashamed to be seen eating such food for fear he would be looked upon as a sissy or a softy.

Another story about a cook who attempted to please the boys with variety is the one told about "Peggy John" Fleming of the Spur Ranch.

"One morning about eleven o'clock, John entered 'The Dive' to see how many had shown up for dinner. After a few minutes he said:

" 'Boys, I'm goin' to give you a treat for dinner.'

" 'What is it?' we all cried out.

" 'Saratogy chips,' said John as he returned to the kitchen.

"When the dinner bell rang, we all hurried to the mess room. The table was set pretty much as usual, fried steaks, beans, potatoes, vinegar roll, and biscuits 'better than mother used to make.' The spuds were thinly sliced and fried a golden brown. I had a suspicion that they might be John's Saratogy chips; however, I said nothing.

" 'John, bring on your Saratogy chips.'

[2] Oren Arnold and John P. Hale, *Hot Irons* (New York, The Macmillan Co., 1940), 210–11.

"John thought we were giving him a game and said, 'How did you like 'em?'

" 'But we ain't had any yet,' Frank replied.

" 'Yes you did, and you've eaten 'em all up,' John answered. 'How did you like the potatoes done that way? That's what the cook book calls Saratogy chips.'

" 'Ah, John, quit fooling us that way; them was just fried potatoes,' said some disappointed boy."[3]

Butter, a luxury the cowhand rarely saw except occasionally at a spread where the woman of the ranch insisted on a few milch cows, was called by the various names of "cow grease," "axle grease," and "skid grease." The usual substitute for butter, called "Charlie Taylor," was a mixture of sorghum and bacon grease.

On occasion the cook might make what was called "Colorado stew with dumplings." For this he cut bacon into pieces, covered it with water, and boiled until done. Diced potatoes and onions were then added and cooked some more. The dumplings were made the same way as baking powder biscuits, pinched off into small pieces, then placed on top of the stew and cooked until done. Here was a whole meal in one kettle.

"Camp potatoes" comprised another dish the cowman liked when he could get it. First the cook diced a generous portion of bacon into a skillet and fried it to a light brown. He then added diced raw potatoes, salt and pepper, and covered them with water. When the mixture had simmered until all the moisture had been absorbed, it was ready to eat.

[3] W. J. Elliott, *The Spurs* (Privately printed, 1909), 68–71.

On rare occasions some near-by nester might raise sweet potatoes which he would trade the cowman for beef. The cook would bake these in hot ashes and the change was enjoyed by the cowboys. Because of their gaseous effects, they soon acquired the name of "music roots."

Some wagons furnished mixed pickles as an added luxury. These were left in the keg and a long-handled fork was supplied to let each man spear his own. The cook, making his own rules of deportment, allowed no one to stand and "pick around" trying to get a favorite or larger piece. Whatever he brought to light—cucumber, onion, or cauliflower—he had to keep. The cook's orders were, "Take 'em as they come and no throw backs."

Oysters, which the cowboy rarely saw, except the canned variety and then only when he went to town, were called "sea plums." Most of the food served in town cafés and hotels was called "soft grub."

At the ranch the cook had more conveniences, better equipment, and usually fewer men to cook for. He might serve pancakes, or "hen fruit stir," if there were eggs. "Splatter dabs" and "saddle blankets" were other names given pancakes. Or the cook might make a batch of sourdough flapjacks. The sourdough was made into a sponge at night and allowed to rise until morning, when some soda and a little bacon grease were added, along with a sprinkling of sugar to make the cakes brown.

The cook used a long-handled skillet and never needed a pancake turner. Tossing a cake into the air with a twist so that it turned bottom side up, he caught it coming down with the skill of an expert. He either sprinkled cakes with a little sugar or served them with "Charlie Taylor."

On rare occasions, if time hung heavily on his hands and he was filled with good cheer, the cook would "fry up" some doughnuts—"bear sign," he called them. This was indeed a treat for the boys, and an outfit which had a cook who could and would make an occasional batch of "bear sign" was the envy of the entire range.

If any of the boys were at the house when this event was taking place, they crowded around to watch these tasty rings of dough browning in the bubbling grease until they became a tantalizing brown. Scarcely had the cook forked them from the grease and placed them in a waiting pan when eager hands reached out to empty it. The grunts of admiration, the smacking of lips, and the licking of grease from fingertips was music to the cook. He let the boys consume the first three or four fryings without comment, but

118

when he thought they had had enough, he moved the pan where he would be between it and the boys.

"That's 'nough, boys," he'd say. "Don't make a damned hawg of yo'self. Save some for the other boys."

As he shooed them from the kitchen, there would be some mild grumbling, but beneath it all was a deep satisfaction, for a "bear sign" fry was indeed an occasion which made the boys love old coosie with a fierce loyalty.

At the ranch kitchen, too, the cook made a dish called "Lumpy Dick." It resembled the blancmange of the housewife, except that water was used instead of milk and he had no eggs. The pudding was boiled over an open fire and whatever he had in spice and flavoring were used to make it more palatable. It was difficult to make it smooth without milk, hence the name.

When the cook had an accumulation of left-overs and wanted to "clean up the kitchen," he gathered his odds and ends of cooked meat, cold potatoes, canned corn, beans, and other things, threw them into a pot, seasoned the stuff highly, and boiled the mixture into what he called a "homogeneous mass." "Mulligan" was cooked much in the same way.

This brings us to a story J. Evetts Haley told about an LIT cook:

"Another noted cook on the ranch was Jack Martin, an outstanding character on the range, as cow-camp cooks usually are. His greatest failing was not in his cooking, but his drinking, and once when Phelps White was completely and commendably angry, and being hungry besides, he "ate Jack out."

" 'Well, what you want me to cook?' Jack complained.

" 'Oh, just a little of everything,' said Phelps, as he went back to the herd. Now cowpuncher cooks can be thoroughly literal, and next day when the outfit came in to eat, Jack had one pot filled with a awful conglomeration of food—beans, rice, and beef and currants—'just a little of everything' he explained."[4]

In different sections of the cow country there was a difference in grub. Some were farther from shipping points and had an unvaried menu, but all had plenty of what they did serve. As a whole there was no stinting of food in the West. When the owner began to skimp, his hands drifted to other wagons. Experience taught him that plenty of substantial food kept his men satisfied and better workers.

[4] J. Evetts Haley, *George W. Littlefield, Texan* (Norman, University of Oklahoma Press, 1943), 115–16.

When ridin' into camp, my friend, don't raise no dust an' sand, ole Cookie's fixin' supper an' sech acts he shore won't stand. Jes' ease around the down-wind side an' loosen up yore cinch; the water barrel is handy to the washpan on the bench. The riders will be in 'bout dark so get yourself all set, a tired an' hungry lot they'll be, it was early when they et.

Now when the boys is ready an' Ole Cookie calls out "Chuck," jes' fall in line behind 'em an' partake of our pot-luck. An' when y'u've et, don't hurry, be shore y'u scrape yore plate, an help ole Cookie wash 'em up an' tell 'im that he's great. Y'u're always welcome, podner, an' we hope y'u like our chuck, when "down our way" again some day, stop by an' look us up.

Tex Taylor

CHAPTER 9 *Chuck Wagon Etiquette*

"Most men are like a bob-wire fence—they have their good points."

To the layman, eating in the open is a novelty, and poor food can be eaten with relish once or twice; but the cowboy who worked and lived in the open day after day demanded that the food be good. There was no romance or novelty for him in outdoor eating. He followed the wagon five months of the year.

Breakfast and the midday meal on roundup were hasty affairs. There was work to be done, and a good hand did not dilly-dally when he had a job to do. The one important and leisurely meal of the day was supper. A group of cowboys settling down to eat that meal was a sight to see. Having selected his plate, cup, knife, and fork from the chuckbox lid at the wagon, the cowhand went from pot to skillet and helped himself to food and coffee. Here was the original cafeteria, and its operation went on for years before the idea struck the city. Later, when cafeterias were well established in the city, you would never see a cowboy patroniz-

123

ing one of them. He was "fed up" with waiting on himself at the wagon. In the city he wanted a pretty girl in a nice white apron to bring his food to him.

After selecting a suitable spot on the prairie upon which to eat, he executed a marvelous, expert scissoring-down into a genuine Turkish squat, with both hands full, yet never spilling a drop from either cup or plate. Balancing his meal with his hands, he crossed his feet while still standing, then let his knees move outward so that the calves of his legs could bear the burden of his weight as he gradually sank to the ground. This lowering of the body looks simple, but is a difficult stunt if one has never practiced it.

The calves of the cowboy's folded legs then formed the table for his plate. From long practice he learned to balance it there even while carving his steak. His cup of coffee was placed on the ground by his side. He took all he thought he could eat at his first helping, for there were no waiters to bring him a second, though there was no rule against his getting one himself. The cook might even throw him an extra biscuit if he called for one. No matter how big his appetite, a fat cowboy was rare. He could store away an amazing amount of food, but the riding and rough work he did seemed to keep him on the lean side. As a rule he ate all he could every meal because he never knew when his work would cause him to miss the next one.

He ate with his hat on, for if he laid it on the ground, it was apt to be stepped on or some fellow puncher might spill beans or coffee or gravy into it. Besides, he was usually eating in the sun. When he ate in the rain, his hat was pushed back so that the water in the wide brim would not run into his plate.

No matter how hot the food had been when he helped himself at the steaming pots, it seemed that the tallow from the beef would "set" on his plate more quickly than he could ease himself down to start eating.

Even though he lived in savage surroundings, the cowboy was not without his code of etiquette at the chuck wagon. And although conditions on the range have undergone vast changes, modern cowboys still follow these well-established precepts. Good social deportment is not peculiar to drawing rooms and dress suits. After all, etiquette is nothing more or less than an observation of the proprieties, a conventional decorum. The cowboy, perhaps more

of a savage and not so cultured as his Eastern brother, never-theless had his own code of etiquette. The clubman might laugh at the cowboy's behavior in cultured surroundings, but place the clubman in a cow camp and he would be just as ignorant of proper conduct.

While the polished clubman is held to highly conventionalized conduct, the cowboy was bound no less severely by his own code. He followed certain rules, not as a display of breeding, as is so often the case with his Eastern brother, but in consideration of others. You will note that all the rules of the cowboy's code are a manifestation of this quality.

As the man of culture has no greater opportunity to show his good breeding than at the dinner table, so the cowman has no greater occasion to show his experience and character than at the chuck-wagon meal. In a cultured home, with the announcement, "Dinner is served," there are rules to be observed. This is equally true at the chuck wagon. When "Come an' get it" is shouted, there are rules of gentlemanly conduct as surely as in a banker's home.

Contrary to Eastern custom, every cowhand began to eat as soon as he reached the chuck wagon, without waiting for the others—that is, if the meal's readiness had been announced. He did so in order not to be in the way of the others as he went from pot to pan filling his plate and cup with the victuals around the fire. Another reason was that the sooner he finished eating, caught and saddled a fresh horse, and was ready to go back to work, the better hand was he. Cowboys ate because they were hungry and did not assemble at a meal as a social gathering. Even when they came in together, there was no crowding, no rushing, no overreaching. These would be breaches not tolerated.

Consideration of others was uppermost in the cowboy's mind. When he lifted the Dutch-oven lid for a helping, he was careful not to place it where the under part would touch sand. If the wind was blowing, he was careful to go around on the lee side so that none of the dust he might stir up would fly into another's plate. If he took a pot off the fire, he was careful to replace it when through so that its contents would keep hot for others.

No man took the last piece of anything unless he was sure the rest were through eating. No man left food in his plate. In the first place, usually he had an appetite sufficient to consume his helpings, but if he did not, the rules demanded that he scrape his scraps to the chipmunks and birds, or rake them into the fire or "squirrel can" to prevent flies.

Under the mess-box lid the cook always placed a huge dishpan, sometimes two. This pan was as has been said before, known all over the range as the "wreck pan" or "roundup pan." The ignorant tenderfoot who did not drop his dirty dishes into it, but set them in a neat pile on the mess-box lid, was in for a "cussin'" from the cook, and those old "dough wranglers" could scorch the atmosphere.

It was a breach of etiquette for the cowboy to tie his horse to a wheel of the chuck wagon, or to ride into camp so that the wind blew dust into the food the cook was preparing. No one liked horse hair in his beans.

It was against the rules for one to jump into chuck until the cook called that it was ready—he wouldn't do it the second time. It was also contrary to custom for one to run a horse into camp or to saddle or unsaddle a horse near the wagon. There was no scuffling or kicking up dust around the chuck wagon during a meal or when food and cooking utensils were exposed.

If one went near the water bucket and found it empty, he was duty-bound to fill it immediately. If, during the meal, a man got up to refill his cup with coffee and another yelled, "Man at the pot," he was obliged to go around with the pot and fill all the cups held out to him. If one lingered too long in helping himself, thus blocking those behind him an unnecessarily long time, someone was apt to yell, "Fire an' fall back," at him.

The cowboy must be called only once to get up in the morning. For that matter a second call was unnecessary. Life in the crisp Western air expelled somnolence and produced appetites that were keen. It still does, for that matter.

Although, when at the chuck wagon the cowboy had all outdoors in which to eat, he was thoughtful of others and did not sprawl all over the ground. For a cowboy to leave the wagon with his bed not rolled and packed when camp was to be moved constituted an almost unpardonable breach of etiquette. If he committed this offense the second time, the cook was apt to drive off and leave it behind, or, if he was reckless and unafraid of consequences, he might tie the bed to a rear axle and drag it to ribbons.

At night around the campfire it was practically an unwritten law that a song or a fiddle piece or a story might not be interrupted—unless the talk was a general discussion.

If a cowboy took pride in being a "hand," he also took pride in proper conduct around the chuck wagon. He did nothing which would break the unmapped rules of range etiquette. He had as much to live up to as the man who ate his meals from linen-covered tables.

The unwritten law of Western hospitality made the stranger welcome at the wagon. He could turn his horse loose, grab a set of "eatin' irons" and help himself at the pots and pans, squat in the circle of silent diners, and no longer be a stranger.

The man forced by circumstances to ride the grub line while hunting a job was welcome because he brought news from other ranges or could tell of recent happenings in the town which he had left a short time before. But the man known as a professional chuck-line rider looking only for a free meal was frowned upon. After a meal, if the drifter, or anyone not working with the outfit, failed to grab a flour-sack towel and help with the dishes, his welcome received a jolt. Don't think the cook would fail to notice and appreciate the stranger's help with the dishes. First off, it told him that here was a man familiar with the code.

One day a stranger came riding into a wagon at a horse-killing pace, brought his mount to a slithering halt some distance from the wagon, and unsaddled. The boys were nearly through eating as he came up with his saddle over his shoulder. Nodding to the cook, he helped himself to food and squatted a short distance away from the others.

Between hasty bites he kept his eyes nervously on the horizon.

When the hands had finished, dropped their dirty dishes into the "wreck pan," caught fresh horses, and ridden back to work, the stranger washed his last mouthful down with a hasty gulp of coffee. The cook had started washing the dishes while the wrangler was still lingering over his last cup of coffee.

The stranger found a dish towel and proceeded to dry the dishes as the cook washed them. For the first time the cook noticed the visitor's nervousness and the close watch he kept on the horizon. He said nothing, but began watching the sky line also. It was not long before he saw two small specks approaching in the distance. The stranger saw them, too, and began hastening his task. The nearer they approached, the more he watched, but there was no panic. He had a job to do, an obligation to fulfill.

Finally the cook dried his hands on his apron, yelled to the wrangler to come finish the dishes, got a rope from the wagon, and went out to the horse herd. Being an old cowhand and knowing horses, he roped the fastest one in the remuda and led it back to the wagon, where he threw on the stranger's saddle and cinched it up for a fast ride. There was a look of gratitude from the stranger, but still he dried dishes. By the time he was through, the approaching riders were within rifle shot. He pulled his hat down for a fast ride, shook the cook's hand in silent gratitude and mutual understanding, mounted, and was away before the approaching law knew what was going on.

130

The cook had never seen this man before; he did not know what crime had placed him beyond the law, but he did know that here was a man who had risked his freedom to uphold one of the unwritten codes of the wagon, so he could not have been all bad. His crime would have had to have been a heinous one for the cook to have refused help and admiration.

There was etiquette at the ranch house also. The West was and is still noted for its open hospitality. There were no signs spelling "Welcome" upon the door mats. It was acted, not made in signs. It was real, not sham. All men were welcome at the ranch, and no questions were asked of them. The outlaw might sit at the table beside the circuit rider and receive the same courteous treatment if he behaved himself.

Every visitor went to the table without invitation when the meal was announced, and there all men ate in silence. In this region where news was the scarcest of commodities, idle gossip was unknown. When the time came for the visitor to take his departure, if he was acquainted with the custom and etiquette of ranch life, he did not think of offering pay, no matter whether his stay had been for days, weeks, or months. No pay was expected of any guest. For one to offer it was very close to an insult and aroused the ire of every man of the outfit. The guest simply mounted, said, "S'long," and rode away without looking back. The taciturn foreman said, "S'long," and went back to work.

It was almost unheard of for a host to ask pay for a meal. The guest would have despised him for it, and so would the outfit for which he rode. His outfit would never again, if gathering stock and seeing one of a penurious host's steers, throw it over on his home range. They would likely kill it for food to be sure of getting back that money. There is a case on record in which a rancher, disregarding this well-established rule of the range, charged a visiting rider for a meal, and for long afterward every time any of this rider's outfit found one of the rancher's animals, they branded it with the word "MEALS" in large letters.

Bob Kinnon told me a similar story. He and a friend rode to a ranch in Texas when they were just boys. They got there at dinner time. After they had eaten, they asked for a job. The boss not only refused them work, but charged them for their dinner.

When they rode away, they were broke and not in the best humor. Bob's friend, Hugh, suggested that they "advertise the outfit." They roped a three-year-old steer, tied him down, built a fire, and put a saddle ring to heat. When the ring got hot, Hugh took two sticks and burned "MEALS —50CTS" on the steer's ribs. He did a good job, and the steer ran the range for years, a living advertisement of the policy of the outfit.

In the sections of the cattle country which modern civilization had not invaded, there were no locks on the doors. Every visitor had the vested right to enter a ranch house at any time, whether the regular occupants were present or absent, and to expect food and shelter for as long as necessary if he did not abuse this privilege.

Although every passer-by had the same right to enter

a house, it was his bounden duty first to ascertain whether any of the occupants were at home and, if so, to await their welcome before attempting to pass through the door. If the visitor was mounted and a follower of convention, he would remain ahorse until requested to dismount. It was extremely discourteous to quit one's mount before receiving an invitation to do so.

If forced by circumstance to travel on and if in actual distress, the visitor might, in the occupant's absence, help himself to food requisite for the journey to his next prospective shelter. The code demanded that he leave a written note in which he stated his name, what he had taken, and why. This writing was not exacted with any idea of assuring a refund to the particular rancher who unwittingly furnished the supplies; it was to impress upon the public that it should borrow only what it needed, and that whenever once more affluent, it should repay—not to the original lender, but to some traveler who was in the same predicament. Besides, when an absent rancher returned home, it might have worried him to see strange tracks, and a note dispelled any anxiety.

It was a courtesy of the land for one to remove his gun before seating himself at the dining table. He did not necessarily remove his hat unless ladies were present. Behatted heads were common at the dining table, but guns were not in evidence. It was polite for a stranger at a ranch to leave his belt and gun hanging on the horn of his saddle or lay them aside when entering the house. This was delicate proof that he was not "lookin' for someone."

The cowboy had many other rules of etiquette which I will not mention here because they do not belong to a discussion of cooks and eating. The cowboy might not have acquired the polish of a refined deportment, but he made his own rules and observed them. His code fitted the life he lived and had as high a standard as that of cultured society. It originated from the principles of men who followed a life in the open—a life free from sham and hypocrisy.[1]

[1] Adapted from an address delivered by the author to the Denver Westerners, June, 1949, at Denver. Full text published in the Denver Westerners' *Brand Book*, 1949.

PART III
A Day with the Cook

When the outfit's in headquarters an' the wagon's in the shed, Ole Cookie has an easy time, he even sleeps in bed. He's got a stove to cook upon, dry wood always at hand; water, coffee, flour, an' sech are at his quick command. He does his fancy cookin' now an' tries out a surprise, an' when the boss brings company, the boys bug out their eyes.

Don't think Ole Cookie's gittin' soft or easin' off the rules, it's jes' that cookin's easier when he's got more food an' tools. He still arises early, I mean while it is black, an' when he yells, "It's ready," y'u had better git yore stack. All hands had better be on time, eat, an' scrape their plate; the boss kin bring the company an' come a little late. But city folks, take my advice in case y'u craves some food, when Cookie hits that breakfast gong, be in a happy mood.

Tex Taylor

Chapter 10 *At the Ranch*

*"Snow on the roof don't mean
it's cold inside."*

W HEN COOKING at the ranch, the Sultan of the Skillets
was no less autocratic than at the wagon. However, at this
time he was usually in a better humor, because he had a
stove to cook upon and did not have to contend with wind,
dust, and rain. Then, too, his supply of fuel was more de-
pendable. Also, at the ranch he usually had a smaller crew
to cook for, just a few hands kept on in winter to keep
things in shape.

The ranch personnel at this time was more like a small
family. Most ranch owners, unless they were married and
had a family of their own, ate with their cowboys. There
was no distinction between boss and hired hand except that
the boss usually sat at the head of the table. If the ranch
was a partnership venture, the senior member was ceded
this honor. Some of the English and Scottish outfits set a
separate table for their employees, a practice that caused
no little resentment among the cowboys. The West was
very democratic and the cowboy felt himself to be as good
as anyone, and no English lord was his superior.

139

A story about Charlie Russell well illustrates the attitude of the normal Westerner toward foreign grandees:

"Russell had hired out as a hunting guide to an English lord recently arrived in Montana. When camp was made the first night, Charlie hobbled the horses, made a fire, and cooked the meal. He then called his Lordship to 'fall to' and began to help himself.

"His Lordship was astonished.

" 'Bah Jove, my man,' he said, 'I'm not accustomed to eating with mah servants, y'know.'

"Charlie had his mouth full of food, and after washing it down with a gulp of hot coffee, coolly surveyed his Lordship.

" 'All right,' he said, 'jes' wait till I get through then.'

"In the free West no man was judged by birth, something over which he had no control, but by his own actions and behavior. One man was as good as another until he proved himself otherwise. For this reason the cowboy did not think much of the English outfits."[1]

Ranchmen did not make a formality of a meal. It was strictly business with no time for idle gossip. Consequently, meals lasted only a short time. The cook had his dishwashing chores after the meal, and the diners were considerate of him—perhaps from having heard him admonish some loiterer to "swaller an' git out" in a voice that meant business. Any cowhand arriving after the meal was over received no sympathy, but only a grin from the cook and a

[1] Ramon F. Adams and Homer E. Britzman, *Charles M. Russell, the Cowboy Artist* (Pasadena, Trail's End Publishing Co., 1948), 110–11.

140

wave of the hand toward the bean pot accompanying the words, "Beans, help yo'self."

Although the cook might be indifferent about satisfying the appetite of a regular hand who was late, he shared the boss' hospitality if an outside guest happened to arrive after the meal hour. Through force of habit he might grumble a little at the added labor, but he has been known to prepare several suppers, one after the other, when guests have stopped. When the boss said, "Put yo' best foot in the soup, Cookie, there's goin' to be company for supper," he did his best to uphold his reputation as a good cook. One hospitable cook of Wyoming, when he saw a horseman at any time on the horizon riding toward the ranch, would throw a lunch together, even though supper would be served twenty minutes after the rider's arrival.

The Western ranchman has always had a reputation for hospitality. No one ever approached the old-time ranch without receiving such invitations as "Light an' line yo' flue with chuck," "Crawl off an' feed yo' tapeworm," "Climb down an' eat a bean," "Get down an' rest yo' hat," or "Come in an' cool yo' saddle." If no one was at home, as has been explained before, the visitor found the latch-string on the outside of an unlocked door, and was welcome to help himself to food for himself and his horse.

Always an early riser, even in winter when daylight came late, the cook crawled out of his bunk—usually in a room next to the kitchen—slipped his feet into his cold shoes, and went into the kitchen to light a coal-oil lamp and shiver until he got his fire going. Breakfasts were served early on the ranch as well as on the roundup. The late Frank Hastings, manager of the Swensen SMS Ranch, once told a story about a cowboy from another ranch who arrived at the old Spur headquarters about ten o'clock one night. He was called to breakfast the next morning about three. As he rode away after breakfast, he was heard to say, "A man can sure stay all night quick at this ranch."

Another cowboy was forced to stay overnight at a ranch where the owners had the habit of rising unusually early. When he got back to his home ranch, some of the boys asked him how this spread fed their hands.

"They serve two suppers ever' night," answered the homecomer, "one about dark and the second one long 'fore daylight."

The eating place on the ranch, especially if it was a separate building, was called by such slang names as the "cook shack," "feed-bag," "feed trough," "grub house," "mess house," "nose-bag," and "swaller-an'-git-out trough."

The furnishings of the ranch dining room were sparse and crude. There was a long pine table, with equally long wooden benches on each side, or a collection of cheap chairs, most of them with cowhide bottoms. Many of them were wired up in one place or another—evidence of efforts to repair past abuse. The table was either bare or covered with oilcloth.

The cook's beating upon a triangle brought the men from the bunkhouse, the corral, or wherever they happened to be. One of the cook's rules was promptness. I know of one Texas cook who got wrathy when one or two of the

boys were late. He strapped on a six-gun, stood at the corner of the table, and declared his rules. When the boss and
his wife got back from Fort Worth, where they had gone
on business, they found the cook a regular walking arsenal
and the boys afraid to step sideways. The cook swore he'd
drop the first man that came into the mess-room late. Nobody did. They either came early or lost their appetite.

Although eating was a business with little idle conversation, now and then one might hear such inelegant praise
as "Throw yo' lip over this puddin'. It's plumb larrapin'."

Or some impatient diner might direct another further up the table with this statement: "When y'u get through pawin' over that beef, send the remains down this way." Usually, however, the hands depended upon the long reach of their arms to help themselves, or the cook would hover about to see that the various dishes were placed in strategic locations.

Once in a while a ranch would use a woman cook. Of course, the boys had to be more careful of their language and manners, but a woman repaid their consideration by looking after their comfort more cheerfully than a man cook. If she was young and unattached, she had no trouble keeping her wood-box filled with fuel. The cowboys vied with each other to stand well in her favor. The male cook was forced to call upon his authority and profanity to keep the supply of fuel adequate for his needs. "No fuel—no food" was his slogan.

After supper, if the cook had had an agreeable day, he did not object to the boys' pushing back their chairs and loitering for a short "bull session." In fact, if the talk lasted long enough for him to finish his dishes, he might join them. Many of the old cooks were good storytellers and could tell as big lies as the next man. In the Texas Panhandle there was an old cook known as Piebiter, who had a reputation all over that section as a good teller of stories. Many of the old cooks liked to relate their past experiences and brag of their prowess.

When he had finished with his observations at such a session, the cook went back into the kitchen to prepare his flapjack batter for the next morning or to perform some other needed duty. His exit was a signal for the loiterers to retire to the bunkhouse, because the cook was an early riser. Since his bunk was in the dining room, the kitchen, or in an adjoining room, the noise of their talk would disturb his slumber. Rarely were late hours kept at a ranch unless there was a dance in progress. Men were too tired and the nights too short for late hours.

Food at the ranch, as on roundup, was hauled in from the outside, bought in wholesale quantities. The cook might not be able to provide many different kinds of food, but he could certainly have plenty of what he did serve. It was a good many years before the ranchman lowered his dignity enough to grow vegetables. He prided himself upon being a cattle raiser, not a truck gardener.

Yet some of the pioneer ranchers, like John Chisum, planted orchards and had fresh fruit in addition to the dried variety. Some of the early ranchers were as far as two hundred miles away from their base of supply. They had huge freight wagons to haul supplies to the ranch, and since the trip sometimes consumed two weeks or more, they bought enough at one time to last a while.

Some of the earlier ranchmen had time to hunt to vary the menu and conserve their beef. Game was plentiful and varied—buffalo, deer, antelope, bear, and sometimes elk within easy distance. But as game became scarcer and the cattle business expanded to occupy more and more of the rancher's time, wild game was found on his table less and less.

In spite of the monotony of an unvaried bill of fare and the sameness of his days and nights, the cowboy would live no other life. His good health brought him the joy of living in spite of dull routine. After the fall roundup the majority of the hands rolled their beds and rode off to spend the winter elsewhere. But in the spring they returned like meadowlarks with the first hint of soft skies and green grass, eager to hear the bawl of cattle and to gorge themselves on Cookie's unstinted meals, especially when they knew him to be a good cook.

Something about the freedom of his life, his vigorous good health, and the occasional exciting incidents of his work held the cowboy. All men were equal and known by their first names, or, more commonly, by nicknames. It was a land where your business was your own. No one cared what you once had been, or asked personal questions about your past. Your present behavior was all they were interested in.

Many of the early ranch cooks were men whose tempers had placed them beyond the law in some other locality. Some of them, perhaps, had a price upon their heads, but as long as they behaved themselves in their chosen new location and could cook, no questions were asked.

When the wagon's on the trail, Ole Cookie cracks the whip, an' them dun mules with zebra legs has got marks on their hip. He's got to get 'way up ahead an' find some wood an' water, set the dough, an' heat the pot, the herd is shore to foller. He moves the wagon twice each day an' cooks three meals to boot, he drives through sand or mud or dust, but he don't give a whoop. Rocks an' gullies, rivers wide, creeks an' hills an' plain, fog or sunshine, wind or rain, he gets there jes' the same.

He stops an' cooks, they eat; he packs, again he's on the move, the herd eats grass along the way but cowboys must have food. So day by day, along the way, from Texas, where we start, the trail herd slowly moves along an' each man plays his part. The part our cookie plays, my friends, is one that's hard to beat, jes' try to ride a hoss all day without a bite to eat.

Tex Taylor

CHAPTER 11 *On the Trail*

*"Look out for the cow's feet and
the hoss' backs an' let the waddies
and the cook look out for
themselves."*

THE EXPERIENCED TRAIL BOSS selected his cook with
care. He wanted a man who could be depended on in a
crisis, a man who could cook well enough to keep a crew
of hungry men satisfied for a period of months, a man who
could economize between supply points and exercise diplomacy in handling the troublesome Indians who begged
for food along the trail. The term "Supaway John," which
the Indians used when begging for food, was all too familiar to the trail cook.

On the trail the safety of the wagon was a matter of
great concern to all. In case of a breakdown everyone
stopped to lend a hand at repairs. If a river was "big swim-
min'," a raft was built to ferry the wagon across. The cracks
in the wagon bed were calked, ropes were laced back and
forth from the bows, making a kind of basket as high as
the sideboards. Flour and other perishables were piled on
this lacing with wagon sheets under them. Sometimes the

supplies were loaded on a separate raft and floated over. Usually the horses were unhitched and forced to swim across. A long cable, made by tying several ropes together, was fastened to the wagon, and riders on the other side pulled the wagon over by their saddle horns.

While the cook on his wagon could cross high and dry, the other hands, either in the saddle or being ferried over by holding their horses' tails, emerged on the other side dripping wet. Occasionally some envious cowboy saw that the cook got a ducking, if only by "accident."

My old trail-driver friend of long standing, Jack Potter, told me what happened when one trail outfit had to cross the Canadian in the early eighties. A raft of logs was built and the wagon run on to it. Ropes were tied on and the raft pulled into the river. When it hit the middle, the current was swift. The boys on the other side could see trouble ahead, so wrapped the rope around a stump. When the raft took up the slack, it was drifting "like a bat outta hell," and the rope snapped like a fishing line.

Ten miles down river the raft was washed up on a little island. The cook was riding high and dry. He did not worry. He found a quart of whiskey in the boss' saddle pocket; he had all the food and beds. All he had to do was sit there and enjoy himself. He knew the boys would find him.

Crossing rivers was no easy task. High water, quicksands, and treacherous banks offered plenty of hazards. Many a cowboy has lost his life crossing one of the many rivers on the old cattle trails. Muscular cramps, suck-holes, undercurrents, swift water, floating logs—any number of

150

things could take the life of even the best swimmer. Many a young carefree boy has gone up the trail "to see the world" only to find his final resting place in an unmarked grave near where his bloated body had been found washed ashore or caught in a tangle farther down the river.

Watering a trail herd was a science. Cattle were watered only once a day, usually in the evening, but it was a job for the experienced. Charles Goodnight once said that "the science of the trail was in grazing and watering the cattle, but the watering was the more important of the two."

Watering meant more than heading the cattle toward the water and letting them go. A good trail boss would slow up his herd long before he hit the river. He would endeavor to cut the cattle into small bunches and let each drink, or

he would throw them up or down stream as they came to the water, thus letting all get a clear drink. When the herd hit the stream all at once, the leaders were crowded out before getting sufficient water and the drags got a muddy drink.

In the morning the herd moved out to graze its way toward its destination, leaving the wagon to be the last to break camp. The trail boss loped far ahead to search out water and the noon camping location. Soon the wagon, followed by the saddle horses, swung wide around the slowly moving herd and gained its position in the lead.

Having selected a suitable camp site, the trail boss rode back and gave directions to the cook, whereupon this worthy whipped his teams into a gallop. When he arrived at the chosen location, camp was made and the routine of cooking began again. While the men ate, the herd was allowed to scatter somewhat to graze and rest. One-half of the men ate while the other half held the cattle. Eating on the trail was done in shifts thus slowing up the cook's work somewhat. True, he could wash the dirty dishes of the first shift while the second ate and in this way gain some time.

Then camp was moved toward the location chosen for the night. The trail boss tried to get the wagon to the night camp site somewhere around five o'clock in the afternoon. The bed ground was selected with care. A good trail boss was particular to avoid a site near timber, washouts, or ravines. He never knew when cattle might stampede, and natural obstacles such as these were dangerous.

Getting a herd in order for its night's rest was no job

for a novice. It required a careful and gradual forming of the herd, not too closely crowded, nor yet scattered over too much territory.

For night guarding the crew was divided into shifts, each shift having its own name, such as "cocktail guard," "killpecker guard," "graveyard shift," and "bob-tail guard." At each shift, two men rode around the herd in opposite directions crooning to the cattle like a mother singing to her baby. Perhaps the cowboy "couldn't carry a tune in a corked jug" and his voice was anything but soothing, but it at least gave the cattle confidence to hear a human voice.

Each sleeping man staked his night horse near by, so that he would be prepared for his shift on guard duty or for a stampede. "Boys, the cattle's runnin'" was an electric, but dreaded, sentence which sent the sleepers to pulling on boots and fumbling in the dark for their picket ropes. It was a standing rule to awaken a trail man by speech and not by touch. His jumpy nerves might make him come alive with a gun in his hand.

The cook was the only man without a horse. In case of a stampede he had to take his chances by crawling into the wagon. Although wagons and camps have been wrecked by stampedes, the cowboy did his best to keep the frenzied cattle headed away from their food supply.

Somewhere, years ago, I read or heard a story of an old trail cook who had fought with Quantrill in the Civil War and who was still a rabid rebel. At one of the trail towns the outfit had passed through the boss had bought a case of canned peaches to give the boys a treat.

153

One evening the cook built up a big fire in order to have plenty of coals for his cooking. He opened the case of peaches with great care, knowing how pleased the boys would be. When he took out a can and saw the picture of Abraham Lincoln and read the label, "Abe Lincoln Peaches," his hatred for the recently victorious Yankees overcame all desire for fruit. With an oath he threw the whole case into the fire, and the explosion that followed scattered peaches over the prairie, the wagon, and not a few of the boys' beards. But he had no regrets—he had stuck to his principles.

A good cook kept the coffeepot on the hot coals during the night, so that men going on night guard could help themselves to this needed stimulant and men coming in could drink a warming cup to take the chill of the night from their bones.

One of the cook's last duties of the night was to turn the wagon tongue toward the North Star so that directions could be taken from it the following morning. It served as the trail man's compass. On the end of the tongue a lighted lantern was hung to guide the night shifts back to camp.

On the trail a good cook always had his eyes on the wood supply. If wood happened to be plentiful in a camp, he would get the wrangler to snake up a big log or two and hoist them on top of his wagon after the other camp plunder had been loaded. He watched his water barrel the same way. If he happened upon a good spring, he would stop, empty the stale water, and refill his barrel.

On the trail the cook's wagon was the place where the

trail cutters made their arrangements for "cuttin' the herd";
it was where the wayfarer sought a job or a square meal;
it was where the cattle thief came to size up the outfit and
judge its fighting strength; it was where the Indians gathered to beg for flour, coffee, and tobacco and to demand
"wohaw." "Which way's the wagon?" indeed became a
common inquiry.

The redskins along the trail were great beggars, and
the cook had to exercise diplomacy when it was difficult to
give them the things they asked for. Usually a trail outfit
traveled light, and the mess-wagon carried only enough
supplies to last until they reached the next supply point.

If the wagon boss ran short of supplies through accident or overgenerosity, he sent the wagon ahead into the
next town for replenishments. In those days he needed no
checkbook. The brand burned upon his wagon and horses
was sufficient endorsement for credit.

Cooks lost their lives on the trail, too—perhaps not
from drowning or from stampedes and falling horses, but
from pitting their surliness against the nerve-frayed tempers of touchy cowboys. When hot lead settled the argu-
ment, it was the final word. When a group of cowmen found
themselves without a cook, no matter by what circumstance, a serious situation resulted. Usually a cowboy who
was known to possess rudimentary knowledge of cooking
was appointed to take the cook's place until another could
be located. There was a standing rule on the range that
anyone making derogatory remarks about the substitute's
cooking should himself be made to swap places with the

one he had criticized. This custom has provided many anecdotes, most of them varied as far as circumstances are concerned, and all of them almost too old to bear repeating.

For example, one substitute cook didn't like his job and did his best to prepare such poor food that it would provoke criticism. One night a cowboy grimaced over the sourdough he was trying to eat and said, "Such sinkers! Burnt on the bottom, soggy in the middle, and salty as hell." Seeing the hopeful look on the cook's face, he quickly added, "But gosh, that's jes' the way I like 'em."

After weeks on the trail, when eyes became bleary from loss of sleep and lips were parched from the heat and alkali, or the cowboy had been saturated by cold rains or covered with river mud or worn out from stampedes and Indian troubles, nerves became taut and only through the diplomacy of the trail boss or the cook was peace kept in the family.

Small wonder hell broke loose when they hit the town of their destination at the end of the trail. It was but the breaking loose of exuberant spirits too long confined by months of monotonous trail work. The cook, though usually a drinking man, was older in years and experience, thus less demonstrative. He was content to absorb his liquor in peace and quiet.

Of course, this was not always the case. There are exceptions to all rules. Some cooks have been known to be affected by liquor much in the same manner as an Indian. It brought out the savage in them, making them murderous and hostile with the world. And many of them had a weakness for alcohol.

One such cook, in spite of his pride in having his meals on time, couldn't resist temptation when the boss brought a pint of lemon extract from town for flavoring stewed apples. When the boys came in for supper, no meal was ready and the wild cook made every effort to chase them from the wagon with a butcher knife. Those sharp and ever ready butcher knives that he always kept handy could make him a dangerous man. Before they could subdue him, he had to be roped and dragged to the creek for a sobering ducking. Needless to say, supper was late and scanty that night, though the cook did have some lemon-flavored apple pies ready. Those pies had been the agent of his temptation and downfall.

Fall roundup an' bad weather 'way back in early time, had the hands an' all the hosses in an ugly frame of mind. Hosses pitched that never usta, an' the rough string shore went wild, an' Ole Cookie acted bronky, like a spoiled an' pompered child. The boss was even techy an' the wrangler soakin' wet; when he rounded the remuda, there was hell to pay, y'u bet.

Fire wood wet an' water muddy made Ole Cookie's job a pain; when the boys came in fer supper, they was ready to complain. Cookie knowed the boys was hungry, tired, an' wet an' galded too, but he dared 'em with a pothook, jes' one gripe about the stew.

Without a word they et their supper an' drank their coffee black, rolled a smoke an' eased around to dry their feet an' back. Ole Cookie prowled around the fire an' poked the bed of coals, an' told 'em what a time he'd had with chuck an' beddin' rolls.

He also loudly told 'em, if they didn't like his chuck, he'd quit that very minnit; let some cowpoke try his luck.

Tex Taylor

CHAPTER 12 *On Roundup*

"There's no room at the chuck wagon for a quitters blankets."

With spring came the roundup and the return of wandering punchers, eager to feel the saddle beneath them, to hear the worried bawl of the cattle, to see the campfires, and smell the pungent scent of sagebrush branding fires. Nothing stirred the heart of a cowboy like preparation for the spring roundup.

After a winter of inactivity, he looked forward to the roundup like a kid to circus day. This was the time he made new friends and renewed old acquaintances; the time he could expend the energy too long held in by forced inertia. He might be just as glad to get back to the home ranch after a summer of hard work under sun, cloud, and rain. His body might be stiff from drenching rains and sleeping in wet blankets, but right now he was filled with zeal for the call of the roundup.

When spring was in the air, he was as full of vim and vinegar as the horses being driven in from their winter idleness. With the shedding of winter hair and the coming of spring grass, each and every horse seemed filled with a rough playfulness which taxed the rider's ability to stay in the saddle.

During the pandemonium of whistling ropes and bucking horses as the animals were roped and ridden, the sober-faced cook went about his business of checking his supplies and putting the final touches to the packing of his wagon. When everything was ready, the wagon boss gave the signal and the whole cavalcade moved out with a rush, as if it had been held down too long. The cook kicked the brake free, popped his blacksnake, gave a yell, and urged his frisky teams into a run. He was followed by the remuda in charge of the wrangler and flanked on each side by the riders, some of them still fighting it out with their fresh and kinky horses.

At the appointed meeting place other wagons gathered. With the mingling of horses and men greeting old friends, all would seem confusion to an outlander, yet from all this seemingly turbulent disorder, things settled down to disciplined routine.

The roundup was strictly a business proposition in spite of the noise and hilarity displayed by the cowboys. The wagon bosses of the various outfits met with the round-up captain to talk over plans, appoint lieutenants, and discuss sections of the range to be worked.

The cooks, in the meantime, were "throwin' the big pot into the little one" and trying to outdo each other in preparing their first meal of the roundup. If a cook had a reputation for good food, he was likely to have more than his share of company for supper.

No work was done this first day. The time after supper

was given over to rough frolicking and horseplay. Usually there was a "kangaroo court" where cowboys were tried on ridiculous charges, invariably found guilty, and assessed punishments. This was a period when overgrown boys could "ketch up" on their love of a practical joke and give vent to their rough sense of humor. Tomorrow, they knew, would mean settling down to serious business, so on this first night they "turned themselves loose." This boisterous horseplay, however, did not last long, for a cowboy's nights were short and he knew he would be routed out before daylight the next morning for a hard day's work.

The cook's day started about three o'clock in the morning, long before the horizon toward the east began to redden. He was awakened either by the night hawk, a herder who had been keeping his eyes on the stars while riding around the herd, by an alarm clock, or by force of habit. He had to get his fires going and prepare breakfast so that the riders could be at work by daylight.

Out on the darkened prairie he could see his "boys" lying scattered about wrapped in their tarps, looking like so many huge cocoons. Kicking the coals of his yesterday's fire to life, he added new fuel, and as this caught, the flames caused his legs to throw shadows which resembled two huge grotesque columns. If the outfit used no night hawk, he walked over to the sleeping day wrangler and delivered a kick where it would do the most good to arouse him. The kick was usually accompanied with some such remark as, "Pile out Wrang. It'll soon be light 'nough to bring the hosses in."

The noise of clattering pots and pans and the delicious aroma of coffee on the morning air soon awakened the sleeping figures on the ground. They began to stir, stretch, and pull on boots. One by one they rolled their beds and dumped them near the wagon, then made their way to the washpan to get the sleep from their eyes.

One old cook had a novel way of waking the boys. From somewhere in the wagon he would pull out a pair of huge spurs with drag rowels, fasten them on his heels, and tramp among the sleeping forms on the ground. When men are lying with ears close to the ground, sounds carry easily and to hear someone tramping about with spurs creates a disagreeable sensation. In semi-wakefulness each man fancies the next step will bring the walker's heel upon his face. This method of waking the crew was quiet, but effective.

By the time the cook gave his call, appetites were

thoroughly whetted. The savory incense sent up by the Dutch oven and coffeepot through the crisp air still does something to a man's gastric juices for that matter.

Breakfast over, the camp again presented a scene of vigorous activity. There was the dull thunder of hoofs on soft earth as the wranglers brought the horse herd in on the run. Ropes cut the air from all directions as each cowboy roped his own mount for the morning drive, or an appointed "ketch hand" did the job for him. Saddling was quickly accomplished. Here and there some rider had trouble staying atop his high-spirited horse.

The cook was a disinterested observer of a better "pitchin' hoss contest" than the city man who paid money to attend a rodeo ever had the opportunity to see. The wilder horses were saddled for the morning circle, and often their pitching was so vicious that riders, as one cowhand observed, were "fallin' off like wormy apples in a high wind." The cool of the morning always put a kink in the horses' backs, especially when they were fresh from the winter range. On rainy mornings there was always the dangerous job of mounting bad horses with muddy boots and slippery stirrups, when crackling slickers frightened the horses and handicapped the riders' efforts to mount.

But from all this confusion the men soon moved out to the spot where their lieutenants would "tell off the riders" and give instructions about the territory to be worked on the drive.

The cook had not been idle during this time. He went about his business with grim industry and a sureness of judgment from thorough knowledge of his profession. He had washed the dishes, pots, and kettles and noisily stowed them in the wagon. Bedrolls and other camp plunder had been loaded, the water barrel filled, and water poured upon the fires, filling the air with the stench of wet wood ashes and greasy dish water. His teams were hooked up by a couple of punchers anxious to be away to join the other riders and be clear of camp.

His job was no small task. There were many little things to attend to. He must see that the coffeepot was emptied, the molasses can securely fastened, and anything else likely to spill tied down so that there would be no danger of upsetting or leakage on beds and other objects.

Like other kings, he had his aspirations. To beat the other cooks to the next camp location and have his wagon set up in the choicest spot was his idea of accomplishment. To do this, he tried to get an early start in the wild chuckwagon race across the prairies. On occasion he left behind a trail of scattered pans and pots which he had been careless in tying down, but which he dared not stop to pick up. Perhaps the cowboys did so later with the pride of belonging to the victorious wagon. Cooks for important ranches were intensely jealous of each other. Each was constantly trying to outdo the other.

Arriving at the new location, the cook skillfully swung his teams so that his wagon would be headed into the wind. This gave him a windbreak for his fires and put the chuck box at the rear in handy reach. He dug his fire trenches directly behind the wagon, never to one side. Juggling his pots

164

and pans with systematic skill, he called loudly on the horse wrangler for wood and water.

For a time there was much hurrying to and fro, with the clamor of wood-chopping, unpacking, and all the man-made noises of setting up camp for cooking. Fires were built in the trenches, and extending lengthwise over the fire pits were placed the steel racks upon which the vessels were hung. As soon as the fires burned down to coals, vessels were put on to heat. Grease was put in to melt for the steaks and into the Dutch ovens for the bread. No movement was wasted, no time lost. The men must be fed on time, and, as at breakfast, there was no lingering at the noon meal. While the coffee boiled, the cook mixed his bread and set it in a warm place to rise. Steaks were sliced and put into the hot grease, and while the food was cooking, he went from one duty to another, from arranging the "eatin' tools" upon the chuck-box lid to placing the "wreck pan" in a handy place.

By the time the meal was ready, the morning's "drive" was approaching the "holding spot" and the cowboys came trooping into camp in a wild race, leaving behind only enough men to hold the herd. After unsaddling and stop-ping just long enough to watch their horses roll to see if they rolled completely over, they stood about joshing and joking like noisy, heavy-bodied, but light-hearted school-boys, waiting for the cook's call of "come an' get it."

Dinner was hastily eaten, and the first boys through caught fresh horses and rode out to relieve the other herders so that they might come in and eat. After all had eaten, the routine of moving camp was repeated, for all the world like a circus moving after each performance. Camp was not always moved in the afternoon, since this time was usually spent branding the calves brought in on the morning drive. But when the outfit had moved on, the timid little prairie animals—the gopher, the prairie dog, mice, and rabbits—crept out to sniff suspiciously at the tainted air of man-made scars.

At the evening camp there was no hurry. Although the cook strove to have supper on time, it was not so imperative since there was little work to be done afterward. He started his meal early, however, because he usually served a greater variety of food than at noon. He baked his pies first, if they were to be dessert, and set them on the chuck-box lid to cool.

To watch a roundup cook prepare a meal was an interesting sight to those not familiar with camp life. After his several fires had burned down, he scraped away the gray ashes which covered his fire hole until he exposed the bed of red coals underneath.

He patted the beds of hot coals down smoothly and then placed his Dutch ovens on them to heat. After his bread was made and in the ovens, he dragged from the bed of the wagon a hind-quarter of a yearling, laid it on the chuck-box lid, and cut slabs of steaks from it. These he cut into pieces the size of his hand, pounded them to tenderize, and dropped them into the pan of flour left from his bread making. As he dropped each piece into the hot, crackling grease, it made a most tantalizing searing sound as it cooked to a delicious golden brown.

166

Mixed with all the other odors was the strong but not unpleasant one of wood smoke. The cook busily made his way from one vessel to another, turning steaks, watching the beans or the browning of his sourdoughs. Quite often he cast an anxious glance toward the place where the herd was being worked. He could hear the continual bawl of the worried cattle and see the clouds of dust they stirred up. As he watched for the break of the riders, he was hoping his meal would be ready when the work was finished and the riders came storming in.

This was the one important meal of the day, and the only one over which the cowboys could linger. After it came the day's moment of relaxation. It was at this time that the chuck wagon became the cowhand's social center. Lolling about in any position suitable to his personal comfort, he could now roll and leisurely smoke a cigarette while he talked of the day's happenings. Stories could be told if short and well seasoned. Songs could be sung, verses composed and added to, and some puncher might drag out a mouth organ, knock the loose tobacco crumbs from it, and join in with an accompaniment.

One might dig from the warbag in his bedroll a greasy deck of cards, spread a saddle blanket near the fire, and start shuffling. There would always be a few willing to try their luck and skill in a game of seven-up or draw poker. Usually there was no money in circulation, and dried beans were used for chips, but the winners could count on the losers' paying up at the end of the roundup. If the cook happened to be in a bad humor, he would take his seat on the bean bag and refuse all comers the use of this commodity for poker chips.

The cook built up his fire to cheery proportions as he and his swamper washed and dried the dishes. There always seemed to be an enchanting atmosphere created by its genial glow.

One of the cook's night duties was to see that the wagon tongue was propped up with a neck-yoke, his harness hung upon it in orderly array and covered with a tarpaulin to keep off the night's dew. As the fire died down, bringing the encircling darkness closer and closer, the weird night noises could be heard clearer in accents appealing to men who love the life of the wilds.

Before the fire was low and the cowboys began drifting out to their bedrolls, there was a session of good-natured kidding and rich humor which would put a vaudeville show to shame. But as the fire slowly died, conversation died with it, and one by one the faces of the men disappeared as darkness moved in. The pulsing red glow of cigarettes spotted the darkness, this alone revealing the position of the men behind them. One by one they rubbed the fire from their cigarettes on a boot heel and left to seek their soogans, stopping to stamp the ground to rout out the insects and reptiles before spreading their beds. Soon all was dark and quiet save for the occasional yipping of a coyote, the nicker of a horse out with the remuda, and the low night songs of the men on herd duty. These were the moments which, after he became too old to ride, held the fondest memories for the cowhand. Here he was close to the soil, and the tales he told, the songs he sang, and his sometimes coarse but always delightful humor reflected his simple code.

And so it went through the long days of the roundup season. But not all the days were pleasant. Under scorching sun and chilling rain the work went on. When the winds came to blow the heat of his fires from his pots, or the rains came to wet his wood and send chilling water down his neck, the cook muttered profanely as he cursed his own imbecility for choosing such a profession. Near by he could hear the wrangler cursing the remuda as the horses stamped thin mud in his face, or the hoodlum swearing at the rain which soaked his beds. Yet he never hesitated to do his best under these trying conditions.

Present-day dietitians, with their knowledge of calories, vitamins, and other new-fangled ideas, are shocked at the cowboy's consumption of starches, coffee, proteins, and fried foods. Yet most of the old-time cowhands, unless they were killed by a falling horse or in a shooting scrape, lived to a ripe old age. Today, with all our supposedly improved food and dietary habits, business and professional men are dropping off between the ages of forty-five and fifty-five at an alarming rate.

Perhaps it was due to the cowboy's life in the open, the jarring of the horse, and his carefree attitude of mind which kept his digestive organs healthy. No one ever heard of him having ulcers or other digestive disorders in spite of the gargantuan meals he consumed, and his good health certainly could not be attributed to the alkaline or scummy, germ-laden water he drank.

Too much credit cannot be given the old wagon cook for the cowboy's contentment with life. A good cook strove to have plenty of well-cooked food, and many cooks possessed an ingenuity for variety in spite of having access to limited supplies. Many a cook went to great trouble to prepare desserts so that the boys would always remember him for the sweet taste he had left in their mouths. And so, in telling you something of his trials and tribulations, his character and his cookery, I hope I have left with you the "sweet taste" richly due this unique American character whose always welcome call was "Come an' get it!"